Ayn Rand was the bestselling author of *The Fountainhead* and *Atlas Shrugged,* among other enduring works of fiction. Objectivism, her unique philosophy, has gained a worldwide audience. The fundamentals of her philosophy are set forth in five nonfiction books: *Introduction to Objectivist Epistemology, For the New Intellectual, The Virtue of Selfishness, Capitalism: The Unknown Ideal,* and *The Romantic Manifesto*. Ayn Rand died in 1982.

Peter Schwartz has an M.A. in journalism from Syracuse University. He is the founding editor and publisher of *The Intellectual Activist* magazine and the author of *The Battle for Laissez-faire Capitalism*. He is the Chairman of the Board of the Ayn Rand Institute and is director of its writing program.

4/5/99

To Gary,

Best wishes,

Peter [illegible]

RETURN OF THE PRIMITIVE
THE ANTI-INDUSTRIAL REVOLUTION

AYN RAND

NEW EXPANDED EDITION OF
The New Left: The Anti-Industrial Revolution

Edited and with an Introduction and Additional Articles by
Peter Schwartz

A MERIDIAN BOOK

MERIDIAN
Published by the Penguin Group
Penguin Putnam Inc., 375 Hudson Street, New York, New York 10014, U.S.A.
Penguin Books Ltd, 27 Wrights Lane, London W8 5TZ, England
Penguin Books Australia Ltd, Ringwood, Victoria, Australia
Penguin Books Canada Ltd, 10 Alcorn Avenue, Toronto, Ontario, Canada M4V 3B2
Penguin Books (N.Z.) Ltd, 182–190 Wairau Road, Auckland 10, New Zealand

Penguin Books Ltd, Registered Offices: Harmondsworth, Middlesex, England

First published by Meridian, an imprint of Dutton NAL,
a member of Penguin Putnam Inc.

Original edition published as *The New Left: The Anti-Industrial Revolution* by Signet in 1971. "Racism" appeared in *The Objectivist Newsletter* and later in Ayn Rand's *The Virtue of Selfishness: A New Concept of Egoism,* published by Signet in 1964, and "Global Balkanization" was first published in the book *The Voice of Reason*.

First Printing, January, 1999
10 9 8 7 6 5 4 3 2 1

Library of Congress Cataloging-in-Publication Data:

Rand, Ayn.
[Selections. 1998]
Return of the primitive : the anti-industrial revolution / Ayn Rand ; edited and with an introduction and additional articles by Peter Schwartz.
p. cm.
ISBN 0-452-01184-1
1. New Left—United States 2. Technology and civilization.
I. Schwartz, Peter. II. Title.
HN90.R3R362 1999
303.4—dc21 98-24523
CIP

Printed in the United States of America
Set in Times New Roman
Designed by Leonard Telesca

Contents

INTRODUCTION

When the original version of this book was published in 1971, it seemed that the ramparts of civilization were about to be breached. It was the time of the New Left—a time of organized violence, militant emotionalism, and open, pervasive nihilism. It was a time when college campuses were being forcibly shut down by student thugs brandishing "Free Speech" banners. It was a time when corporate buildings and military-recruitment offices were being invaded by guerrillas demanding "Peace Now!" It was a time of psychedelic "flower children" and "people's armies," of Timothy Leary and Abbie Hoffman and Charles Manson, of the Theater of the Absurd and the Black Panthers.

Spearheading this mindlessness was a movement that resisted definition. Its enemies were anyone and anything American, its heroes were dictatorial killers like Ho Chi Minh and Fidel Castro, its goal was indiscriminate destruction—yet its leaders were hailed by cultural commentators as idealistic defenders of the individual against an oppressive state.

American society was under dizzying siege. It was in retreat, uncertain whether to embrace or repel this onslaught—an onslaught launched in the name of a cause no one could name.

Ayn Rand proceeded to name it.

In her essays in this book, she identified its ideological essence. She explained how the "revolutionaries" of that movement were faithful practitioners of every important idea their elders had taught them. She showed that the New Left was the offspring of the Establishment's philosophers and of their anti-reason, anti-individualism, anti-capitalism doctrines.

Those doctrines were fused, in the 1960s, into an overwhelming hostility toward one distinctively Western target: industrialization. The New Left declared that the West was corrupt and that its influence had to be eliminated through the renunciation of technology. People were exhorted to give up their automobiles and shopping centers, their air conditioners and nuclear power plants.

This was the distinguishing characteristic of the New Left. It brazenly advocated what prior collectivists had been reluctant to acknowledge—even to themselves—as inherent in their philosophy. "The activists of the New Left," Ayn Rand wrote, "are closer [than those of the Old Left] to revealing the truth of their motives: they do not seek to take over industrial plants, they seek to destroy technology."

While the New Left did not triumph in its "anti-industrial revolution," it did pave the way for an ongoing assault on the rational mind and its products. Writing about the New Left's campus commandos, Ayn Rand said that "even though the student rebellion has not aroused much public sympathy, the most ominous aspect of the situation is the fact that it has not met any *ideological opposition,*" that it has shown "the road ahead is empty, with no intellectual barricades in sight" and that the "battle is to continue."

That battle is indeed continuing.

It is being waged today by two cultural movements virulently opposed to the advances—material and intellectual—created by Western civilization. One movement is environmentalism; the other, multiculturalism. Both seek to enshrine a new primitivism.

Primitive, according to the *Oxford English Dictionary,* means: "Of or belonging to the first age, period or stage; pertaining to early times . . ." With respect to human development, primitivism is a pre-rational stage. It is a stage in which man lives in fearful awe of a universe he cannot understand. The primitive man does not grasp the law of causality. He does not comprehend the fact that the world is governed by natural laws and that nature can be ruled by any man who discovers those laws. To a primitive, there is only a mysterious *super*natural. Sunshine, darkness, rainfall, drought, the clap of thunder, the hooting of a spotted owl—all are inexplicable, portentous, and sacrosanct to him. To this non-conceptual mentality, man is metaphysically subordinate to nature, which is never to be commanded, only meekly obeyed.

This is the state of mind to which the environmentalists want us to revert.

If primitive man regards the world as unknowable, how does he decide what to believe and how to act? Since such knowledge is not innate, where does primitive man turn for guidance? To his tribe. It is membership in a collective that infuses such a person with his sole sense of identity. The tribe's edicts thus become his unquestioned absolutes, and the tribe's welfare becomes his fundamental value.

This is the state of mind to which the multiculturalists want us to revert. They hold that the basic unit of existence is the tribe, which they define by the crudest, most primitive, most anti-conceptual criteria (such as skin color). They consequently reject the view that the achievements of Western—i.e., individualistic—civilization represent a way of life superior to that of savage tribalism.

Both environmentalism and multiculturalism wish to destroy the values of a rational, industrial age. Both are scions of the New Left, zealously carrying on its campaign of sacrificing progress to primitivism.

It is for the purpose of analyzing the philosophic progeny of the New Left that this expanded edition of *The New Left* has been compiled.

I have retained everything from the original edition and added essays of my own on environmentalism, multiculturalism, and feminism. Because multiculturalists have fostered enormous confusion about the nature of racism and of "ethnicity," I have also added two Ayn Rand articles on these subjects—"Racism" and "Global Balkanization"—even though they have previously been published elsewhere (the first in *The Virtue of Selfishness,* the second in *The Voice of Reason*).

The result is a collection of essays identifying, explaining, and evaluating different manifestations of the same anti-industrial revolution.

It is eye-opening to see how much of the New Left's once-radical agenda not only has been adopted by today's society, but is no longer even controversial. The trappings of the New Left are gone, but its substance has endured.

For example, in the 1960s there were repeated, charged confrontations between corporations and "back-to-nature" hippies over such matters as pollution and recycling. Now, Earth Day is an annual cultural event—promoted by big business; now, countless products advertise themselves as "ecology friendly" (such as McDonald's hamburgers, which the company boasts come from no cows that graze at the expense of the planet's "rain forests"); now, the major villains in children's cartoon programs are not criminals, but greedy tree-loggers; and now, most states, according to a news report in the *New York Times,* "require schools to incorporate environmental concepts into virtually every subject in all grade levels."

In the 1960s, college students forcibly occupied administration buildings, demanding courses in "black studies." Today, every major university features full *departments* (and even some designated dormitories and cafeterias) for a variety of ethnic excogitations. Today, instead of violent sit-ins, there has been a quiet coup by "diversity committees," whose authoritarian thought-police reign on campuses and who banish "politically incorrect" dissenters to the dungeons of re-education seminars.

This devolution has been the result, not of the intellectual persuasiveness of its defenders, but of the intellectual emptiness of its opponents. The anti-industrial revolutionaries have been winning only by default. As Ayn Rand said: "The uncontested absurdities of today are the accepted slogans of tomorrow. They come to be accepted by degrees, by dint of constant pressure on one side and constant retreat on the other—until one day when they are suddenly declared to be the country's official ideology. That is the way welfare statism came to be accepted in this country."

It is also the way multiculturalism and environmentalism have come to be accepted. But this insidious process does not have to continue. The absurdities that have become today's primitivism can, and urgently need to, be challenged. But they cannot be fought by the typically conservative method of arguing that they are good ideas that "unfortunately, go too far." This battle requires an uncompromising loyalty to rational values—and a repudiation of the new primitivism as fundamentally irrational.

Perhaps this book will help people acquire the intellectual means and the moral conviction to mount such a battle.

—Peter Schwartz
January 1998

Foreword to the First Edition

About a year ago, I received the following letter from a reader whom I have not met:

> Dear Miss Rand:
>
> I am a graduate student in sociology at Northern Illinois University and a student of Objectivism. . . .
>
> Actually, what I want to discuss with you is your writings on the New Left. I have read them all and, in my opinion, they offer the best critical analysis that has ever been written on this movement. Your recent articles: "The Left: Old and New"; "Apollo and Dionysus"; and your recent article in *The New York Times Sunday Magazine*, "The New Left Represents an Intellectual Vacuum," were superb. I recently reread your article, "The Cashing-In: The Student 'Rebellion,' " published in 1965, and I was struck by how accurate and prophetic your analysis was at that time.
>
> After reading these articles it occurred to me that, if they were all collected together and published (i.e., mass-distributed in paperback by Signet), they could have a tremendous impact on the culture and especially on the college campuses.
>
> It is my fervent hope that you will seriously consider issuing such a book, Miss Rand. Believe me, there are no other analyses of the New Left that measure up to those published by *The Objectivist.* If the book was issued in paperback by Signet, . . . as your other books have [been], it would be on almost every newsstand and in every college bookstore. In fact, most college bookstores devote a section

of their space to books dealing with the New Left and campus turmoil. Your book would therefore be displayed prominently. The publication and distribution of such a book to college students could mark a turning point for the students who read it. It would be a voice of reason for students to turn to. It would give them the intellectual ammunition that they could find nowhere else. . . .

Sincerely,
G.M.B.

As a rule, I do not like practical suggestions from readers. But this was such a good idea so convincingly presented that I showed the letter to my publishers, who agreed with its writer wholeheartedly. Such was the origin of this book—with my thanks to Mr. G. M. B.

The purpose of the book is clearly stated in the letter: this book is intended for college students—for those among them who *are* seeking "a voice of reason to turn to." It is intended also for all those who are concerned about college students and about the state of modern education.

I delayed the publication of the book in order to include two articles I was planning at the time, which belong in this collection ("The Anti-Industrial Revolution" and "The Comprachicos"). I have included "The Cashing-In: The Student 'Rebellion' " (originally published in *The Objectivist Newsletter*) in order to let readers judge for themselves the accuracy of my understanding of the activist movement's philosophical meaning, goals and sources.

All the other articles in this book, with one exception, appeared originally in my magazine *The Objectivist.* The date at the end of each article indicates the specific issue. The exception is a brief piece which appeared as part of a symposium in *The New York Times Magazine.*

—Ayn Rand
New York City
April 1971

The Schools

The Cashing-In: The Student "Rebellion"

The so-called student "rebellion," which was started and keynoted at the University of California at Berkeley, has profound significance, but not of the kind that most commentators have ascribed to it. And the nature of the misrepresentations is part of its significance.

The events at Berkeley began, in the fall of 1964, ostensibly as a student protest against the University administration's order forbidding political activity—specifically, the recruiting, fund-raising and organizing of students for political action off-campus—on a certain strip of ground adjoining the campus, which was owned by the University. Claiming that their rights had been violated, a small group of "rebels" rallied thousands of students of all political views, including many "conservatives," and assumed the title of the "Free Speech Movement." The Movement staged "sit-in" protests in the administration building, and committed other acts of physical force, such as assaults on the police and the seizure of a police car for use as a rostrum.

The spirit, style and tactics of the rebellion are best illustrated by one particular incident. The University administration called a mass meeting, which was attended by eighteen thousand students and faculty members, to hear an address on the situation by the University President, Clark Kerr; it had been expressly announced that no student speakers would be allowed to address the meeting. Kerr attempted to end the rebellion by capitulating: he promised to grant most of the rebels' demands; it looked as if he had won the audience to his side. Whereupon, Mario Savio, the rebel leader, seized the microphone, in an attempt to take over the meeting, ignoring the rules and the fact that the meeting had been adjourned. When he was—properly—dragged off the platform, the leaders of the F.S.M. admitted, openly and jubilantly, that they had almost lost their battle, but had saved it by provoking the administration to an act of "violence" (thus admitting that the victory of their publicly proclaimed goals was not the goal of their battle).

What followed was nationwide publicity, of a peculiar kind. It was a sudden and, seemingly, spontaneous out-pouring of articles, studies, surveys, revealing a strange unanimity of approach in several basic aspects: in ascribing to the F.S.M. the importance of a national movement, unwarranted by the facts—in blurring the facts by means of unintelligible generalities—in granting to the rebels the status of spokesmen for American youth, acclaiming their "idealism" and "commitment" to political action, hailing them as a symptom of the "awakening" of college students from "political apathy." If ever a "puff-job" was done by a major part of the press, this was it.

In the meantime, what followed at Berkeley was a fierce, three-cornered struggle among the University administration, its Board of Regents and its faculty, a struggle so sketchily reported in the press that its exact nature remains fogbound. One can gather only that the Regents were, apparently, demanding a "tough" policy toward the rebels, that the majority of the faculty were on the rebels' side and that the administration was caught in the "moderate" middle of the road.

The struggle led to the permanent resignation of the University's Chancellor (as the rebels had demanded)—the temporary resignation, and later reinstatement, of President Kerr—and, ultimately, an almost complete capitulation to the F.S.M., with the administration granting most of the rebels' demands. (These included the right to advocate illegal acts and the right to an unrestricted freedom of speech *on campus.*)

To the astonishment of the naive, this did not end the rebellion: the more demands were granted, the more were made. As the administration intensified its efforts to appease the F.S.M., the F.S.M. intensified its provocations. The unrestricted freedom of speech took the form of a "Filthy Language Movement," which consisted of students carrying placards with four-letter words, and broadcasting obscenities over the University loudspeakers (which Movement was dismissed with mild reproof by most of the press, as a mere "adolescent prank").

This, apparently, was too much even for those who sympathized with the rebellion. The F.S.M. began to lose its following—and was, eventually, dissolved. Mario Savio quit the University, declaring that he "could not keep up with the *undemocratic* procedures that the administration is following" (italics mine)—and departed, reportedly to organize a nationwide revolutionary student movement.

This is a bare summary of the events as they were reported by the press. But some revealing information was provided by volunteers, outside the regular news channels, such as in the letters-to-the-editor columns.

An eloquent account was given in a letter to *The New York Times* (March 31, 1965) by Alexander Grendon, a biophysicist in the Donner Laboratory, University of California:

> The F.S.M. has always applied coercion to insure victory. One-party "democracy," as in the Communist countries or the lily-white portions of the South, corrects opponents of the party line by punishment. The punishment of the recalcitrant university administration (and more than 20,000 students who avoided participation in the conflict) was to "bring the university to a grinding halt" by physical force.
>
> To capitulate to such corruption of democracy is to teach students that these methods are right. President Kerr capitulated repeatedly. . . .
>
> Kerr agreed the university would not control "advocacy of illegal acts," an abstraction until illustrated by examples: In a university lecture hall, a self-proclaimed anarchist advises students how to cheat to escape military service; a nationally known Communist uses the university facilities to condemn our Government in vicious terms for its action in Vietnam, while funds to support the Vietcong are illegally solicited; propaganda for the use of marijuana, with instructions where to buy it, is openly distributed on campus.
>
> Even the abstraction "obscenity" is better understood when one hears a speaker, using the university's amplifying equipment, describe in vulgar words his experiences in group sexual intercourse and homosexuality and recommend these practices, while another suggests students should have the same sexual freedom on campus as dogs. . . .

> Clark Kerr's "negotiation"—a euphemism for surrender—on each deliberate defiance of orderly university processes contributes not to a liberal university but to a lawless one.

David S. Landes, professor of history, Harvard University, made an interesting observation in a letter to *The New York Times* (December 29, 1964). Stating that the Berkeley revolt represents potentially one of the most serious assaults on academic freedom in America, he wrote:

"In conclusion, I should like to point out the deleterious implications of this dispute for the University of California. I know personally of five or six faculty members who are leaving, not because of lack of sympathy with 'free speech' or 'political action,' but because, as one put it, who wants to teach at the University of Saigon?"

The clearest account and most perceptive evaluation were offered in an article in the *Columbia University Forum* (Spring 1965), entitled "What's Left at Berkeley," by William Petersen, professor of sociology at the University of California at Berkeley. He writes:

> The first fact one must know about the Free Speech Movement is that it has little or nothing to do with free speech. . . . If not free speech, what then is the issue? In fact, preposterous as this may seem, the real issue is the seizure of power. . . .
>
> That a tiny number, a few hundred out of a student body of more than 27,000, was able to disrupt the campus is the consequence of more than vigor and skill in agitation. This miniscule group could not have succeeded in getting so many students into motion without three other, at times unwitting, sources of support: off-campus assistance of various kinds, the University administration and the faculty.
>
> Everyone who has seen the efficient, almost military organization of the agitators' program has a reasonable basis for believing that skilled personnel and money are being dispatched into the Berkeley battle. . . . Around the Berkeley community a dozen "*ad hoc* committees to support" this or that element of the student revolt sprang up spontaneously, as though out of nowhere.

> The course followed by the University administration . . . could hardly have better fostered a rebellious student body if it had been devised to do so. To establish dubious regulations and when they are attacked to defend them by unreasonable argument is bad enough; worse still, the University did not impose on the students any sanctions that did not finally evaporate. . . . Obedience to norms is developed when it is suitably rewarded, and when noncompliance is suitably punished. That professional educators should need to be reminded of this axiom indicates how deep the roots of the Berkeley crisis lie.
>
> But the most important reason that the extremists won so many supporters among the students was the attitude of the faculty. Perhaps their most notorious capitulation to the F.S.M. was a resolution passed by the Academic Senate on December 8, by which the faculty notified the campus not only that they supported all of the radicals' demands but also that, in effect, they were willing to fight for them against the Board of Regents, should that become necessary. When that resolution passed by an overwhelming majority—824 to 115 votes—it effectively silenced the anti-F.S.M. student organizations. . . .
>
> The Free Speech Movement is reminiscent of the Communist fronts of the 1930's, but there are several important differences. The key feature, that a radical core uses legitimate issues ambiguously in order to manipulate a large mass, is identical. The core in this case, however, is not the disciplined Communist party, but a heterogeneous group of radical sects.

Professor Petersen lists the various socialist, Trotskyist, communist and other groups involved. His conclusion is: "The radical leaders on the Berkeley campus, like those in Latin American or Asian universities, are not the less radical for being, in many cases, outside the discipline of a formal political party. They are defined not by whether they pay dues to a party, but by their actions, their vocabulary, their way of thinking. The best term to describe them, in my opinion, is Castroite." This term, he explains, applies primarily to their choice of tactics, to the fact that "in critical respects all of them imitate the Castro movement. . . .

"At Berkeley, provocative tactics applied not against a dictatorship but against the liberal, divided, and vacillating University administration proved to be enormously effective. Each provocation and subsequent victory led to the next."

Professor Petersen ends his article on a note of warning: "By my diagnosis . . . not only has the patient [the University] not recovered but he is sicker than ever. The fever has gone down temporarily, but the infection is spreading and becoming more virulent."

Now let us consider the ideology of the rebels, from such indications as were given in the press reports. The general tone of the reports was best expressed by a headline in *The New York Times* (March 15, 1965): "The New Student Left: Movement Represents Serious Activists in Drive for Changes."

What kind of changes? No specific answer was given in the almost full-page story. Just "changes."

Some of these activists "who liken their movement to a 'revolution,' want to be called radicals. Most of them, however, prefer to be called 'organizers.' "

Organizers—of what? Of "deprived people." For what? No answer. Just "organizers."

"Most express contempt for any specific labels, and they don't mind being called cynics. . . . The great majority of those questioned said they were as skeptical of Communism as they were of any other form of political control. . . . 'You might say we're a-Communist,' said one of them, 'just as you might say we're amoral and a-almost everything else.' "

There are exceptions, however. A girl from the University of California, one of the leaders of the Berkeley revolt, is quoted as saying: "At present the socialist world, even with all its problems, is moving closer than any other countries toward the sort of society I think should exist. In the Soviet Union, it has almost been achieved."

Another student, from the City College of New York, is quoted as concurring: " 'The Soviet Union and the whole Socialist bloc are on the right track,' he said."

In view of the fact that most of the young activists were active in the civil rights movement, and that the Berkeley rebels had started by hiding behind the issue of civil rights (attempting, unsuccessfully, to smear all opposition as of "racist" origin), it is interesting to read that: "There is little talk among the activists about racial integration. Some of them consider the subject passé. They declare that integration will be almost as evil as segregation if it results in a complacent, middle-class interracial society."

The central theme and basic ideology of all the activists is: *anti-ideology.* They are militantly opposed to all "labels," definitions and theories; they proclaim the supremacy of the immediate moment and commitment to action—to subjectively, emotionally motivated action. Their anti-intellectual attitude runs like a stressed leitmotif through all the press reports.

"The Berkeley mutineers did not seem political in the sense of those student rebels in the Turbulent Thirties," declares an article in *The New York Times Magazine* (Feb. 14, 1965), "they are too suspicious of all adult institutions to embrace wholeheartedly even those ideologies with a stake in smashing the system. An anarchist or I.W.W. strain seems as pronounced as any Marxist doctrine. 'Theirs is a sort of political existentialism,' says Paul Jacobs, a research associate at the university's Center for the Study of Law and Society, who is one of the F.S.M.'s applauders. 'All the old labels are out. . . .' "

And: "The proudly immoderate zealots of the F.S.M. pursue an activist creed—that only commitment can strip life of its emptiness, its absence of meaning in a great 'knowledge factory' like Berkeley."

An article in *The Saturday Evening Post* (May 8, 1965), discussing the various youth groups of the left, quotes a leader of Students for a Democratic Society:

"We began by rejecting the old sectarian left and its ancient quarrels, and with a contempt for American society, which we saw as depraved. We are interested in direct action and specific issues. We do not spend endless hours debating the nature of Soviet Russia or whether Yugoslavia is a degenerate workers' state." And: "With sit-ins we saw for the first time the chance for direct participation in meaningful social revolution."

"In their off-picket-line hours," states the same article, "the P.L. [Progressive Labor] youngsters hang out at the experimental theaters and coffee shops of Manhattan's East Village. Their taste in reading runs more to Sartre than to Marx."

With an interesting touch of unanimity, a survey in *Newsweek* (March 22, 1965) quotes a young man on the other side of the continent: " 'These students don't read Marx,' said one Berkeley Free Student Movement leader, 'they read Camus.' "

"If they are rebels," the survey continues, "they are rebels without an ideology, and without long-range revolutionary programs. They rally over issues, not philosophies, and seem unable to formulate or sustain a systematized political theory of society, either from the left or right."

"Today's student seeks to find himself through what he does, not what he thinks," the survey declares explicitly—and quotes some adult authorities in sympathetic confirmation. " 'What you have now, as in the 30's,' says *New York Post* editor James A. Wechsler, 'are groups of activists who really want to function in life.' But not ideologically. 'We used to sit around and debate Marxism, but students now are working for civil-rights and peace.' " Richard Unsworth, chaplain at Dartmouth, is quoted as saying: "In the world of today's campus 'the avenue now is doing and then reflecting on your doing, instead of reflecting, then deciding, and then doing, the way it was a few years ago.' " Paul Goodman, described as writer, educator and "one of the students' current heroes," is quoted as hailing the Berkeley movement because: "The leaders of the insurrection, he says, 'didn't play it cool, they took risks, *they were willing to be confused,* they didn't know whether it all would be a success or a failure. Now they don't want to be cool any more, they want to take over.' " (Italics mine. The same tribute could be paid to any drunken driver.)

The theme of "taking over" is repeated again and again. The immediate target, apparently, is the takeover of the universities. *The New York Times Magazine* article quotes one of the F.S.M. leaders: "Our idea is that the university is composed of faculty, students, books and ideas. In a literal sense, the administration is merely there to make sure the sidewalks are kept clean. It should be the servant of the faculty and the students."

The climax of this particular line was a news-story in *The New York Times* (March 29, 1965) under the heading: "Collegians adopt a 'Bill of Rights.' "

"A group of Eastern college students declared here [in Philadelphia] this weekend that college administrators should be no more than housekeepers in the educational community.

"The modern college or university, they said, should be run by the students and the professors; administrators would be 'maintenance, clerical and safety personnel whose purpose is to enforce the will of faculty and students.' "

A manifesto to this effect was adopted at a meeting held at the University of Pennsylvania and attended by 200 youths "from 39 colleges in the Philadelphia and New York areas, Harvard, Yale, the University of California at Berkeley, and from schools in the Midwest."

"A recurring theme in the meeting was that colleges and universities had become servants of the 'financial, industrial, and military establishment,' and that students and faculty were being 'sold down the river' by administrators.

"Among the provisions of the manifesto were declarations of freedom to join, organize or hold meetings of any organization . . . abolition of tuition fees; control of law enforcement by the students and faculty; an end to the Reserve Officer Training Corps; abolition of loyalty oaths; student-faculty control over curriculum. . . ."

The method used to adopt that manifesto is illuminating: "About 200 students attended the meeting, 45 remaining until the end when the 'Student Bill of Rights' was adopted." So much for "democratic procedures" and for the activists' right to the title of spokesmen for American youth.

What significance is ascribed to the student rebellion by all these reports and by the authorities they choose to quote? Moral courage is not a characteristic of today's culture, but in no other contemporary issue has moral cowardice been revealed to such a naked, ugly extent. Not only do most of the commentators lack an independent evaluation of the events, not only do they take their cue from the rebels, but of all the rebels' complaints, it is the most superficial, irrelevant and, therefore, the *safest,* that they choose to support and to accept as the cause of the rebellion: the complaint that the universities have grown "too big."

As if they had mushroomed overnight, the "bigness" of the universities is suddenly decried by the consensus as a national problem and blamed for the "unrest" of the students, whose motives are hailed as youthful "idealism." In today's culture, it has always been safe to attack "bigness." And since the meaningless issue of mere *size* has long served as a means of evading real issues, on all sides of all political fences, a new catch phrase has been added to the list of "Big Business," "Big Labor," "Big Government," etc.: "Big University."

For a more sophisticated audience, the socialist magazine *The New Leader* (Dec. 21, 1964) offers a Marxist-Freudian appraisal, ascribing the rebellion primarily to "alienation" (quoting Savio: "Somehow people are being separated off from something") and to "generational revolt" ("Spontaneously the natural idiom of the student political protest was that of sexual protest against the forbidding university administrator who ruled *in loco parentis*").

But the prize for expressing the moral-intellectual essence of today's culture should go to Governor Brown of California. Remember that the University of California is a state institution, that its Regents are appointed by the Governor and that he, therefore, was the ultimate target of the revolt, including all its manifestations, from physical violence to filthy language.

"Have we made our society safe for students with ideas?" said Governor Brown at a campus dinner. (*The New York Times,* May 22, 1965.) "We have not. Students have changed but the structure of the university and its attitudes towards its students have not kept pace with that change.

"Therefore, some students felt they had the right to go outside the law to force the change. But in so doing, they displayed the height of *idealistic hypocrisy.* [Italics mine.] On the one hand, they held up the Federal Constitution, demanding their rights of political advocacy. But at the same time, they threw away the principle of due process in favor of direct action.

"In doing so, they were as wrong as the university. This, then, is the great challenge that faces us, the challenge of change."

Consider the fact that Governor Brown is generally regarded as a powerful chief executive and, by California Republicans, as a formidable opponent. Consider the fact that "according to the California Public Opinion Poll, 74 percent of the people disapprove of the student protest movement in Berkeley." (*The New Leader,* April 12, 1965.) Then observe that Governor Brown did not dare denounce a movement led or manipulated by a group of 45 students—and that he felt obliged to qualify the term "hypocrisy" by the adjective "idealistic," thus creating one of the weirdest combinations in today's vocabulary of evasion.

Now observe that in all that mass of comments, appraisals and interpretations (including the ponderous survey in *Newsweek* which offered statistics on every imaginable aspect of college life) not one word was said about the *content* of modern education, about *the nature of the ideas* that are being inculcated by today's universities. Every possible question was raised and considered, except: *What are the students taught to think?* This, apparently, was what no one dared discuss.

This is what we shall now proceed to discuss.

If a dramatist had the power to convert philosophical ideas into real, flesh-and-blood people and attempted to create the walking embodiments of modern philosophy—the result would be the Berkeley rebels.

These "activists" are so fully, literally, loyally, devastatingly the products of modern philosophy that someone should cry to all the university administrations and faculties: "Brothers, you asked for it!"

Mankind could not expect to remain unscathed after decades of exposure to the radiation of intellectual fission-debris, such as: "Reason is impotent to know things as they are—reality is unknowable—certainty is impossible—knowledge is mere probability—truth is that which works—mind is a superstition—logic is a social convention—ethics is a matter of subjective commitment to an arbitrary postulate"—and the consequent mutations are those contorted young creatures who scream, in chronic terror, that they know nothing and want to rule everything.

If that dramatist were writing a movie, he could justifiably entitle it "Mario Savio, Son of Immanuel Kant."

With rare and academically neglected exceptions, the philosophical "mainstream" that seeps into every classroom, subject and brain in today's universities, is: epistemological agnosticism, avowed irrationalism, ethical subjectivism. Our age is witnessing the ultimate climax, the cashing-in on a long process of destruction, at the end of the road laid out by Kant.

Ever since Kant divorced reason from reality, his intellectual descendants have been diligently widening the breach. In the name of reason, Pragmatism established a range-of-the-moment view as an enlightened perspective on life, context-dropping as a rule of epistemology, expediency as a principle of morality, and collective subjectivism as a substitute for metaphysics. Logical Positivism carried it further and, in the name of reason, elevated the immemorial psycho-epistemology of shyster lawyers to the status of a scientific epistemological system—by proclaiming that knowledge consists of linguistic manipulations. Taking this seriously, Linguistic Analysis declared that the task of philosophy is, not to identify universal principles, but to tell people what they mean when they speak, which they are otherwise unable to know (which last, by that time, was true—in philosophical circles). This was the final stroke of philosophy breaking its moorings and floating off, like a lighter-than-air balloon, losing any semblance of connection to reality, any relevance to the problems of man's existence.

No matter how cautiously the proponents of such theories skirted any reference to the relationship between theory and practice, no matter how coyly they struggled to treat philosophy as a parlor or classroom game—the fact remained that young people went to college for the purpose of acquiring *theoretical* knowledge to guide them in *practical* action. Philosophy teachers evaded questions about the application of their ideas to reality, by such means as declaring that "reality is a meaningless term," or by asserting that philosophy has no purpose other than the amusement of manufacturing arbitrary "constructs," or by urging students to temper every theory with "common sense"—the common sense they had spent countless hours trying to invalidate.

As a result, a student came out of a modern university with the following sediment left in his brain by his four to eight years of study: existence is an uncharted, unknowable jungle, fear and uncertainty are man's permanent state, skepticism is the mark of maturity, cynicism is the mark of realism and, above all, the hallmark of an intellectual is the denial of the intellect.

When and if academic commentators gave any thought to the practical results of their theories, they were predominantly united in claiming that uncertainty and skepticism are socially valuable traits which would lead to tolerance of differences, flexibility, social "adjustment" and willingness to compromise. Some went so far as to maintain explicitly that intellectual certainty is the mark of a dictatorial mentality, and that chronic *doubt*—the absence of firm convictions, the lack of absolutes—is the guarantee of a peaceful, "democratic" society.

They miscalculated.

It has been said that Kant's dichotomy led to two lines of Kantian philosophers, both accepting his basic premises, but choosing opposite sides: those who chose reason, abandoning reality—and those who chose reality, abandoning reason. The first delivered the world to the second.

The collector of the Kantian rationalizers' efforts—the receiver of the bankrupt shambles of sophistry, casuistry, sterility and abysmal triviality to which they had reduced philosophy—was *Existentialism.*

Existentialism, in essence, consists of pointing to modern philosophy and declaring: "Since *this* is reason, to hell with it!"

In spite of the fact that the pragmatists-positivists-analysts had obliterated reason, the existentialists accepted them as reason's advocates, held them up to the world as examples of rationality and proceeded to reject reason altogether, proclaiming its impotence, rebelling against its "failure," calling for a return to reality, to the problems of human existence, to values, to action—to subjective values and mindless action. In the name of reality, they proclaimed the moral supremacy of "instincts," urges, feelings—and the cognitive powers of stomachs, muscles, kidneys, hearts, blood. It was a rebellion of headless bodies.

The battle is not over. The philosophy departments of today's universities are the battleground of a struggle which, in fact, is only a family quarrel between the analysts and the existentialists. Their progeny are the activists of the student rebellion.

If these activists choose the policy of "doing and then reflecting on your doing"—hasn't Pragmatism taught them that truth is to be judged by consequences? If they "seem unable to formulate or sustain a systematized political theory of society," yet shriek with moral righteousness that they propose to achieve their social goals by physical force—hasn't Logical Positivism taught them that ethical propositions have no cognitive meaning and are merely a report on one's feelings or the equivalent of emotional ejaculations? If they are savagely blind to everything but the immediate moment—hasn't Logical Positivism taught them that nothing else can be claimed with certainty to exist? And while the Linguistic Analysts are busy demonstrating that "The cat is on the mat" does *not* mean that "the mat" is an attribute of "the cat," nor that "on-the-mat" is the genus to which "the cat" belongs, nor yet that "the-cat" equals "on-the-mat"—is it any wonder that students storm the Berkeley campus with placards inscribed "Strike now, analyze later"? (This slogan is quoted by Professor Petersen in the *Columbia University Forum.*)

On June 14, CBS televised a jumbled, incoherent, unintelligible—and for these very reasons, authentic and significant—documentary entitled "The Berkeley Story." There is method in every kind of madness—and for those acquainted with modern philosophy, that documentary was like a display of sideshow mirrors throwing off twisted reflections and random echoes of the carnage perpetrated in the academic torture-chambers of the mind.

"Our generation has no ideology," declared the first boy interviewed, in the tone of defiance and hatred once reserved for saying: "Down with Wall Street!"—clearly projecting that the enemy now is not the "Robber Barons," but *the mind.* The older generation, he explained scornfully, had "a neat little pill" to solve everything, but the pill didn't work and they merely "got their hearts busted." "We don't believe in pills," he said.

"We've learned that there are no absolute rules," said a young girl, hastily and defensively, as if uttering an axiom—and proceeded to explain inarticulately, with the help of gestures pointing inward, that "we make rules for ourselves" and that what is right for *her* may not be right for others.

A girl described her classes as "words, words, words, paper, paper, paper"—and quietly, in a tone of authentic despair, said that she stopped at times to wonder: "What am I doing here? I'm not learning anything."

An intense young girl who talked volubly, never quite finishing a sentence nor making a point, was denouncing society in general, trying to say that since people are social products, society has done a bad job. In the middle of a sentence, she stopped and threw in, as a casual aside: "Whatever way I turn out, I still am a product," then went on. She said it with the simple earnestness of a conscientious child acknowledging a self-evident fact of nature. It was not an act: the poor little creature meant it.

The helpless bewilderment on the face of Harry Reasoner, the commentator, when he tried to sum up what he had presented, was an eloquent indication of why the press is unable properly to handle the student rebellion. "Now—immediacy—any situation must be solved *now,*" he said incredulously, describing the rebels' attitude, neither praising nor blaming, in the faintly astonished, faintly helpless tone of a man unable to believe that he is seeing savages running loose on the campus of one of America's great universities.

Such are the products of modern philosophy. They are the type of students who are too intelligent not to see the logical consequences of the theories they have been taught—but not intelligent nor independent enough to see through the theories and reject them.

So they scream their defiance against "The System," not realizing that they are its most consistently docile pupils, that theirs is a rebellion against the status quo by its archetypes, against the intellectual "Establishment" by its robots who have swallowed every shopworn premise of the "liberals" of the 1930's, including the catchphrases of altruism, the dedication to "deprived people," to such a safely *conventional* cause as "the war on poverty." A rebellion that brandishes banners inscribed with bromides is not a very convincing nor very inspiring sight.

As in any movement, there is obviously a mixture of motives involved: there are the little shysters of the intellect who have found a gold mine in modern philosophy, who delight in arguing for argument's sake and stumping opponents by means of ready-to-wear paradoxes—there are the little role-players who fancy themselves as heroes and enjoy defiance for the sake of defiance—there are the nihilists who, moved by a profound hatred, seek nothing but destruction for the sake of destruction—there are the hopeless dependents who seek to "belong" to any crowd that would have them—and there are the plain hooligans who are always there, on the fringes of any mob action that smells of trouble. Whatever the combination of motives, *neurosis* is stamped in capital letters across the whole movement, since there is no such thing as rejecting reason through an innocent error of knowledge. But whether the theories of modern philosophy serve merely as a screen, a defense-mechanism, a rationalization of neurosis or are, in part, its cause—the fact remains that modern philosophy has destroyed the best in these students and fostered the worst.

Young people do seek a comprehensive view of life, i.e., a philosophy, they do seek meaning, purpose, ideals—and most of them take what they get. It is in their teens and early twenties that most people seek philosophical answers and set their premises, for good or evil, for the rest of their lives. Some never reach that stage; some never give up the quest; but the majority are open to the voice of philosophy for a few brief years. These last are the permanent, if not innocent, victims of modern philosophy.

They are not independent thinkers nor intellectual originators; they are unable to answer or withstand the flood of modern sophistries. So some of them give up, after one or two unintelligible courses, convinced that thinking is a waste of time—and turn into lethargic cynics or stultified Babbitts by the time they reach twenty-five. Others accept what they hear; they accept it blindly and *literally;* these are today's activists. And no matter what tangle of motives now moves them, every teacher of modern philosophy should cringe in their presence, if he is still open to the realization that it is by means of the best within them, by means of their twisted, precarious groping for ideas, that he has turned them into grotesque little monstrosities.

Now what happens to the better minds in modern universities, to the students of above average intelligence who are actually eager to learn? What they find and have to endure is a long, slow process of psycho-epistemological torture.

Directly or indirectly, the influence of philosophy sets the epistemological standards and methods of teaching for all departments, in the physical sciences as well as in the humanities. The consequence, today, is a chaos of subjective whims setting the criteria of logic, of communication, demonstration, evidence, proof, which differ from class to class, from teacher to teacher. I am not speaking of a difference in viewpoint or content, but of the absence of *basic epistemological principles* and the consequent difference in the method of functioning required of a student's mind. It is as if each course were given in a different language, each requiring that one *think* exclusively in that language, none providing a dictionary. The result—to the extent that one would attempt to comply—is intellectual disintegration.

Add to this: the opposition to "system-building," i.e., to the integration of knowledge, with the result that the material taught in one class contradicts the material taught in the others, each subject hanging in a vacuum and to be accepted out of context, while any questions on how to integrate it are rejected, discredited and discouraged.

Add to this: the arbitrary, senseless, haphazard conglomeration of most curricula, the absence of any hierarchical structure of knowledge, any order, continuity or rationale—the jumble of courses on out-of-context minutiae and out-of-focus surveys—the all-pervading unintelligibility—the arrogantly self-confessed irrationality—and, consequently, the necessity to memorize, rather than learn, to recite, rather than understand, to hold in one's mind a cacophony of undefined jargon long enough to pass the next exam.

Add to this: the professors who refuse to answer questions—the professors who answer by evasion and ridicule—the professors who turn their classes into bull-sessions on the premise that "we're here to mull things over together"—the professors who *do* lecture, but, in the name of "anti-dogmatism," take no stand, express no viewpoint and leave the students in a maze of contradictions with no lead to a solution—the professors who *do* take a stand and invite the students' comments, then penalize dissenters by means of lower grades (particularly in political courses).

Add to this: the moral cowardice of most university administrations, the policy of permanent moral neutrality, of compromising on anything, of evading any conflict at any price—and the students' knowledge that the worst classroom injustice will remain uncorrected, that no appeal is practicable and no justice is to be found anywhere.

Yes, of course, there are exceptions—there *are* competent educators, brilliant minds and rational men on the university staffs—but they are swallowed in the rampaging "mainstream" of irrationality and, too often, defeated by the hopeless pessimism of bitter, long-repressed frustration.

And further: most professors and administrators are much more competent and rational as individuals than they are in their collective performance. Most of them realize and, privately, complain about the evils of today's educational world. But each of them feels individually impotent before the enormity of the problem. So they blame it on some nameless, disembodied, almost mystical power, which they designate as "The System"—and too many of them take it to be a *political* system, specifically *capitalism.* They do not realize that there is only one human discipline which enables men to deal with large-scale problems, which has the power to integrate and unify human activities—and that that discipline is *philosophy,* which they have set, instead, to the task of disintegrating and destroying their work.

What does all this do to the best minds among the students? Most of them endure their college years with the teeth-clenched determination of serving out a jail sentence. The psychological scars they acquire in the process are incalculable. But they struggle as best they can to preserve their capacity to think, sensing dimly that the essence of the torture is an assault on their mind. And what they feel toward their schools ranges from mistrust to resentment to contempt to hatred—intertwined with a sense of exhaustion and excruciating boredom.

To various extents and various degrees of conscious awareness, these feelings are shared by the entire pyramid of the student body, from intellectual top to bottom. *This* is the reason why the handful of Berkeley rebels was able to attract thousands of students who did not realize, at first, the nature of what they were joining and who withdrew when it became apparent. Those students were moved by a desperate, incoherent frustration, by a need to protest, not knowing fully against what, by a blind desire to strike out at the university somehow.

I asked a small group of intelligent students at one of New York's best universities—who were ideologically opposed to the rebels—whether they would fight for the university administration, if the rebellion came to their campus. All of them shook their heads, with faint, wise, bitter smiles.

The philosophical impotence of the older generation is the reason why the adult authorities—from the Berkeley administration to the social commentators to the press to Governor Brown—were unable to take a firm stand and had no rational answer to the Berkeley rebellion. Granting the premises of modern philosophy, logic was on the side of the rebels. To answer them would require a *total* philosophical re-evaluation, down to basic premises—which none of those adults would dare attempt.

Hence the incredible spectacle of brute force, hoodlum tactics and militantly explicit irrationality being brought to a university campus—and being met by the vague, uncertain, apologetic concessions, the stale generalities, the evasive platitudes of the alleged defenders of academic law and order.

In a civilized society, a student's declaration that he rejects reason and proposes to act outside the bounds of rationality, would be taken as sufficient grounds for immediate expulsion—let alone if he proceeded to engage in mob action and physical violence on a university campus. But modern universities have long since lost the moral right to oppose the first—and are, therefore, impotent against the second.

The student rebellion is an eloquent demonstration of the fact that when men abandon reason, they open the door to physical force as the only alternative and the inevitable consequence.

The rebellion is also one of the clearest refutations of the argument of those intellectuals who claimed that skepticism and chronic doubt would lead to social harmony. "When men reduce their virtues to the approximate, then evil acquires the force of an absolute, when loyalty to an unyielding purpose is dropped by the virtuous, it's picked up by scoundrels—and you get the indecent spectacle of a cringing, bargaining, traitorous good and a self-righteously uncompromising evil." (*Atlas Shrugged*)

Who stands to profit by that rebellion? The answer lies in the nature and goals of its leadership.

If the rank-and-file of the college rebels are victims, at least in part, this cannot be said of their leaders. Who are their leaders? Any and all of the statist-collectivist groups that hover, like vultures, over the remnants of capitalism, hoping to pounce on the carcass—and to accelerate the end, whenever possible. Their minimal goal is just "to make trouble"—to undercut, to confuse, to demoralize, to destroy. Their ultimate goal is to take over.

To such leadership, the college rebels are merely cannon-fodder, intended to stick their headless necks out, to fight on campuses, to go to jail, to lose their careers and their future—and eventually, if the leadership succeeds, to fight in the streets and lose their "non-absolute" lives, paving the way for the absolute dictatorship of whoever is the bloodiest among the thugs scrambling for power. Young fools who refuse to look beyond the immediate *"now,"* have no way of knowing whose long-range goals they are serving.

The communists are involved, among others; but, like the others, they are merely the manipulators, not the cause, of the student rebellion. This is an example of the fact that whenever they win, they win by default—like germs feeding on the sores of a disintegrating body. They did not create the conditions that are destroying American universities—they did not create the hordes of embittered, aimless, neurotic teenagers—but they *do* know how to attack through the sores which their opponents insist on evading. They are professional ideologists and it is not difficult for them to move into an intellectual vacuum and to hang the cringing advocates of "anti-ideology" by their own contradictions.

For its motley leftist leadership, the student rebellion is a trial balloon, a kind of cultural temperature-taking. It is a test of how much they can get away with and what sort of opposition they will encounter.

For the rest of us, it is a miniature preview—in the microcosm of the academic world—of what is to happen to the country at large, if the present cultural trend remains unchallenged.

The country at large is a mirror of its universities. The practical result of modern philosophy is today's mixed economy with its moral nihilism, its range-of-the-moment pragmatism, its anti-ideological ideology and its truly shameful recourse to the notion of "Government by Consensus." (See my article in the May and June 1965 issues of *The Objectivist Newsletter.*)

Rule by pressure groups is merely the prelude, the social conditioning for mob rule. Once a country has accepted the obliteration of moral principles, of individual rights, of objectivity, of justice, of reason, and has submitted to the rule of legalized brute force—the elimination of the concept "legalized" does not take long to follow. Who is to resist it—and in the name of what?

When numbers are substituted for morality, and no individual can claim a right, but any gang can assert any desire whatever, when *compromise* is the only policy expected of those in power, and the preservation of the moment's "stability," of peace at any price, is their only goal—the winner, necessarily, is whoever presents the most unjust and irrational demands; the system serves as an open invitation to do so. If there were no communists or other thugs in the world, such a system would create them.

The more an official is committed to the policy of compromise, the less able he is to resist anything: to give in, is his "instinctive" response in any emergency, his basic principle of conduct, which makes him an easy mark.

In this connection, the extreme of naive superficiality was reached by those commentators who expressed astonishment that the student rebellion had chosen Berkeley as its first battleground and President Kerr as its first target *in spite of* his record as a "liberal" and as a renowned mediator and arbitrator. "Ironically, some of the least mature student spokesmen . . . tried to depict Mr. Kerr as the illiberal administrator," said an editorial in *The New York Times* (March 11, 1965). "This was, of course, absurd in view of Mr. Kerr's long and courageous battle to uphold academic freedom and students' rights in the face of those right-wing pressures that abound in California." Other commentators pictured Mr. Kerr as an innocent victim caught between the conflicting pressures of the "conservatives" on the Board of Regents and the "liberals" on the faculty. But, in fact and in logic, the middle of the road can lead to no other final destination—and it is clear that the rebels chose Clark Kerr as their first target, not *in spite of,* but *because of* his record.

Now project what would happen if the technique of the Berkeley rebellion were repeated on a national scale. Contrary to the fanatical belief of its advocates, compromise does not satisfy, but *dissatisfies* everybody; it does not lead to general fulfillment, but to general frustration; those who try to be all things to all men, end up by not being anything to anyone. And more: the partial victory of an unjust claim, encourages the claimant to try further; the partial defeat of a just claim, discourages and paralyzes the victim. If a determined, disciplined gang of statists were to make an assault on the crumbling remnants of a mixed economy, boldly and explicitly proclaiming the collectivist tenets which the country had accepted by tacit default—what resistance would they encounter? The dispirited, demoralized, embittered majority would remain lethargically indifferent to any public event. And many would support the gang, at first, moved by a desperate, incoherent frustration, by a need to protest, not knowing fully against what, by a blind desire to strike out somehow at the suffocating hopelessness of the status quo.

Who would feel morally inspired to fight for Johnson's "consensus"? Who fought for the aimless platitudes of the Kerensky government in Russia—of the Weimar Republic in Germany—of the Nationalist government in China?

But no matter how badly demoralized and philosophically disarmed a country might be, it has to reach a certain psychological turning point before it can be pushed from a state of semi-freedom into surrender to full-fledged dictatorship. And *this* was the main ideological purpose of the student rebellion's leaders, whoever they were: *to condition the country to accept force as the means of settling political controversies.*

Observe the ideological precedents which the Berkeley rebels were striving to establish: all of them involved the abrogation of rights and the advocacy of force. These notions have been publicized, yet their meaning has been largely ignored and left unanswered.

1. The main issue was the attempt to make the country accept *mass civil disobedience* as a proper and valid tool of political action. This attempt has been made repeatedly in connection with the civil rights movement. But there the issue was confused by the fact that the Negroes *were* the victims of legalized injustice and, therefore, the matter of breaching legality did not become unequivocally clear. The country took it as a fight for justice, not as an assault on the law.

Civil disobedience may be justifiable, in some cases, when and if an individual disobeys a law in order to bring an issue to court, as a test case. Such an action involves respect for legality and a protest directed only at a particular law which the individual seeks an opportunity to prove to be unjust. The same is true of a group of individuals when and if the risks involved are their own.

But there is no justification, in a civilized society, for the kind of mass civil disobedience that involves the violation of the rights of others—regardless of whether the demonstrators' goal is good or evil. The end does *not* justify the means. No one's rights can be secured by the violation of the rights of others. Mass disobedience is an assault on the concept of rights: it is a mob's defiance of legality as such.

The forcible occupation of another man's property or the obstruction of a public thoroughfare is so blatant a violation of rights that an attempt to justify it becomes an abrogation of morality. An individual has no right to do a "sit-in" in the home or office of a person he disagrees with—and he does not acquire such a right by joining a gang. Rights are not a matter of numbers—and there can be no such thing, in law or in morality, as actions forbidden to an individual, but permitted to a mob.

The only power of a mob, as against an individual, is greater muscular strength—i.e., plain, brute physical force. The attempt to solve social problems by means of physical force is what a civilized society is established to prevent. The advocates of mass civil disobedience admit that their purpose is intimidation. A society that tolerates intimidation as a means of settling disputes—the *physical* intimidation of some men or groups by others—loses its moral right to exist as a social system, and its collapse does not take long to follow.

Politically, mass civil disobedience is appropriate only as a prelude to civil war—as the declaration of a total break with a country's political institutions. And the degree of today's intellectual chaos and context-dropping was best illustrated by some "conservative" California official who rushed to declare that he objects to the Berkeley rebellion, but respects civil disobedience as a valid American tradition. "Don't forget the Boston Tea Party," he said, forgetting it.

If the meaning of civil disobedience is somewhat obscured in the civil rights movement—and, therefore, the attitude of the country is inconclusive—that meaning becomes blatantly obvious when a sit-in is staged on a university campus. If the universities—the supposed citadels of reason, knowledge, scholarship, civilization—can be made to surrender to the rule of brute force, the rest of the country is cooked.

2. To facilitate the acceptance of force, the Berkeley rebels attempted to establish a special distinction between *force* and *violence:* force, they claimed explicitly, is a proper form of social action, but violence is not. Their definition of the terms was as follows: coercion by means of a *literal* physical contact is "violence" and is reprehensible; any other way of violating rights is merely "force" and is a legitimate, peaceful method of dealing with opponents.

For instance, if the rebels occupy the administration building, that is "force"; if policemen drag them out, that is "violence." If Savio seizes a microphone he has no right to use, that is "force"; if a policeman drags him away from it, that is "violence."

Consider the implications of that distinction as a rule of social conduct: if you come home one evening, find a stranger occupying your house and throw him out bodily, he has merely committed a peaceful act of "force," but *you* are guilty of "violence" and *you* are to be punished.

The theoretical purpose of that grotesque absurdity is to establish a moral inversion: to make the *initiation* of force moral, and *resistance* to force immoral—and thus to obliterate *the right of self-defense.* The immediate practical purpose is to foster the activities of the lowest political breed: the provocateurs, who commit acts of force and place the blame on their victims.

3. To justify that fraudulent distinction, the Berkeley rebels attempted to obliterate a legitimate one: the distinction between

ideas and *actions.* They claimed that freedom of speech means freedom of action and that no clear line of demarcation can be drawn between them.

For instance, if they have the right to advocate any political viewpoint—they claimed—they have the right to organize, on campus, any off-campus activities, even those forbidden by law. As Professor Petersen put it, they were claiming the right "to use the University as a sanctuary from which to make illegal raids on the general community."

The difference between an exchange of ideas and an exchange of blows is self-evident. The line of demarcation between freedom of speech and freedom of action is established by the ban on the initiation of physical force. It is only when that ban is abrogated that such a problem can arise—but when that ban is abrogated, no political freedom of any kind can remain in existence.

At a superficial glance, the rebels' "package-deal" may seem to imply a sort of anarchistic extension of freedom; but, in fact and in logic, it implies the exact opposite—which is a grim joke on those unthinking youths who joined the rebellion in the name of "free speech." If the freedom to express ideas were equated with the freedom to commit crimes, it would not take long to demonstrate that no organized society can exist on such terms and, therefore, that the expression of ideas has to be curtailed and some ideas have to be forbidden, just as criminal acts are forbidden. Thus the gullible would be brought to concede that the right of free speech is undefinable and "impracticable."

4. An indication of such a motive was given by the rebels' demand for unrestricted freedom of speech on campus—with the consequent "Filthy Language Movement."

There can be no such thing as the right to an unrestricted freedom of speech (or of action) *on someone else's property.* The fact that the university at Berkeley is owned by the state, merely complicates the issue, but does not alter it. The owners of a state university are the voters and taxpayers of that state. The university administration, appointed (directly or indirectly) by an elected official, is, theoretically, the agent of the owners—and has to act as such, so long as state universities exist. (Whether they *should* exist, is a different question.)

In any undertaking or establishment involving more than one man, it is the owner or owners who set the rules and terms of appropriate conduct; the rest of the participants are free to go elsewhere and seek different terms, if they do not agree. There can be no such thing as the right to act on whim, to be exercised by some participants at the expense of others.

Students who attend a university have the right to expect that they will not be subjected to hearing the kind of obscenities for which the owner of a semi-decent barroom would bounce hoodlums out onto the street. The right to determine what sort of language is permissible, belongs to the administration of a university—fully as much as to the owner of a barroom.

The technique of the rebels, as of all statists, was to take advantage of the principles of a free society in order to undercut them by an alleged demonstration of their "impracticability"—in this case, the "impracticability" of the right of free speech. But, in fact, what they have demonstrated is a point farthest removed from their goals: that *no rights of any kind can be exercised without property rights.*

It is only on the basis of property rights that the sphere and application of individual rights can be defined in any given social situation. Without property rights, there is no way to solve or to avoid a hopeless chaos of clashing views, interests, demands, desires and whims.

There was no way for the Berkeley administration to answer the rebels except by invoking property rights. It is obvious why neither modern "liberals" nor "conservatives" would care to do so. It is not the contradictions of a free society that the rebels were exposing and cashing-in on, but the contradictions of a mixed economy.

As to the question of what ideological policy should properly be adopted by the administration of a state university, it is a question that has no answer. There are no solutions for the many contradictions inherent in the concept of "public property," particularly when the property is directly concerned with the dissemination of ideas. This is one of the reasons why the rebels would choose a state university as their first battleground.

A good case could be made for the claim that a state university has no right to forbid the teaching or advocacy of any political viewpoint whatever, as, for instance, of communism, since some of the taxpaying owners may be communists. An equally good case could be made for the claim that a state university has no right to permit the teaching and advocacy of any political viewpoint which (as, for instance, communism) is a direct threat to the property, freedom and lives of the majority of the taxpaying owners. Majority rule is not applicable in the realm of ideas; an individual's convictions are not subject to a majority vote; but neither an individual nor a minority nor a majority should be forced to support their own destroyers.

On the one hand, a government institution has no right to forbid the expression of any ideas. On the other hand, a government institution has no right to harbor, assist and finance the country's enemies (as, for instance, the collectors of funds for the Vietcong).

The source of these contradictions does not lie in the principle of individual rights, but in their violation by the collectivist institution of "public property."

This issue, however, has to be fought in the field of constitutional law, not on campus. As students, the rebels have no greater rights in a state university than in a private one. As taxpayers, they have no greater rights than the millions of other California taxpayers involved. If they object to the policies of the Board of Regents, they have no recourse except at the polls at the next election—if they can persuade a sufficient number of voters. This is a pretty slim chance—and this is a good argument *against* any type of "public property." But it is not an issue to be solved by physical force.

What is significant here is the fact that the rebels—who, to put it mildly, are *not* champions of private property—refused to abide by the kind of majority rule which is inherent in public ownership. *That* is what they were opposing when they complained that universities have become servants of the "financial, industrial and military establishment." It is the rights of these particular groups of taxpayers (the right to a voice in the management of state universities) that they were seeking to abrogate.

If anyone needs proof of the fact that the advocates of public ownership are not seeking "democratic" control of property by majority rule, but control by dictatorship—this is one eloquent piece of evidence.

5. As part of the ideological conditioning for that ultimate goal, the rebels attempted to introduce a new variant on an old theme that has been the object of an intense drive by all statist-collec-

tivists for many years past: the obliteration of the difference between private action and government action.

This has always been attempted by means of a "package-deal" ascribing to private citizens the specific violations constitutionally forbidden to the government, and thus destroying individual rights while freeing the government from any restrictions. The most frequent example of this technique consists of accusing private citizens of practicing "censorship" (a concept applicable only to the government) and thus negating their right to disagree. (See my article on "Man's Rights" in the April 1963 issue of *The Objectivist Newsletter.*)

The new variant provided by the rebels was their protest against alleged "double jeopardy." It went as follows: if the students commit illegal acts, they will be punished by the courts and must not, therefore, be penalized by the university for the same offense.

"Double jeopardy" is a concept applicable only to *one* branch of the government, the judiciary, and only to a specific judiciary action: it means that a man must not be put on trial twice for the same offense.

To equate private judgment and action (or, in this context, a government official's judgment and action) with a court trial, is worse than absurd. It is an outrageous attempt to obliterate the right to moral judgment and moral action. It is a demand that a lawbreaker suffer no *civil* consequences of his crime.

If such a notion were accepted, individuals would have no right to evaluate the conduct of others nor to act according to their evaluation. They would have to wait until a court had decreed whether a given man was guilty or innocent—and even after he was pronounced guilty, they would have no right to change their behavior toward him and would have to leave the task of penalizing him exclusively to the government.

For instance, if a bank employee were found guilty of embezzlement and had served his sentence, the bank would have no right to refuse to give him back his former job—since a refusal would constitute "double jeopardy."

Or: a government official would have no right to watch the legality of the actions of his department's employees, nor to lay down rules for their strict observance of the law, but would have to wait until a court had found them guilty of law-breaking—and would have to reinstate them in their jobs, after they had served their sentences for influence-peddling or bribe-taking or treason.

The notion of *morality as a monopoly of the government* (and of a single branch or group within the government) is so blatantly a part of the ideology of a dictatorship that the rebels' attempt to get away with it is truly shocking.

6. The rebels' notion that universities should be run by students and faculties was an open, explicit assault on the right attacked implicitly by all their other notions: the right of private property. And of all the various statist-collectivist systems, the one they chose as their goal is, politico-economically, the least practical; intellectually, the least defensible; morally, the most shameful: *Guild Socialism.*

Guild socialism is a system that abolishes the exercise of individual ability by chaining men into groups according to their line of work, and delivering the work into the group's power, as its exclusive domain, with the group dictating the rules, standards and practices of how the work is to be done and who shall or shall not do it.

Guild socialism is the concrete-bound, routine-bound mentality of a savage, elevated into a social theory. Just as a tribe of savages seizes a piece of jungle territory and claims it as a monopoly by reason of the fact of being there—so guild socialism grants a monopoly, not on a jungle forest or water hole, but on a factory or a university—not by reason of a man's ability, achievement or even "public service," but by reason of the fact that he is there.

Just as savages have no concept of causes or consequences, of past or future, and no concept of efficacy beyond the muscular power of their tribe—so guild socialists, finding themselves in the midst of an industrial civilization, regard its institutions as phenomena of nature and see no reason why the gang should not seize them.

If there is any one proof of a man's incompetence, it is the stagnant mentality of a worker (or of a professor) who, doing some small, routine job in a vast undertaking, does not care to look beyond the lever of a machine (or the lectern of a classroom), does not choose to know how the machine (or the classroom) got there or what makes his job possible, and proclaims that the management of the undertaking is parasitical and unnecessary. Managerial work—the organization and integration of human effort into purposeful, large-scale, long-range activities—is, in the realm of action, what man's conceptual faculty is in the realm of cognition. It is beyond the grasp and, therefore, is the first target of the self-arrested, sensory-perceptual mentality.

If there is any one way to confess one's own mediocrity, it is the willingness to place one's work in the absolute power of a group, particularly a group of one's *professional colleagues.* Of any forms of tyranny, this is the worst; it is directed against a single human attribute: the mind—and against a single enemy: the innovator. The innovator, by definition, is the man who challenges the established practices of his profession. To grant a professional monopoly to any group, is to sacrifice human ability and abolish progress; to advocate such a monopoly, is to confess that one has nothing to sacrifice.

Guild socialism is the rule of, by and for mediocrity. Its cause is a society's intellectual collapse; its consequence is a quagmire of stagnation; its historical example is the guild system of the Middle Ages (or, in modern times, the fascist system of Italy under Mussolini).

The rebels' notion that students (along with faculties) should run universities and determine their curricula is a crude absurdity. If an ignorant youth comes to an institution of learning in order to acquire knowledge of a certain science, by what means is he to determine what is relevant and how he should be taught? (In the process of learning, he can judge only whether his teacher's presentation is clear or unclear, logical or contradictory; he cannot determine the proper course and method of teaching, ahead of any knowledge of the subject.) It is obvious that a student who demands the right to run a university (or to decide who should run it) has no knowledge of the concept of knowledge, that his demand is self-contradictory and disqualifies him automatically. The same is true—with a much heavier burden of moral guilt—of the professor who taught him to make such demands and who supports them.

Would you care to be treated in a hospital where the methods of therapy were determined by a vote of doctors and patients?

Yet the absurdity of these examples is merely more obvious—not more irrational nor more vicious—than the standard collectivist claim that workers should take over the factories created by men whose achievement they can neither grasp nor equal. The basic epistemological-moral premise and pattern are the same: the obliteration of reason obliterates the concept of reality, which obliterates the concept of achievement, which obliterates the concept of the distinction between *the earned* and *the unearned.* Then the incompetent can seize factories, the ignorant can seize universities, the brutes can seize scientific research laboratories—and nothing is left in a human society but the power of whim and fist.

What makes guild socialism cruder than (but not different from) most statist-collectivist theories is the fact that it represents the other, the usually unmentioned, side of altruism: it is the voice, not of the givers, but of the receivers. While most altruistic theorists proclaim "the common good" as their justification, advocate self-sacrificial service to the "community" and keep silent about the exact nature or identity of the recipients of sacrifices—guild socialists brazenly declare themselves to be the recipients and present their claims to the community, demanding its services. If they want a monopoly on a given profession, they claim, the rest of the community must give up the right to practice it. If they want a university, they claim, the community must provide it.

And if "selfishness" is taken, by the altruists, to mean the sacrifice of others to self, I challenge them to name an uglier example of it than the pronouncement of the little Berkeley collectivist who declared: "Our idea is that the university is composed of faculty, students, books and ideas. In a literal sense, the administration is merely there to make sure the sidewalks are kept clean. It should be the servant of the faculty and the students."

What did that little disembodied mystic omit from his idea of a university? Who pays the salaries of the faculty? Who provides the livelihood of the students? Who publishes the books? Who builds the classrooms, the libraries, the dormitories—and the sidewalks? Leave it to a modern "mystic of *muscle*" to display the kind of contempt for "vulgar material concerns" that an old-fashioned mystic would not quite dare permit himself.

Who—besides the university administration—is to be the voiceless, rightless "servant" and sidewalk-sweeper of the faculty and students? No, not only the men of productive genius who create the material wealth that makes universities possible, not only the "tycoons of big business," not only the "financial, industrial, and military establishment"—but every taxpayer of the state of California, every man who works for a living, high or low, every human being who earns his sustenance, struggles with his budget, pays for what he gets, and does not permit himself to evade the reality of "vulgar material concerns."

Such is the soul revealed by the ideology of the Berkeley rebellion. Such is the meaning of the rebels' demands and of the ideological precedents they were trying to establish.

Observe the complexity, the equivocations, the tricks, the twists, the intellectual acrobatics performed by these avowed advocates of unbridled feelings—and the ideological consistency of these activists who claim to possess no ideology.

The first round of the student rebellion has not gone over too well. In spite of the gratuitous "puff-job" done by the press, the attitude of the public is a mixture of bewilderment, indifference and antagonism. Indifference—because the evasive vagueness of the press reports was self-defeating: people do not understand what it is all about and see no reason to care. Antagonism—because the American public still holds a profound respect for universities (as they might be and ought to be, but are not any longer), and the commentators' half-laudatory, half-humorous platitudes about the "idealism of youth" have not succeeded in whitewashing the fact that brute physical force was brought to a university campus. That fact has aroused a vague sense of uneasiness in people, a sense of undefined, apprehensive condemnation.

The rebellion's attempt to invade other campuses did not get very far. There were some disgraceful proclamations of appeasement by some university administrators and commencement orators this spring, but no discernible public sympathy.

There were a few instances of a proper attitude on the part of university administrations—an attitude of firmness, dignity and uncompromising severity—notably at Columbia University. A commencement address by Dr. Meng, president of Hunter College, is also worth noting. Declaring that the violation of the rights of others "is intolerable" in an academic community and that any student or teacher guilty of it deserves "instant expulsion," he said: "Yesterday's ivory tower has become today's foxhole. The leisure of the theory class is increasingly occupied in the organization of picket lines, teach-ins, think-ins, and stakeouts of one sort or another." (*The New York Times,* June 18, 1965.)

But even though the student rebellion has not aroused much public sympathy, the most ominous aspect of the situation is the fact that it has not met any *ideological opposition,* that the implications of the rebels' stand have neither been answered nor rejected, that such criticism as it did evoke was, with rare exceptions, evasively superficial.

As a trial balloon, the rebellion has accomplished its leaders' purpose: it has demonstrated that they may have gone a bit too far, bared their teeth and claws a bit too soon, and antagonized many potential sympathizers, even among the "liberals"—but that the road ahead is empty, with no intellectual barricades in sight.

The battle is to continue. The long-range intentions of the student rebellion have been proclaimed repeatedly by the same activists who proclaim their exclusive dedication to the immediate moment. The remnants of the "Free Speech Movement" at Berkeley have been reorganized into a "Free Student Union," which is making militant noises in preparation for another assault. No matter how absurd their notions, the rebels' assaults are directed at the most important philosophical-political issues of our age. These issues cannot be ignored, evaded or bribed away by compromise. When brute force is on the march, compromise is the red carpet. When reason is attacked, common sense is not enough.

Neither a man nor a nation can exist without some form of philosophy. A man has the free will to think or not; if he does not, he takes what he gets. The free will of a nation is its intellectuals; the rest of the country takes what they offer; they set the terms, the values, the course, the goal.

In the absence of intellectual opposition, the rebels' notions will gradually come to be absorbed into the culture. The uncontested absurdities of today are the accepted slogans of tomorrow. They come to be accepted by degrees, by precedent, by implication, by erosion, by default, by dint of constant pressure on one side and constant retreat on the other—until the day when they are suddenly declared to be the country's official ideology. That is the way welfare statism came to be accepted in this country.

What we are witnessing today is an acceleration of the attempts to cash in on the ideological implications of welfare statism and to push beyond it. The college rebels are merely the commandos, charged with the task of establishing ideological beachheads for a full-scale advance of all the statist-collectivist forces against the remnants of capitalism in America; and part of their task is the takeover of the ideological control of America's universities.

If the collectivists succeed, the terrible historical irony will lie in the fact that what looks like a noisy, reckless, belligerent confidence is, in fact, a hysterical bluff. The acceleration of collectivism's advance is not the march of winners, but the blind stampede of losers. Collectivism has lost the battle for men's minds; its advocates know it; their last chance consists of the fact that no one else knows it. If they are to cash in on decades of philosophical corruption, on all the gnawing, scraping, scratching, burrowing to dig a maze of philosophical rat-holes which is about to cave in, it's now or never.

As a cultural-intellectual power and a moral ideal, collectivism died in World War II. If we are still rolling in its direction, it is only by the inertia of a void and the momentum of disintegration. A social movement that began with the ponderous, brain-cracking, dialectical constructs of Hegel and Marx, and ends up with a horde of morally unwashed children, each stamping his foot and shrieking: "I want it *now!*"—is through.

All over the world, while mowing down one helpless nation after another, collectivism has been steadily losing the two elements that hold the key to the future: the brains of mankind and its youth. In regard to the first, observe Britain's "brain drain." In regard to the second, consider the fact (which was not mentioned in the press comments on the student rebellion) that in a predominant number of American universities, the political views of the faculty are perceptibly more "liberal" than those of the student body. (The same is true of the youth of the country at large—as against the older generation, the 35 to 50 age bracket, who were reared under the New Deal and who hold the country's leadership, at present.) That is one of the facts which the student rebellion was intended to disguise.

This is not to say that the anti-collectivists represent a *numerical* majority among college students. The passive supporters of the status quo are always the majority in any group, culture, society or age. But it is not by passive majorities that the trends of a nation are set. Who sets them? Anyone who cares to do so, if he has the intellectual ammunition to win on the battlefield of ideas, which belongs to those who *do* care. Those who don't, are merely social ballast by their own choice and predilection.

The fact that the "non-liberals" among college students (and among the youth of the world) can be identified at present only as "anti-collectivists" is the dangerous element and the question mark in today's situation. They are the young people who are not ready to give up, who want to fight against a swamp of evil, but do not know what is the good. They have rejected the sick, worn platitudes of collectivism—(along with all of its cultural manifestations, including the cult of despair and depravity—the studied mindlessness of jerk-and-moan dancing, singing or acting—the worship of anti-heroes—the experience of looking up to the dissection of a psychotic's brain, for inspiration, and to the bare feet of an inarticulate brute, for guidance—the stupor of reduction to sensory stimuli—the sense of life of a movie such as *Tom Jones*)—but they have found, as yet, no direction, no consistent philosophy, no rational values, no long-range goals. Until and unless they do, their incoherent striving for a better future will collapse before the final thrust of the collectivists.

Historically, we are now in a kind of intellectual no-man's-land—and the future will be determined by those who venture out of the trenches of the status quo. Our direction will depend on whether the venturers are crusaders fighting for a new Renaissance or scavengers pouncing upon the wreckage left of yesterday's battles. The crusaders are not yet ready; the scavengers are.

That is why—in a deeper sense than the little zombies of college campuses will ever grasp—"Now, now, now!" is the last slogan and cry of the ragged, bearded stragglers who had once been an army rallied by the promise of a *scientifically* (!) planned society.

The two most accurate characterizations of the student rebellion, given in the press, were: "Political Existentialism" and "Castroite." Both are concepts pertaining to intellectual bankruptcy: the first stands for the abdication of reason—the second, for that state of hysterical panic which brandishes a fist as its sole recourse.

In preparation for its published survey (March 22, 1965), *Newsweek* conducted a number of polls among college students at large, on various subjects, one of which was the question of who are the students' heroes. The editors of *Newsweek* informed me that my name appeared on the resultant list, and sent an interviewer to question me about my views on the state of modern universities. For reasons best known to themselves, they chose not to publish any part of that interview. What I said (in briefer form) was what I am now saying in this article—with the exception of the concluding remarks which follow and which I want to address most particularly to those college students who chose me as one of their heroes.

Young people are constantly asking what they can do to fight today's disastrous trends; they are seeking some form of action, and wrecking their hopes in blind alleys, particularly every four years, at election time. Those who do not realize that the battle is ideological, had better give up, because they have no chance. Those who do realize it, should grasp that the student rebellion offers them a chance to train themselves for the kind of battle they will have to fight in the world, when they leave the university; a chance, not only to train themselves, but to win the first rounds of that wider battle.

If they seek an important cause, they have the opportunity to fight the rebels, to fight *ideologically,* on *moral-intellectual* grounds—by identifying and exposing the meaning of the rebels' demands, by naming and answering the basic principles which the rebels dare not admit. The battle consists, above all, of providing the country (or all those within hearing) with *ideological answers*—a field of action from which the older generation has deserted under fire.

Ideas cannot be fought except by means of better ideas. The battle consists, not of opposing, but of exposing; not of denouncing, but of disproving; not of evading, but of boldly proclaiming a full, consistent and radical alternative.

This does not mean that rational students should enter debates with the rebels or attempt to convert them: one cannot argue with self-confessed irrationalists. The goal of an ideological battle is to enlighten the vast, helpless, bewildered majority in the universities—and in the country at large—or, rather, the minds of those among the majority who are struggling to find answers or those who, having heard nothing but collectivist sophistries for years, have withdrawn in revulsion and given up.

The first goal of such a battle is to wrest from a handful of beatniks the title of "spokesmen for American youth," which the press is so anxious to grant them. The first step is to make oneself heard, on the campus and outside. There are many civilized ways to do it: protest-meetings, public petitions, speeches, pamphlets, letters-to-editors. It is a much more important issue than picketing the United Nations or parading in support of the House Un-American Activities Committee. And while such futile groups as Young Americans for Freedom are engaged in such undertakings, they are letting the collectivist vanguard speak in their name—in the name of American college students—without any audible sound of protest.

But in order to be heard, one must have something to say. To have that, one must know one's case. One must know it fully, logically, consistently, all the way down to philosophical fundamentals. One cannot hope to fight nuclear experts with Republican pea-shooters. And the leaders behind the student rebellion *are* experts at their particular game.

But they are dangerous only to those who stare at the issues out of focus and hope to fight ideas by means of faith, feelings and fund-raising. You would be surprised how quickly the ideologists of collectivism retreat when they encounter a confident, *intellectual* adversary. Their case rests on appealing to human confusion, ignorance, dishonesty, cowardice, despair. Take the side they dare not touch: appeal to human intelligence.

Collectivism has lost the two crucial weapons that raised it to world power and made all of its victories possible: intellectuality and idealism, or reason and morality. It had to lose precisely at the height of its success, since its claim to both was a fraud: the full, actual reality of socialist-communist-fascist states has demonstrated the brute irrationality of collectivist systems and the inhumanity of altruism as a moral code.

Yet reason and morality are the only weapons that determine the course of history. The collectivists dropped them, because they had no right to carry them. Pick them up; you have.

(*July–September 1965*)

The Chickens' Homecoming

A microcosmic version of what is wrong with today's world, including the cause and the exact mechanics of how it got that way, was enacted at the annual business meeting of the Eastern Division of the American Philosophical Association on December 28, 1969. Like an old-fashioned morality play, the event had an awe-inspiring element of justice: it would be hard to find a group of men who had done more to deserve what they got.

The central debate of the occasion was triggered by some philosophers, described only as "radical," who demanded that the meeting pass a resolution they had drafted. The resolution condemned the war in Vietnam, in blatantly Marxist terms, declaring that it is "a direct consequence of [America's] foreign policy whose basic aim is to make and keep a large part of the world safe for American enterprise"; that American foreign aid, "particularly in underdeveloped countries, amounts to the exploitation of the peoples of these countries" and that it "necessitates the suppression of popular rebellions."

An allegedly conservative group opposed the resolution. According to *The New York Times* (December 29, 1969): "The academics, including some of the nation's best-known thinkers, filled the Grand Ballroom of the Waldorf-Astoria Hotel with hisses and shouts in debating the issue . . .

"While Vietnam was the ostensible subject of debate, the central issue was two conflicting views of the task of philosophy—that the discipline's job is to train minds and advance thought dispassionately and aloof from politics, and that philosophy should bring its talents to bear on the issues of the day. [This is a correct summary of the state of today's philosophy;

note the nature of the false dichotomy, which we shall discuss later.]

"The debate was symptomatic of the uneasiness of many young students and professors in recent years who contend that philosophy has lost touch with American life, being concerned instead with sterile quibbles over abstractions. [This is generosity on the part of the reporter: it is not over *abstractions* that today's philosophers are quibbling.] It is a common saying that philosophy now devotes itself to the problems of philosophy, not the problems of men."

How did the "dispassionate mind-trainers" oppose the radicals? They did as well, and with the same results, as their former students do in comparable situations, such as the conservatives when opposing the liberals, or the liberals when opposing the socialists, or the socialists when opposing the communists, or college administrators when opposing campus thugs: they steadfastly abstained from mentioning any essentials or referring to any fundamental principles.

First, they tried to resort to a typically modern weapon: evasion. "The opponents [of the resolution] made an early attempt to postpone discussion of the issue indefinitely," writes *The New York Times,* "and lost by a vote of 120 to 78."

"I hope," declared the leader of the radicals, "that we are not going to construe ourselves as a narrow professional organization. Our duty as people must take priority over our alleged duty as 'professionals.' "

"This can only damage our association," declared a leader of the opposition. "I plead with you as philosophers to suspend judgment on some of the horrendous things in this resolution." (Ethics, apparently, is not part of philosophy and, in the face of a horrendous resolution, a philosopher must not attempt to discover the truth or falsehood of its allegations: he must not pass judgment, but suspend it.)

If such tactics are futile even in the realm of practical politics (with fifty years of evidence to demonstrate the failure), what could they be expected to achieve in the realm of philosophy? Just exactly what they did achieve. The opponents of the radicals' resolution did not win, they did not walk out, they did not resign: they *compromised.*

The meeting passed an amended resolution that kept the first and last paragraphs of the original virtually intact, but omitted all the rest. It omitted the Marxist evaluation of American foreign policy and condemned the war in Vietnam without reasons or explanations. In other words, it discarded Marxist theory, but accepted its product as if it were a self-evident primary requiring no proof or discussion.

The quality and stature of the amendments may be gauged by the following:

The first paragraph of the original resolution stated that the war in Vietnam constitutes "a moral and political problem." The amendment changed it to "a moral problem" (in the hope that no one would accuse the A.P.A. of taking a *political* stand—even though the resolution deals with the war in Vietnam).

The last paragraph of the original resolution read: "Therefore, it is the sense of the American Philosophical Association that we oppose both the Vietnamization of the war and the claim that the United States has any right to negotiate the future of the Vietnamese people, and we advocate instead the total withdrawal from Vietnam of all American forces as fast as the boats and planes can carry them."

The last paragraph of the amended resolution reads: "It is the sense of the Eastern Division of the American Philosophical Association that we oppose both the policy of bombing villages to compensate for partial withdrawal of U.S. troops and the claim that the U.S. has any right to negotiate the future of the Vietnamese people, and we advocate instead the total withdrawal from Vietnam of all American forces as soon as physically possible."

Just as politicians feel it safe to take a firm stand in favor of motherhood, so their equivalents in philosophy felt it safe to take a stand against the bombing of villages. The implication, in their resolution, that such bombing is not a military necessity, but a deliberate, senseless atrocity on the part of the U.S. would be clear to a schoolboy, but, apparently, not to modern philosophers. Nor would it occur to them that viewing the war in Vietnam as a *moral* problem and condemning the U.S., without a word about the nature, methods and atrocities of the enemy, is a moral obscenity—particularly in view of the fact that the U.S. has nothing to gain from that suicidal war and undertook it only in compliance with these same philosophers' morality of altruism.

Apparently for fear of having succeeded at creating confusion and being misunderstood, the author of the amended resolution wrote a letter to the Editor of *The New York Times* (February 7, 1970) to correct its report: "The story and headlines present the event as a victory of right-wing over left while, in fact, it was a victory for the moderate left. After all, the Putnam resolution was passed, although with my moderating amendment." So it was, which made matters much worse for the American Philosophical Association—which is always the case when the moderates deal with moral issues, morality being a realm where no compromise is possible.

(An extra touch of grim justice: the author of the amended resolution had been a graduate philosophy student under one of the leaders of the conservative opposition.)

The original resolution was more honest than the amended one, and more philosophical: it stated its theoretical base. That base (Marxism) is false as hell, but its very falsehood defeats it and works to protect the unwary: when people know the theoretical grounds of any given stand, they are able to check it, to judge and to decide whether they agree or not. To name one's principles is to open one's declarations to serious critical appraisal. But the evasion of theory, the enunciation of arbitrary inexplicable pronouncements, is an act of destruction that no Marxist theories could match: it destroys *epistemology.* It undercuts the principles of rationality, invalidates the processes of a civilized discussion, discards logic and replaces it with the "Sez you—Sez I" method of communication—which the campus activists are using to great advantage.

If you wonder how it came about that the American people were never given a chance to vote on the question of whether they want to adopt socialism, yet virtually the entire program of *The Communist Manifesto* has been enacted into law in this country—you have seen that process reenacted at a philosophical convention.

To discard a theory, yet accept its product—to discard (or to hide) the Marxist means, but adopt and propagate its end—is contemptible, even for politicians. When philosophers do it, it amounts to a declaration that philosophy is dead and that it died of unemployment.

By way of an autopsy, examine the false dichotomy mentioned earlier, the "two conflicting views of the task of philosophy." One side holds that the task is "to train minds and advance thought" and that politics is not philosophy's concern; the other side holds that it is, and that philosophy must deal with "the issues of the day." What subject is omitted from this dichotomy? *Politics*—in the full, exact, *philosophical* meaning of the term.

Politics is the study of the principles governing the proper organization of society; it is based on *ethics,* the study of the proper values to guide man's choices and actions. Both ethics and politics, necessarily, have been branches of philosophy from its birth.

Philosophy is the science that studies the fundamental aspects of the nature of existence. The task of philosophy is to provide man with a comprehensive view of life. This view serves as a base, a frame of reference, for all his actions, mental or physical, psychological or existential. This view tells him the nature of the universe with which he has to deal (metaphysics); the means by which he is to deal with it, i.e., the means of acquiring knowledge (epistemology); the standards by which he is to choose his goals and values, in regard to his own life and character (ethics)—and in regard to society (politics); the means of concretizing this view is given to him by esthetics.

It is not a question of whether man chooses to be guided by a comprehensive view: he is not equipped to survive without it. The nature of his consciousness does not permit him an animal's percept-guided, range-of-the-moment form of existence. No matter how primitive his actions, he needs to project them into the future and to weigh their consequences; this requires a *conceptual* process, and a conceptual process cannot take place in a vacuum: it requires a *context.* Man's choice is not whether he needs a comprehensive view of life, but only whether his view is true or false. If it is false, it leads him to act as his own destroyer.

In the early stages of mankind's development, that view was provided by religion, i.e., by mystic fantasy. Man's psycho-epistemological need is the reason why even the most primitively savage tribes always clung to some form of religious belief; the mystic (i.e., anti-reality) nature of their view was the cause of mankind's incalculably long stagnation.

Man came into his own in Greece, some two-and-a-half thousand years ago. The birth of philosophy marked his adulthood; not the *content* of any particular system of philosophy, but deeper: the *concept* of philosophy—the realization that a comprehensive view of existence is to be reached by man's *mind.*

Philosophy is the goal toward which religion was only a helplessly blind groping. The grandeur, the reverence, the exalted purity, the austere dedication to the pursuit of truth, which are commonly associated with religion, should properly belong to the field of philosophy. Aristotle lived up to it and, in part, so did Plato, Aquinas, Spinoza—but how many others? It is earlier than we think.

If you observe that ever since Hume and Kant (mainly Kant, because Hume was merely the Bertrand Russell of his time) philosophy has been striving to prove that man's mind is impotent, that there's no such thing as reality and we wouldn't be able to perceive it if there were—you will realize the magnitude of the treason involved.

The task of philosophy requires the total best of a mind's capacity; the responsibility is commensurate. Most men are unable to form a comprehensive view of life: some, because their ability is devoted to other professions; a great many, because they lack the ability. But all need that view and, consciously or subconsciously, directly or indirectly, they accept what philosophy offers them.

The integration of factual data, the maintenance of a full context, the discovery of principles, the establishment of causal connections and thus the implementation of a long-range vision—these are some of the tasks required of a philosopher in every branch of his profession and, today, particularly in *politics*.

In the space of a single lifetime, two world wars have devastated the entire civilized world; two major dictatorships, in Russia and Germany, have committed such atrocities that most men are unable fully to believe it—and the bloody rise of rule by brute force is spreading around the globe. Something is obviously wrong with mankind's political ideas, and needs urgent attention. To declare—in such circumstances—that politics is not the concern of philosophy is so unspeakable a default that it can be compared only to the stand of a doctor declaring, in the midst of a bubonic plague epidemic, that health or disease is not the concern of medicine.

It is political philosophy that sets the goals and determines the course of a country's practical politics. But political philosophy means: abstract theory to identify, explain and evaluate the trend of events, to discover their causes, project their consequences, define the problems and offer the solutions.

Yet for many decades past, there has been no interest in political theory among academic philosophers; there has been no such thing as political philosophy—with the stale exception of Marxism, if one can call it a philosophy.

Bearing this in mind, evaluate the dichotomy displayed at the A.P.A. convention.

If the conservative philosophers assert that their job is "to train minds and advance thought, aloof from politics," how do they propose to do it? To train minds—in what skill? To advance thought—about what? Apparently, a man's mind is to be trained to think with no reference to man's problems and, therefore, with the implicit knowledge that his thinking is of no consequence whatever to the events taking place in the world around him or to his own life, goals and actions. If so, how long will he choose to think, and what will be his view of thought and of reason? (You can see the answer on any campus in the country.)

On the other hand, if the radical philosophers assert that their job is to deal with "the issues of the day," which day do they mean? Philosophical issues are not of "the day" or even "the year." Where do "the issues of the day" come from? Who originates them? How do philosophers determine which issue to pick up and on which side?

It is obvious that what the radicals mean by political involvement is not professional, i.e., *philosophical* participation in politics, but an unthinking, emotional "commitment" to any slogan or issue of the immediate moment. Enjoying, by default, a monopoly on political philosophy, they are anxious to have it regarded as a subject closed to discussion, and they raise issues only in terms of practical politics, with the Marxist frame of reference to be taken for granted, as dogma.

The major part of the guilt, however, belongs to the conservatives: they *have accepted the radicals' terms.* When they speak of dispassionate aloofness from politics, they mean practical politics, but they discard the wider, philosophical meaning of the term as well. They concede the premise that there is no such thing as political theory and that the realm of politics consists of nothing but random concretes, below the level of philosophy's concern. Which is all that the radicals want them to concede.

The result, at that convention, was the spectacle of a gruesome battle: the advocates of thought divorced from action versus the advocates of action divorced from thought—men armed with concepts in the form of floating abstractions versus men armed with concrete-bound percepts.

The outcome was a double disgrace: (1) that a philosophical association passed a political resolution and (2) the kind of resolution it passed.

1. No professional organization has the right to take an ideological stand in the name of its members. A man's ideas, including political convictions, are exclusively his to determine and cannot be delegated to or prescribed by anyone else. It is not a matter of "professional ethics," but of individual rights. The practice of passing ideological resolutions is a futile and immoral device of pressure-group warfare. For all the very reasons that a philosopher, as a thinking individual, should take a strong stand on political issues, he should not allow it to be taken for him by a collective: he, above all other men, should know that a man's convictions are not to be determined or prescribed by majority vote. (The same moral principles apply to universities that attempt to pass such resolutions.)

2. If movie stars give out interviews criticizing *military tactics,* no one takes it seriously. If drugged adolescents scream demands that the war in Vietnam be ended at once, regardless of means, methods, context or consequences, one wonders about the quality of their educators. But when an association of philosophers does *both,* it is a disgrace.

The nature of our foreign policy is a proper concern of philosophy; the strategy of our military operations is not. The goal of the war in Vietnam is a proper concern of philosophy; the practice or nonpractice of bombing and the choice of targets are not. (If someone squeaks that the bombing of villages is a "moral" issue, let him remember that villages are the enemy's strongholds in Vietnam—a fact which that shameful resolution neglected to mention.)

There is a great deal that philosophers could do about the war in Vietnam, and their services are desperately needed. The whole country, including our soldiers dying in the jungles, is in a state of bewildered confusion about that war and its purpose. But a philosophical approach would consist of tracing the *ideological* history of how we got into that war, what influences or interests pushed us in, what errors of our foreign policy were responsible, what basic premises created that policy and how they should be corrected.

If such a study were made, it would remind the country that the war in Vietnam was started by President Kennedy, who is the idol of all the anti-war protesters; that the basic premises of our foreign policy were set by another idol, President Roosevelt, and reinforced by the United Nations and by every peace and One-World group ever since: the premises that we owe a duty to the rest of the world, that we are responsible for the welfare of any nation anywhere on earth, that *isolationism* is selfish, immoral and impractical in a "shrinking" modern world, etc. Such a study would demonstrate the evil of altruistic "interventionism" or "internationalism," and would define the proper principles (the premises of national self-interest) that should guide America's foreign policy.

This is just a brief suggestion of what a philosopher's task would be in regard to the war in Vietnam, but it is enough to indicate the scale of the alleged conservatives' evasion.

If—with reason, justice, morality, facts and history on their side—they abdicated their leadership as philosophers and had nothing to offer people but the advice to ignore politics, anyone could take over, and did.

Passive resignation to disaster is not a widespread characteristic among men, particularly not among Americans. If, in a desperate situation, one side declares that nothing can be done and the other offers the possibility of action, men will take the action—even if it is some suicidal attempt, such as that resolution.

It must be remembered that "reason," "justice," "morality," "facts," "history" are the things that most of those conservative philosophers had been proclaiming to be nonexistent or nonobjective or unknowable or unprovable or belonging to the realm of arbitrary emotional choice. Through decades of promulgating such doctrines as Pragmatism, Logical Positivism, Linguistic Analysis, they refused to consider the fact that these doctrines would disarm and paralyze the best among men, those who take philosophy seriously, and that they would unleash the worst, those who, scorning philosophy, reason, justice, morality, would have no trouble brushing the disarmed out of the way.

This is the prospect they ignored in regard to the future of the country. It is justice that the blow should strike them first. A tiny minority group took over the leading branch of a profession of some 7,000 members and forced it to slap its own face by a resolution proclaiming that philosophy is a farce.

The brothers had asked for it. To what sort of problems had they been giving priority over the problems of politics? Among the papers to be read at that same convention were: "Pronouns and Proper Names"—"Can Grammar Be Thought?"—"Propositions as the Only Realities."

The only reality, as it usually does, avenged itself at that convention.

(*June 1970*)

The Comprachicos

I

The comprachicos, or comprapequeños, were a strange and hideous nomadic association, famous in the seventeenth century, forgotten in the eighteenth, unknown today. . . .

Comprachicos, as well as comprapequeños, is a compound Spanish word that means "child-buyers."

The comprachicos traded in children.

They bought them and sold them.

They did not steal them. The kidnapping of children is a different industry.

And what did they make of these children?

Monsters.

Why monsters?

To laugh.

The people needs laughter; so do the kings. Cities require side-show freaks or clowns; palaces require jesters. . . .

To succeed in producing a freak, one must get hold of him early. A dwarf must be started when he is small. . . .

Hence, an art. There were educators. They took a man and turned him into a miscarriage; they took a face and made a muzzle. They stunted growth; they mangled features. This artificial production of teratological cases had its own rules. It was a whole science. Imagine an inverted orthopedics. Where God had put a straight glance, this art put a squint. Where God had put harmony, they put deformity. Where God had put perfection, they brought back a botched attempt. And, in the eyes of connoisseurs, it is the botched that was perfect. . . .

The practice of degrading man leads one to the practice of deforming him. Deformity completes the task of political suppression. . . .

The comprachicos had a talent, to disfigure, that made them valuable in politics. To disfigure is better than to kill. There was the iron mask, but that is an awkward means. One cannot populate Europe with iron masks; deformed mountebanks, however, run through the streets without appearing implausible; besides, an iron mask can be torn off, a mask of flesh cannot. To mask you forever by means of your own face, nothing can be more ingenious. . . .

The comprachicos did not merely remove a child's face, they removed his memory. At least, they removed as much of it as they could. The child was not aware of the mutilation he had suffered. This horrible surgery left traces on his face, not in his mind. He could remember at most that one day he had been seized by some men, then had fallen asleep, and later they had cured him. Cured him of what? He did not know. Of the burning by sulphur and the incisions by iron, he remembered nothing. During the operation, the comprachicos made the little patient unconscious by means of a stupefying powder that passed for magic and suppressed pain. . . .

In China, since time immemorial, they have achieved refinement in a special art and industry: the molding of a living man. One takes a child two or three years old, one puts him into a porcelain vase, more or less grotesque in shape, without cover or bottom, so that the head and feet protrude. In the daytime, one keeps this vase standing upright; at night, one lays it down, so that the child can sleep. Thus the child expands without growing, slowly filling the contours of the vase with his compressed flesh and twisted bones. This bottled development continues for several years. At a certain point, it becomes irreparable. When one judges that this has occurred and that the monster is made, one breaks the vase, the child comes out, and one has a man in the shape of a pot. (Victor Hugo, *The Man Who Laughs,* translation mine.)

Victor Hugo wrote this in the nineteenth century. His exalted mind could not conceive that so unspeakable a form of inhumanity would ever be possible again. The twentieth century proved him wrong.

The production of monsters—helpless, twisted monsters whose normal development has been stunted—goes on all around us. But the modern heirs of the comprachicos are smarter and subtler than their predecessors: they do not hide, they practice their trade in the open; they do not buy children, the children are delivered to them; they do not use sulphur or iron, they achieve their goal without ever laying a finger on their little victims.

The ancient comprachicos hid the operation, but displayed its results; their heirs have reversed the process: the operation is open, the results are invisible. In the past, this horrible surgery left traces on a child's face, not in his mind. Today, it leaves traces in his mind, not on his face. In both cases, the child is not aware of the mutilation he has suffered. But today's comprachicos do not use narcotic powders: they take a child before he is fully aware of reality and never let him develop that awareness. Where nature had put a normal brain, they put mental retardation. To make you unconscious for life by means of your own brain, nothing can be more ingenious.

This is the ingenuity practiced by most of today's educators. They are the comprachicos of the mind.

They do not place a child into a vase to adjust his body to its contours. They place him into a "Progressive" nursery school to adjust him to society.

The Progressive nursery schools start a child's education at the age of three. Their view of a child's needs is militantly anti-cognitive and anti-conceptual. A child of that age, they claim, is too young for cognitive training; his natural desire is not to learn, but to play. The development of his conceptual faculty, they claim, is an unnatural burden that should not be imposed on him; he should be free to act on his spontaneous urges and feelings in order to express his subconscious desires, hostilities and fears. The primary goal of a Progressive nursery school is "social adjustment"; this is to be achieved by means of group activities, in which a child is expected to develop both "self-expression" (in the form of anything he might feel like doing) and conformity to the group.

(For a presentation of the essentials of the Progressive nursery schools' theories and practice—as contrasted to the rationality of the Montessori nursery schools—I refer you to "The Montessori Method" by Beatrice Hessen in *The Objectivist,* May–July 1970.)

"Give me a child for the first seven years," says a famous maxim attributed to the Jesuits, "and you may do what you like with him afterwards." This is true of most children, with rare, heroically independent exceptions. The first five or six years of a child's life are crucial to his cognitive development. They determine, not the content of his mind, but its method of functioning, its psycho-epistemology. (Psycho-epistemology is the study of man's cognitive processes from the aspect of the interaction between man's conscious mind and the automatic functions of his subconscious.)

At birth, a child's mind is tabula rasa; he has the potential of awareness—the mechanism of a human consciousness—but no content. Speaking metaphorically, he has a camera with an extremely sensitive, unexposed film (his conscious mind), and an extremely complex computer waiting to be programmed (his subconscious). Both are blank. He knows nothing of the external world. He faces an immense chaos which he must learn to perceive by means of the complex mechanism which he must learn to operate.

If, in any two years of adult life, men could learn as much as an infant learns in his first two years, they would have the capacity of genius. To focus his eyes (which is not an innate, but an acquired skill), to perceive the things around him by integrating his sensations into percepts (which is not an innate, but an acquired skill), to coordinate his muscles for the task of crawling, then standing upright, then walking—and, ultimately, to grasp the process of concept-formation and learn to speak—these are some of an infant's tasks and achievements whose magnitude is not equaled by most men in the rest of their lives.

These achievements are not conscious and volitional in the adult sense of the terms: an infant is not aware, in advance, of the processes he has to perform in order to acquire these skills, and the processes are largely automatic. But they are acquired skills, nevertheless, and the enormous effort expended by an infant to acquire them can be easily observed. Observe also the intensity, the austere, the unsmiling *seriousness* with which an infant watches the world around him. (If you ever find, in an adult, that degree of seriousness about reality, you will have found a great man.)

A child's cognitive development is not completed by the time he is three years old—it is just about to begin in the full, human, conceptual sense of the term. He has merely traveled through the anteroom of cognition and acquired the prerequisites of knowledge, the rudimentary mental tools he needs to begin to learn. His mind is in a state of eager, impatient flux: he is unable to catch up with the impressions bombarding him from all sides; he wants to know everything and at once. After the gigantic effort to acquire his mental tools, he has an overwhelming need to use them.

For him, the world has just begun. It is an intelligible world now; the chaos is in his mind, which he has not yet learned to organize—*this* is his next, *conceptual* task. His every experience is a discovery; every impression it leaves in his mind is new. But he is not able to think in such terms: to him, it is the world that's new. What Columbus felt when he landed in America, what the astronauts felt when they landed on the moon, is what a child feels when he discovers the earth, between the ages of two and seven. (Do you think that Columbus' first desire was to "adjust" to the natives—or that the astronauts' first wish was to engage in fantasy play?)

This is a child's position at about the age of three. The next three or four years determine the brightness or the misery of his future: they program the cognitive functions of his subconscious computer.

The subconscious is an integrating mechanism. Man's conscious mind observes and establishes connections among his experiences; the subconscious integrates the connections and makes them become automatic. For example, the skill of walking is acquired, after many faltering attempts, by the automatization of countless connections controlling muscular movements; once he learns to walk, a child needs no conscious awareness of such problems as posture, balance, length of step, etc.—the mere decision to walk brings the integrated total into his control.

A mind's cognitive development involves a continual process of automatization. For example, you cannot perceive a table as an infant perceives it—as a mysterious object with four legs. You perceive it as a table, i.e., a man-made piece of furniture, serving a certain purpose belonging to a human habitation, etc.; you cannot separate these attributes from your sight of the table, you experience it as a single, indivisible percept—yet all you see is a four-legged object; the rest is an automatized integration of a vast amount of conceptual knowledge which, at one time, you had to learn bit by bit. The same is true of everything you perceive or experience; as an adult, you cannot perceive or experience in a vacuum, you do it in a certain automatized *context*—and the efficiency of your mental operations depends on the kind of context your subconscious has automatized.

"Learning to speak is a process of automatizing the use (i.e., the meaning and the application) of concepts. And more: all learning involves a process of automatizing, i.e., of first acquiring knowledge by fully conscious, focused attention and observation, then of establishing mental connections which make that knowledge automatic (instantly available as a context), thus freeing man's mind to pursue further, more complex knowledge." (*Introduction to Objectivist Epistemology.*)

The process of forming, integrating and using concepts is not an automatic, but a volitional process—i.e., a process which uses both new and automatized material, but which is directed volitionally. It is not an innate, but an acquired skill; it has to be *learned*—it is the most crucially important part of learning—and all of man's other capacities depend on how well or how badly he learns it.

This skill does not pertain to the particular *content* of a man's knowledge at any given age, but to the *method* by which he acquires and organizes knowledge—the method by which his mind deals with its content. The method *programs* his subconscious computer, determining how efficiently, lamely or disastrously his cognitive processes will function. The programming of a man's subconscious consists of the kind of cognitive habits he acquires; these habits constitute his psycho-epistemology.

It is a child's early experiences, observations and subverbal conclusions that determine this programming. Thereafter, the interaction of content and method establishes a certain reciprocity: the method of acquiring knowledge affects its content, which affects the further development of the method, and so on.

In the flux of a child's countless impressions and momentary conclusions, the crucial ones are those that pertain to the nature of the world around him, and to the efficacy of his mental efforts. The words that would name the essence of the long, wordless process taking place in a child's mind are two questions: Where am I?—and: Is it worth it?

The child's answers are not set in words: they are set in the form of certain reactions which become habitual, i.e., automatized. He does not conclude that the universe is "benevolent" and that thinking is important—he develops an eager curiosity about every new experience, and a desire to understand it. Subconsciously, in terms of automatized mental processes, he develops the implicit equivalent of two fundamental premises, which are the cornerstones of his future sense of life, i.e., of his *metaphysics* and *epistemology,* long before he is able to grasp such concepts consciously.

Does a child conclude that the world is intelligible, and proceed to expand his understanding by the effort of conceptualizing on an ever-wider scale, with growing success and enjoyment? Or does he conclude that the world is a bewildering chaos, where the fact he grasped today is reversed tomorrow, where the more he sees the more helpless he becomes—and, consequently, does he retreat into the cellar of his own mind, locking its door? Does a child reach the stage of self-consciousness, i.e., does he grasp the distinction between consciousness and existence, between his mind and the outside world, which leads him to understand that the task of the first is to perceive the second, which leads to the development of his critical faculty and of control over his mental operations? Or does he remain in an indeterminate daze, never certain of whether he feels or perceives, of where one ends and the other begins, which leads him to feel trapped between two unintelligible states of flux: the chaos within and without? Does a child learn to identify, to categorize, to integrate his experiences and thus acquire the self-confidence needed to develop a long-range vision? Or does he learn to see nothing but the immediate moment and the feelings it produces, never venturing to look beyond it, never establishing any context but an emotional one, which leads him eventually to a stage where, under the pressure of any strong emotion, his mind disintegrates and reality vanishes?

These are the kinds of issues and answers that program a child's mind in the first years of his life, as his subconscious automatizes one set of cognitive—psycho-epistemological—habits or the other, or a continuum of degrees of precarious mixtures between the two extremes.

The ultimate result is that by the age of about seven, a child acquires the capacity to develop a vast conceptual context which will accompany and illuminate his every experience, creating an ever-growing chain of automatized connections, expanding the power of his intelligence with every year of his life—or a child shrivels as his mind shrinks, leaving only a nameless anxiety in the vacuum that should have been filled by his growing brain.

Intelligence is the ability to deal with a broad range of abstractions. Whatever a child's natural endowment, the use of intelligence is an acquired skill. It has to be acquired by a child's own effort and automatized by his own mind, but adults can help or hinder him in this crucial process. They can place him in an environment that provides him with evidence of a stable, consistent, intelligible world which challenges and rewards his efforts to understand—or in an environment where nothing connects to anything, nothing holds long enough to grasp, nothing is answered, nothing is certain, where the incomprehensible and unpredictable lurks behind every corner and strikes him at any random step. The adults can accelerate or hamper, retard and, perhaps, destroy the development of his conceptual faculty.

Dr. Montessori's Own Handbook indicates the nature and extent of the help that a child needs at the time he enters nursery school. He has learned to identify objects; he has not learned to abstract attributes, i.e., consciously to identify things such as height, weight, color or number. He has barely acquired the ability to speak; he is not yet able to grasp the nature of this, to him, amazing skill, and he needs training in its proper use (i.e., training in conceptualization). It is psycho-epistemological training that Dr. Montessori had in mind (though this is not her term), when she wrote the following about her method:

"The didactic material, in fact, does not offer to the child the 'content' of the mind, but the *order* for that 'content.' . . . The mind has formed itself by a special exercise of attention, observing, comparing, and classifying.

"The mental attitude acquired by such an exercise leads the child to make ordered observations in his environment, observations which prove as interesting to him as discoveries, and so stimulate him to multiply them indefinitely and to form in his mind a rich 'content' of clear ideas.

"Language now comes to *fix* by means of *exact words* the ideas which the mind has acquired. . . . In this way the children are able to 'find themselves,' alike in the world of natural things and in the world of objects and of words which surround them, for they have an inner guide which leads them to become *active and intelligent explorers* instead of wandering wayfarers in an unknown land." (Maria Montessori, *Dr. Montessori's Own Handbook,* New York, Schocken Books, 1965, pp. 137–138.)

The purposeful, disciplined use of his intelligence is the highest achievement possible to man: it is that which makes him human. The higher the skill, the earlier in life its learning should be started. The same holds true in reverse, for those who seek to stifle a human potential. To succeed in producing the atrophy of intelligence, a state of man-made stupidity, one must get hold of the victim early; a mental dwarf must be started when he is small. This is the art and science practiced by the comprachicos of the mind.

At the age of three, when his mind is almost as plastic as his bones, when his need and desire to know are more intense than they will ever be again, a child is delivered—by a Progressive nursery school—into the midst of a pack of children as helplessly ignorant as himself. He is not merely left without cognitive guidance—he is actively discouraged and prevented from pursuing cognitive tasks. He wants to learn; he is told to play. Why? No answer is given. He is made to understand—by the emotional vibrations permeating the atmosphere of the place, by every crude or subtle means available to the adults whom he cannot understand—that the most important thing in this peculiar world is not to know, but to get along with the pack. Why? No answer is given.

He does not know what to do; he is told to do anything he feels like. He picks up a toy; it is snatched away from him by another child; he is told that he must learn to share. Why? No answer is given. He sits alone in a corner; he is told that he must join the others. Why? No answer is given. He approaches a group, reaches for their toys and is punched in the nose. He cries, in angry bewilderment; the teacher throws her arms around him and gushes that she loves him.

Animals, infants and small children are exceedingly sensitive to emotional vibrations: it is their chief means of cognition. A small child senses whether an adult's emotions are genuine, and grasps instantly the vibrations of hypocrisy. The teacher's mechanical crib-side manner—the rigid smile, the cooing tone of voice, the clutching hands, the coldly unfocused, unseeing eyes—add up in a child's mind to a word he will soon learn: phony. He knows it is a disguise; a disguise hides something; he experiences suspicion—and fear.

A small child is mildly curious about, but not greatly interested in, other children of his own age. In daily association, they merely bewilder him. He is not seeking equals, but cognitive superiors, people who *know.* Observe that young children prefer the company of older children or of adults, that they hero-worship and try to emulate an older brother or sister. A child needs to reach a certain development, a sense of his own identity, before he can enjoy the company of his "peers." But he is thrown into their midst and told to adjust.

Adjust to *what?* To anything. To cruelty, to injustice, to blindness, to silliness, to pretentiousness, to snubs, to mockery, to treachery, to lies, to incomprehensible demands, to unwanted favors, to nagging affections, to unprovoked hostilities—and to the overwhelming, overpowering presence of Whim as the ruler of everything. (Why these and nothing better? Because these are the protective devices of helpless, frightened, unformed children who are left without guidance and are ordered to act as a mob. The better kinds of actions require thought.)

A three-year-old delivered into the power of a pack of other three-year-olds is worse off than a fox delivered to a pack of hounds: the fox, at least, is free to run; the three-year-old is expected to court the hounds and seek their love while they tear him to pieces.

After a while, he adjusts. He gets the nature of the game—wordlessly, by repetition, imitation and emotional osmosis, long before he can form the concepts to identify it.

He learns not to question the supremacy of the pack. He discovers that such questions are taboo in some frightening, supernatural way; the answer is an incantation vibrating with the overtones of a damning indictment, suggesting that he is guilty of some innate, incorrigible evil: "Don't be selfish." Thus he acquires self-doubt, before he is fully aware of a self.

He learns that regardless of what he does—whether his action is right or wrong, honest or dishonest, sensible or senseless—if the pack disapproves, he is wrong and his desire is frustrated; if the pack approves, then anything goes. Thus the embryo of his concept of morality shrivels before it is born.

He learns that it is no use starting any lengthy project of his own—such as building a castle out of boxes—it will be taken over or destroyed by others. He learns that anything he wants must be grabbed today, since there is no way of telling what the pack will decide tomorrow. Thus his groping sense of time-continuity—of the future's reality—is stunted, shrinking his awareness and concern to the range of the immediate moment. He is able (and motivated) to perceive the present; he is unable (and unmotivated) to retain the past or to project the future.

But even the present is undercut. Make-believe is a dangerous luxury, which only those who have grasped the distinction between the real and the imaginary can afford. Cut off from reality, which he has not learned fully to grasp, he is plunged into a world of fantasy playing. He may feel a dim uneasiness, at first: to him, it is not imagining, it is lying. But he loses that distinction and gets into the swing. The wilder his fantasies, the warmer the teacher's approval and concern; his doubts are intangible, the approval is real. He begins to believe his own fantasies. How can he be sure of what is true or not, what is out there and what is only in his mind? Thus he never acquires a firm distinction between existence and consciousness: his precarious hold on reality is shaken, and his cognitive processes subverted.

His desire to know dies slowly; it is not killed—it is diluted and swims away. Why bother facing problems if they can be solved by make-believe? Why struggle to discover the world if you can make it become whatever you wish—by wishing?

His trouble is that the wishing also seems to fade. He has nothing left to guide him, except his feelings, but he is afraid to feel. The teacher prods him to self-expression, but he knows that this is a trap: he is being put on trial before the pack, to see whether he fits or not. He senses that he is constantly expected to feel, but he does not feel anything—only fear, confusion, helplessness and boredom. He senses that these must not be expressed, that there is something wrong with him if he has such feelings—since none of the other children seem to have them. (That they are all going through the same process, is way beyond his capacity to understand.) They seem to be at home—he is the only freak and outcast.

So he learns to hide his feelings, to simulate them, to pretend, to evade—to repress. The stronger his fear, the more aggressive his behavior; the more uncertain his assertions, the louder his voice. From playacting, he progresses easily to the skill of putting on an act. He does so with the dim intention of protecting himself, on the wordless conclusion that the pack will not hurt him if it never discovers what he feels. He has neither the means nor the courage to grasp that it is not his bad feelings, but the good ones, that he wants to protect from the pack: his feelings about anything important to him, about anything he loves—i.e., the first, vague rudiments of his values.

He succeeds so well at hiding his feelings and values from others that he hides them also from himself. His subconscious automatizes his act—he gives it nothing else to automatize. (Years later, in a "crisis of identity," he will discover that there is nothing behind the act, that his mask is protecting a vacuum.) Thus, his emotional capacity is stunted and, instead of "spontaneity" or emotional freedom, it is the arctic wastes of repression that he acquires.

He cannot know by what imperceptible steps he, too, has become a phony.

Now he is ready to discover that he need not gamble on the unpredictable approval of the intangible, omnipotent power which he cannot name, but senses all around him, which is named the will of the pack. He discovers that there are ways to manipulate its omnipotence. He observes that some of the other children manage to impose *their* wishes on the pack, but they never say so openly. He observes that the shifting will of the pack is not so mysterious as it seemed at first, that it is swung by a silent contest of wills among those who compete for the role of pack leaders.

How does one fight in such a competition? He cannot say—the answer would take conceptual knowledge—but he learns by doing: by flattering, threatening, cajoling, intimidating, bribing, deceiving the members of the pack. Which tactics does one use, when and on whom? He cannot say—it has to be done by "instinct" (i.e., by the unnamed, but automatized connections in his mind). What does he gain from this struggle? He cannot say. He has long since forgotten why he started it—whether he had some particular wish to achieve, or out of revenge or frustration or aimlessness. He feels dimly that there was nothing else to do.

His own feelings now swing unpredictably, alternating between capricious fits of domination, and stretches of passive, compliant indifference which he can name only as: "What's the use?" He sees no contradiction between his cynical maneuvering and his unalterable fear of the pack: the first is motivated by and reinforces the second. The will of the pack has been internalized: his unaccountable emotions become his proof of its omnipotence.

The issue, to him, is now *metaphysical.* His subconscious is programmed, his fundamentals are set. By means of the wordless integrations in his brain, the faceless, intangible shape of the pack now stands between him and reality, with the will of the pack as the dominant power. He is "adjusted."

Is this his conscious idea? It is not: he is wholly dominated by his subconscious. Is it a reasoned conviction? It is not: he has not discovered reason. A child needs periods of privacy in order to learn to think. He has had less privacy in that nursery school than a convict in a crowded concentration camp. He has had no privacy even for his bathroom functions, let alone for such an unsocial activity as concept-formation.

He has acquired no incentive, no motive, to develop his intellect. Of what importance can reality be to him if his fate depends on the pack? Of what importance is thought, when the whole of his mental attention and energy are trained to focus on detecting the emotional vibrations of the pack? Reality, to him, is no longer an exciting challenge, but a dark, unknowable threat, which evokes a feeling he did not have when he started: a feeling not of ignorance, but of failure, not of helplessness, but of impotence—a sense of his own malfunctioning mind. The pack is the only realm he knows where he feels at home; he needs its protection and reassurance; the art of human manipulation is the only skill he has acquired.

But humility and hostility are two sides of the same coin. An overwhelming hostility toward all men is his basic emotion, his automatic context for the concept "man." Every stranger he meets is a potential threat—a member of that mystic entity, "others," which rules him—an enemy to appease and to deceive.

What became of his potential intelligence? Every precondition of its use has been stunted; every prop supporting his mind has been cut: he has no self-confidence—no concept of self—no sense of morality—no sense of time-continuity—no ability to project the future—no ability to grasp, to integrate or to apply abstractions—no firm distinction between existence and consciousness—no values, with the mechanism of repression paralyzing his evaluative capacity.

Any one of these mental habits would be sufficient to handicap his mind—let alone the weight of the total, the calculated product of a system devised to cripple his rational faculty.

At the age of five-and-a-half, he is ready to be released into the world: an impotent creature, unable to think, unable to face or deal with reality, a creature who combines brashness and fear, who can recite its memorized lessons, but cannot understand them—a creature deprived of its means of survival, doomed to limp or stumble or crawl through life in search of some nameless relief from a chronic, nameless, incomprehensible pain.

The vase can now be broken—the monster is made. The comprachicos of the mind have performed the basic surgery and mangled the wiring—the connections—in his brain. But their job is not completed; it has merely begun.

II

Is the damage done to a child's mind by a Progressive nursery school irreparable?

Scientific evidence indicates that it is in at least one respect: the time wasted in delaying a child's cognitive development cannot be made up. The latest research on the subject shows that a child whose early cognitive training has been neglected will never catch up, in intellectual progress, with a properly trained child of approximately the same intelligence (as far as this last can be estimated). Thus all the graduates of a Progressive nursery school are robbed of their full potential, and their further development is impeded, slowed down, made much harder.

But the Progressive nursery school does not merely neglect the cognitive training that a child needs in his early years: it stifles his normal development. It conditions his mind to an anti-conceptual method of functioning that paralyzes his rational faculty.

Can the damage be corrected or is the child doomed to a lifetime of conceptual impotence?

This is an open question. No firm answer can be given on the present level of knowledge.

We know that a child's bones are not fully formed at birth: they are soft and plastic up to a certain age, and harden gradually into their final shape. There is a strong likelihood that the same is true of a child's mind: it is blank and flexible at birth, but its early programming may become indelible at a certain point. The body has its own timetable of development, and so, perhaps, has the mind. If some complex skills are not acquired by a certain age, it may become too late to acquire them. But the mind has a wider range of possibilities, a greater capacity to recover, because its volitional faculty gives it the power to control its operations.

Volition, however, does not mean non-identity; it does not mean that one can misuse one's mind indefinitely without suffering permanent damage. But it does mean that so long as a child is not insane, he has the power to correct many faults in his mental functioning, and many injuries, whether they are self-inflicted or imposed on him from the outside. The latter are easier to correct than the former.

The evidence indicates that some graduates of the Progressive nursery schools do recover and others do not—and that their recovery depends on the degree of their "nonadjustment," i.e., the degree to which they rejected the school's conditioning. By "recovery" I mean the eventual development of a rational psycho-epistemology, i.e., of the ability to deal with reality by means of conceptual knowledge.

It is the little "misfits" who have the best chance to recover—the children who do not conform, the children who endure three years of agonizing misery, loneliness, confusion, abuse by the teachers and by their "peers," but remain aloof and withdrawn, unable to give in, unable to fake, armed with nothing but the feeling that there is something *wrong* in that nursery school.

These are the "problem children" who are periodically put

through the torture of the teachers' complaints to their parents, and through the helpless despair of seeing their parents side with the torturers. Some of these children are violently rebellious; others seem outwardly timid and passive, but are outside the reach of any pressure or influence. Whatever their particular forms of bearing the unbearable, what they all have in common is *the inability to fit in,* i.e., to accept the *intellectual* authority of the pack. (Not all "misfits" belong to this category; there are children who reject the pack for entirely different reasons, such as frustrated powerlust.)

The nonconformists are heroic little martyrs who are given no credit by anyone—not even by themselves, since they cannot identify the nature of their battle. They do not have the conceptual knowledge or the introspective skill to grasp that they are unable and unwilling to accept anything without understanding it, and that they are holding to the sovereignty of their own judgment against the terrifying pressure of everyone around them.

These children have no means of knowing that what they are fighting for is the integrity of their minds—and that they will come out of those schools with many problems, battered, twisted, frightened, discouraged or embittered, but it is their rational faculty that they will have saved.

The little manipulators, the "adjusted" little pack leaders, will not.

The manipulators have, in effect, sold out: they have accepted the approval of the pack and/or power over the pack as a value, in exchange for surrendering their judgment. To fake reality at an age when one has not learned fully to grasp it—to automatize a technique of deception when one has not yet automatized the technique of perception—is an extremely dangerous thing to do to one's own mind. It is highly doubtful whether this kind of priority can ever be reversed.

The little manipulators acquire a *vested interest* in evasion. The longer they practice their policies, the greater their fear of reality and the slimmer their chance of ever recapturing the desire to face it, to know, to understand.

The principle involved is clear on an adult level: when men are caught in the power of an enormous evil—such as under the Soviet or Nazi dictatorship—those who are willing to suffer as helpless victims, rather than make terms with the evil, have a good chance to regain their psychological health; but not those who join the G.P.U. or the S.S.

Even though the major part of the guilt belongs to his teachers, the little manipulator is not entirely innocent. He is too young to understand the immorality of his course, but nature gives him an emotional warning: he *does not like himself* when he engages in deception, he feels dirty, unworthy, unclean. This protest of a violated consciousness serves the same purpose as physical pain: it is the warning of a dangerous malfunction or injury. No one can force a child to disregard a warning of this kind; if he does, if he chooses to place some value above his own sense of himself, what he gradually kills is his self-esteem. Thereafter, he is left without motivation to correct his psycho-epistemology; he has reason to dread reason, reality and truth; his entire emotional mechanism is automatized to serve as a defense against them.

The majority of the Progressive nursery schools' graduates represent a mixture of psychological elements, on a continuum between the nonconformist and the manipulator. Their future development depends in large part on the nature of their future education. The nursery schools have taught them the wrong *method* of mental functioning; now they are expected to begin acquiring mental *content,* i.e., ideas, by such means as they possess.

The modern educators—the comprachicos of the mind—are prepared for the second stage of their task: to indoctrinate the children with the kinds of ideas that will make their intellectual recovery unlikely, if not impossible—and to do it by the kind of method that continues and reinforces the conditioning begun in the nursery school. The program is devised to stunt the minds of those who managed to survive the first stage with some remnants of their rational capacity, and to cripple those who were fortunate enough not to be sent to a Progressive nursery. In comprachico terms, this program means: to keep tearing the scabs off the wounds left by the original surgery and to keep infecting the wounds until the child's mind and spirit are broken.

To stunt a mind means to arrest its conceptual development, its power to use abstractions—and to keep it on a concrete-bound, perceptual method of functioning.

John Dewey, the father of modern education (including the Progressive nursery schools), opposed the teaching of theoretical (i.e., conceptual) knowledge, and demanded that it be replaced by concrete, "practical" action, in the form of "class projects" which would develop the students' social spirit.

"The mere absorbing of facts and truths," he wrote, "is so exclusively individual an affair that it tends very naturally to pass into selfishness. There is no obvious social motive for the acquirement of mere learning, there is no clear social gain in success thereat." (John Dewey, *The School and Society,* Chicago, The University of Chicago Press, 1956, p. 15.)

This much is true: the perception of reality, the learning of facts, the ability to distinguish truth from falsehood, are exclusively individual capacities; the mind is an exclusively individual "affair"; there is no such thing as a collective brain. And intellectual integrity—the refusal to sacrifice one's mind and one's knowledge of the truth to any social pressures—is a profoundly and properly *selfish* attitude.

The goal of modern education is to stunt, stifle and destroy the students' capacity to develop such an attitude, as well as its conceptual and psycho-epistemological preconditions.

There are two different methods of learning: by memorizing and by understanding. The first belongs primarily to the perceptual level of a human consciousness, the second to the conceptual.

The first is achieved by means of repetition and concrete-bound association (a process in which one sensory concrete leads automatically to another, with no regard to content or meaning). The best illustration of this process is a song which was popular some twenty years ago, called "Mairzy Doats." Try to recall some poem you had to memorize in grade school; you will find that you can recall it only if you recite the sounds automatically, by the "Mairzy Doats" method; if you focus on the meaning, the memory vanishes. This form of learning is shared with man by the higher animals: all animal training consists of making the animal memorize a series of actions by repetition and association.

The second method of learning—by a process of understanding—is possible only to man. To understand means to focus on the content of a given subject (as against the sensory—visual or auditory—form in which it is communicated), to isolate its essentials, to establish its relationship to the previously known, and to integrate it with the appropriate categories of other subjects. Integration is the essential part of understanding.

The predominance of memorizing is proper only in the first few years of a child's education, while he is observing and gathering perceptual material. From the time he reaches the conceptual level (i.e., from the time he learns to speak), his education requires a progressively larger scale of understanding and progressively smaller amounts of memorizing.

Just as modern educators proclaim the importance of developing a child's individuality, yet train him to conform to the pack, so they denounce memorization, yet their method of teaching ignores the requirements of conceptual development and confines learning predominantly to a process of memorizing. To grasp what this does to a child's mind, project what it would do to a child's body if, at the age of seven, he were not permitted to walk, but were required to crawl and stumble like an infant.

The comprachico technique starts at the base. The child's great achievement in learning to speak is undercut and all but nullified by the method used to teach him to read. The "Look-Say" method substitutes the concrete-bound memorization of the visual shapes of words for the phonetic method which taught a child to treat letters and sounds as abstractions. The senseless memorizing of such a vast amount of sensory material places an abnormal strain on a child's mental capacity, a burden that cannot be fully retained, integrated or automatized. The result is a widespread "reading neurosis"—the inability to learn to read—among children, including many of above average intelligence, a neurosis that did not exist prior to the introduction of the "Look-Say" method. (If the enlightenment and welfare of children were the modern educators' goal, the incidence of that neurosis would have made them check and revise their educational theories; it has not.)

The ultimate result is the half-illiterate college freshmen who are unable to read a book (in the sense of understanding its content, as against looking at its pages) or to write a paper or to spell—or even to speak coherently, which is caused by the inability to organize their thoughts, if any.

When applied to conceptual material, memorizing is the psycho-epistemological destroyer of understanding and of the ability to think. But throughout their grade- and high-school years, memorizing becomes the students' dominant (and, in some cases, virtually exclusive) method of mental functioning. They have no other way to cope with the schools' curricula that consist predominantly of random, haphazard, disintegrated (and unintegratable) snatches of various subjects, without context, continuity or systematic progression.

The material taught in one class has no relation to and frequently contradicts the material taught in another. The cure, introduced by the modern educators, is worse than the disease; it consists in the following procedure: a "theme" is picked at random for a given period of time, during which every teacher presents his subject in relation to that theme, without context or earlier preparation. For instance, if the theme is "shoes," the teacher of physics discusses the machinery required to make shoes, the teacher of chemistry discusses the tanning of leather, the teacher of economics discusses the production and consumption of shoes, the teacher of mathematics gives problems in calculating the costs of shoes, the teacher of English reads stories involving shoes (or the plight of the barefoot), and so on.

This substitutes the accidental concrete of an arbitrarily picked "theme" for the conceptual integration of the content of one discipline with that of another—thus conditioning the students' minds to the concrete-bound, associational method of functioning, while they are dealing with conceptual material. Knowledge acquired in that manner cannot be retained beyond the next exam, and sometimes not even that long.

The indoctrination of children with a mob spirit—under the category of "social adjustment"—is conducted openly and explicitly. The supremacy of the pack is drilled, pounded and forced into the student's mind by every means available to the comprachicos of the classroom, including the contemptible policy of grading the students on their social adaptability (under various titles). No better method than this type of grading could be devised to destroy a child's individuality and turn him into a stale little conformist, to stunt his unformed sense of personal identity and make him blend into an anonymous mob, to penalize the best, the most intelligent and honest children in the class, and to reward the worst, the dull, the lethargic, the dishonest.

Still more evil (because more fundamental) is the "discussion" method of teaching, which is used more frequently in the humanities than in the physical sciences, for obvious reasons. Following this method, the teacher abstains from lecturing and merely presides at a free-for-all or "bull session," while the students express their "views" on the subject under study, which they do not know and have come to school to learn. What these sessions produce in the minds of the students is an unbearable boredom.

But this is much worse than a mere waste of the students' time. They are being taught some crucial things, though not the ostensible subject of study. They are being given a lesson in metaphysics and epistemology. They are being taught, by implication, that there is no such thing as a firm, objective reality, which man's mind must learn to perceive correctly; that reality is an indeterminate flux and can be anything the pack wants it to be; that truth or falsehood is determined by majority vote. And more: that *knowledge* is unnecessary and irrelevant, since the teacher's views have no greater validity than the oratory of the dullest and most ignorant student—and, therefore, that reason, thinking, intelligence and education are of no importance or value. To the extent that a student absorbs these notions, what incentive would he have to continue his education and to develop his mind? The answer may be seen today on any college campus.

As to the content of the courses in the grade and high schools, the anti-rational indoctrination is carried on in the form of slanted, distorted material, of mystic-altruist-collectivist slogans, of propaganda for the supremacy of emotions over reason—but this is merely a process of cashing in on the devastation wrought in the children's psycho-epistemology. Most of the students do graduate as full-fledged little collectivists, reciting the appropriate dogma, but one cannot say that this represents their convictions. The truth is much worse than that: they are incapable of holding *any* convictions of any kind, and they gravitate to collectivism because that is what they have memorized—and also because one does not turn to reason and independence out of fear, helplessness and self-doubt.

III

No matter what premises a child may form in his grade- and high-school years, the educational system works to multiply his inner conflicts.

The graduates of the Progressive nurseries are caught in the clash between their dazed, unfocused, whim-oriented psycho-epistemology and the demands of reality, with which they are not prepared to deal. They are expected to acquire some sort of formal knowledge, to pass exams, to achieve acceptable grades, i.e., to comply with some minimal factual norms—but, to them, it is a metaphysical betrayal. Facts are what they have been trained to ignore; facts cannot be learned by the kind of mental process they have automatized: by an animal-like method of catching the emotional cues emitted by the pack. The pack is still there, but it cannot help them at examination time—which they have to face in a state they have been taught to regard as evil: alone.

The panic of the conflict between their foggy subjectivism and the rudiments of objectivity left in the schools by a civilized past, leads to a nameless resentment in the minds of such children, to a wordless feeling that they are being unfairly imposed upon—they do not know how or by whom—to a growing hostility without object. The comprachicos, in due time, will offer them an object.

Some of the brighter children—those who are mentally active and do want to learn—are caught in a different conflict. Struggling to integrate the chaotic snatches of information taught in their classes, they discover the omissions, the non sequiturs, the contradictions, which are seldom explained or resolved. Their questions are usually ignored or resented or laughed at or evaded by means of explanations that confuse the issue further. A child may give up, in bewilderment, concluding that the pursuit of knowledge is senseless, that education is an enormous pretense of some evil kind which he cannot understand—and thus he is started on the road to anti-intellectuality and mental stagnation. Or a child may conclude that the school will give him nothing, that he must learn on his own—which is the best conclusion to draw in the circumstances, except that it can lead him to a profound contempt for teachers, for other adults and, often, for all men (which is the road to subjectivism).

The "socializing" aspects of the school, the pressure to conform to the pack, are, for him, a special kind of torture. A thinking child cannot conform—thought does not bow to authority. The resentment of the pack toward intelligence and independence is older than Progressive education; it is an ancient evil (among children and adults alike), a product of fear, self-doubt and envy. But Pragmatism, the father of Progressive education, is a Kantian philosophy and uses Kant's technique of cashing in on human weaknesses and fears.

Instead of teaching children respect for one another's individuality, achievements and rights, Progressive education gives an official stamp of moral righteousness to the tendency of frightened half-savages to gang up on one another, to form "in-groups" and to persecute the outsider. When, on top of it, the outsider is penalized or reprimanded for his inability to "get along with people," the rule of mediocrity is elevated into a system. ("Mediocrity" does not mean an average intelligence; it means an average intelligence that resents and envies its betters.) Progressive education has institutionalized an Establishment of Envy.

The thinking child is not antisocial (he is, in fact, the only type of child fit for social relationships). When he develops his first values and conscious convictions, particularly as he approaches adolescence, he feels an intense desire to share them with a friend who would understand him; if frustrated, he feels an acute sense of loneliness. (Loneliness is specifically the experience of this type of child—or adult; it is the experience of those who have something to offer. The emotion that drives conformists to "belong," is not loneliness, but fear—the fear of intellectual independence and responsibility. The thinking child seeks equals; the conformist seeks protectors.)

One of the most evil aspects of modern schools is the spectacle of a thinking child trying to "adjust" to the pack, trying to hide his intelligence (and his scholastic grades) and to act like "one of the boys." He never succeeds, and is left wondering helplessly: "What is wrong with me? What do I lack? What do they *want?*" He has no way of knowing that his lack consists in thinking of such questions. The questions imply that there are reasons, causes, principles, values—which are the very things the pack mentality dreads, evades and resents. He has no way of knowing that one's psycho-epistemology cannot be hidden, that it shows in many subtle ways, and that the pack rejects him because they sense his factual (i.e., judging) orientation, his *psycho-epistemological* self-confidence and lack of fear. (Existentially, such loners lack social self-confidence and, more often than not, are afraid of the pack, but the issue is *not* existential.)

Gradually, the thinking child gives up the realm of human relationships. He draws the conclusion that he can understand science, but not people, that people are unknowable, that they are outside the province of reason, that some other cognitive means are required, which he lacks. Thus he comes to accept a false dichotomy, best designated as *reason versus people,* which his teachers are striving to instill and reinforce.

The conformists, in the face of that dichotomy, give up reason; he gives up people. Repressing his need of friendship, he gives up concern with human values, with moral questions, with social issues, with the entire realm of the humanities. Seeking rationality, objectivity and intelligibility—i.e., a realm where he can function—he escapes into the physical sciences or technology or business, i.e., into the professions that deal primarily with matter rather than with man. (This is a major cause of America's "brain drain," of the appalling intellectual poverty in the humanities, with the best minds running—for temporary protection—to the physical sciences.)

There is nothing wrong, of course, in choosing a career in the physical professions, if such is one's rational preference. But it is a tragic error if a young man chooses it as an escape, because the escape is illusory. Since the dichotomy he accepted is false, since repression is not a solution to anything, but merely an impairment of his mental capacity, the psychological price he pays is nameless fear, unearned guilt, self-doubt, neurosis, and, more often than not, indifference, suspicion or hostility toward people. The result, in his case, is the exact opposite of the social harmony the comprachicos of Progressive education had promised to achieve.

There are children who succumb to another, similar dichotomy: *values versus people.* Prompted by loneliness, unable to know that the pleasure one finds in human companionship is possible only on the grounds of holding the same values, a child may attempt to reverse cause and effect: he places companionship first and tries to adopt the values of others, repressing his own half-formed value-judgments, in the belief that this will bring him friends. The dogma of conformity to the pack encourages and reinforces his moral self-abnegation. Thereafter, he struggles blindly to obtain from people some satisfaction which he cannot define (and which cannot be found), to alleviate a sense of guilt he cannot name, to fill a vacuum he is unable to identify. He alternates between abject compliance with his friends' wishes, and peremptory demands for affection—he becomes the kind of emotional dependent that no friends of any persuasion could stand for long. The more he fails, the more desperately he clings to his pursuit of people and "love." But the nameless emotion growing in his subconscious, never to be admitted or identified, is hatred for people. The result, again, is the opposite of the comprachicos' alleged goal.

No matter what their individual problems or what defenses they choose, all the children—from the "adjusted" to the independent—suffer from a common blight in their grade- and high-school years: boredom. Their reasons vary, but the emotional result is the same. Learning is a conceptual process; an educational method devised to ignore, bypass and contradict the requirements of conceptual development, cannot arouse any interest in learning. The "adjusted" are bored because they are unable actively to absorb knowledge. The independent are bored because they seek *knowledge,* not games of "class projects" or group "discussions." The first are unable to digest their lessons; the second are starved.

The comprachicos succeed in either case. The independent children, who resist the conditioning and preserve some part of their rationality, are predominantly shunted, or self-exiled, into the physical sciences and allied professions, away from social, philosophical or humanistic concerns. The social field—and thus society's future—is left to the "adjusted," to the stunted, twisted, mutilated minds the comprachicos' technique was intended to produce.

The average high-school graduate is a jerky, anxious, incoherent youth with a mind like a scarecrow made of sundry patches that cannot be integrated into any shape. He has no concept of knowledge: he does not know when he knows and when he does not know. His chronic fear is of what he is *supposed* to know, and his pretentious posturing is intended to hide the fact that he hasn't the faintest idea. He alternates between oracular pronouncements and blankly evasive silence. He assumes the pose of an authority on the latest, journalistic issues in politics (part of his "class projects") and recites the canned bromides of third-rate editorials as if they were his original discoveries. He does not know how to read or write or consult a dictionary. He is sly and "wise"; he has the cynicism of a decadent adult, and the credulity of a child. He is loud, aggressive, belligerent. His main concern is to prove that he is afraid of nothing—because he is scared to death of everything.

His mind is in a state of whirling confusion. He has never learned to conceptualize, i.e., to identify, to organize, to integrate the content of his mind. In school and out, he has observed and experienced (or, more precisely, been exposed to) many things, and he cannot tell their meaning or import, he does not know what to make of them, sensing dimly that he should make something somehow. He does not know where to begin; he feels chronically behind himself, unable to catch up with his own mental content—as if the task of untangling it were far beyond his capacity.

Since he was prevented from conceptualizing his cognitive material step by step, as he acquired it, the accumulation of unidentified experiences and perceptual impressions is now such that he feels paralyzed. When he tries to think, his mind runs into a blank wall every few steps; his mental processes seem to dissolve in a labyrinth of question marks and blind alleys. His subconscious, like an unattended basement, is cluttered with the irrelevant, the accidental, the misunderstood, the ungrasped, the undefined, the not-fully-remembered; it does not respond to his mental efforts. He gives up.

The secret of his psycho-epistemology—which baffles those who deal with him—lies in the fact that, as an adult, he has to use concepts, but *he uses concepts by a child's perceptual method.* He uses them as concretes, as the immediately given—without context, definitions, integrations or specific referents; his only context is the immediate moment. To what, then, do his concepts refer? To a foggy mixture of partial knowledge, memorized responses, habitual associations, his audience's reactions and his own feelings, which represent the content of his mind at that particular moment. On the next day or occasion, the same concepts will refer to different things, according to the changes in his mood and in the immediate circumstances.

He seems able to understand a discussion or a rational argument, sometimes even on an abstract, theoretical level. He is able to participate, to agree or disagree after what appears to be a critical examination of the issue. But the next time one meets him, the conclusions he reached are gone from his mind, as if the discussion had never occurred even though he remembers it: he remembers the event, i.e., a discussion, not its intellectual content.

It is beside the point to accuse him of hypocrisy or lying (though some part of both is necessarily involved). His problem is much worse than that: he was sincere, he meant what he said *in and for that moment.* But it ended with that moment. Nothing happens in his mind to an idea he accepts or rejects; there is no processing, no integration, no application to himself, his actions or his concerns; he is unable to use it or even to retain it. Ideas, i.e., abstractions, have no reality to him; abstractions involve the past and the future, as well as the present; nothing is fully real to him except the present. Concepts, in his mind, become percepts—percepts of people uttering sounds; and percepts end when the stimuli vanish. When he uses words, his mental operations are closer to those of a parrot than of a human being. In the strict sense of the word, *he has not learned to speak.*

But there is one constant in his mental flux. The subconscious is an integrating mechanism; when left without conscious control, it goes on integrating on its own—and, like an automatic blender, his subconscious squeezes its clutter of trash to produce a single basic emotion: fear.

He is not equipped to earn a living in a primitive village, but he finds himself in the midst of the brilliant complexity of an industrial, technological civilization, which he cannot begin to understand. He senses that something is demanded of him—by his parents, by his friends, by people at large, and, since he is a living organism, by his own restless energy—something he is unable to deliver.

He has been trained to react, not to act; to respond, not to initiate; to pursue pleasure, not purpose. He is a playboy without money, taste or the capacity of enjoyment. He is guided by his feelings—he has nothing else. And his feelings are only various shades of panic.

He cannot turn for help to his parents. In most cases, they are unable and/or unwilling to understand him; he distrusts them and he is too inarticulate to explain anything. What he needs is rational guidance; what they offer him is their own brand of irrationality. If they are old-fashioned, they tell him that he is too self-indulgent and it's about time he came down to earth and assumed some responsibility; for moral guidance, they say, he ought to go to church. If they are modern, they tell him that he takes himself too seriously and ought to have more fun; for moral guidance, they tell him that nobody is ever fully right or fully wrong, and take him to a cocktail party raising funds for some liberal cause.

His parents are the products of the same educational system, but at an earlier stage, at a time when the school conditioning was furtively indirect, and rational influences still existed in the culture—which permitted them to get away with discarding intellectual concerns and playing the fashionable game of undercutting reason, while believing that somebody else would always be there to provide them with a civilized world.

Of any one group involved, it is not the comprachicos who are the guiltiest, it is the parents—particularly the educated ones who could afford to send their children to Progressive nursery schools. Such parents would do anything for their children, except give them a moment's thought or an hour's critical inquiry into the nature of the educational institutions to be selected. Prompted chiefly by the desire to get the children off their hands and out of their way, they selected schools as they select clothes—according to the latest fashion.

The comprachicos do not hide their theories and methods; they propagate them openly, in countless books, lectures, magazines and school brochures. Their theme is clear: they attack the intellect and proclaim their hatred of reason—the rest is gush and slush. Anyone who delivers a helpless child into their hands, does so because he shares their motives. Mistakes of this size are not made innocently.

There is, however, an innocent group of parents: the hard-working, uneducated ones who want to give their children a better chance in life and a brighter future than their own. These parents spend a lifetime in poverty, struggling, skimping, saving, working overtime to send their children through school (particularly, through college). They have a profound respect for the educated people, for teachers, for learning. They would not be able to conceive of the comprachico mentality—to imagine an educator who works, not to enlighten, but to cripple their children. Such parents are the victims of as vicious a fraud as any recorded in criminal history.

(This last is one of the reasons to question the motives—and the compassion—of those unemployed busy-bodies who flitter about, protecting consumers from oversized breakfast-cereal boxes. What about the consumers of education?)

If you want to grasp what the comprachicos' methods have done to the mind of a high-school graduate, remember that the intellect is often compared to the faculty of sight. Try to project what you would feel if your eyesight were damaged in such a way that you were left with nothing but peripheral vision. You would sense vague, unidentifiable shapes floating around you, which would vanish when you tried to focus on them, then would reappear on the periphery and swim and switch and multiply. *This* is the mental state—and the terror—produced in their students by the comprachicos of Progressive education.

Can such a youth recondition his mental processes? It is possible, but the automatization of a conceptual method of functioning—which, in his nursery-school years, would have been an easy, joyous, natural process—would now require an excruciatingly difficult effort.

As an illustration of the consequences of delaying nature's timetable, consider the following. In our infancy, all of us had to learn and automatize the skill of integrating into percepts the material provided by our various sense organs. It was a natural, painless process which—as we can infer by observing infants—we were eager to learn. But medical science has recorded cases of children who were born blind and later, in their youth or adulthood, underwent an operation that restored their sight. Such persons are not able to see, i.e., they experience sensations of sight, but cannot perceive objects. For example, they recognize a triangle by touch, but cannot connect it to the sight of a triangle; the sight conveys nothing to them. The ability to see is not innate—it is *a skill that has to be acquired.* But the material provided by these persons' other senses is so thoroughly integrated and automatized that they are unable instantly to break it up to add a new element, vision. This integration now requires such a long, difficult process of retraining that few of them choose to undertake it. These few succeed, after a heroically persevering struggle. The rest give up, preferring to stay in their familiar world of touch and sound—to remain sightless for life.

An unusual kind of moral strength and of personal ambition (i.e., of self-esteem) is required to regain one's sight: a profound love of life, a passionate refusal to remain a cripple, an intense dedication to the task of achieving the best within one's reach. The reward is commensurate.

The same kind of dedication and as difficult a struggle are required of a modern high-school graduate to regain his rational faculty. The reward is as great—or greater. In the midst of his chronic anxiety, he is still able to experience some moments of freedom, to catch a few glimpses of what life would be like in a joyous state of self-confidence. And one thing he does know for certain: that there is something wrong with him. He has a springboard—a slender, precarious one, but still a springboard—for an incentive to recapture the use of his mind.

The comprachicos destroy that incentive in the third stage of their job: in college.

IV

Most young people retain some hold on their rational faculty—or, at least, some unidentified desire to retain it—until their early twenties, approximately until their post-college years. The symptom of that desire is their quest for a comprehensive view of life.

It is man's rational faculty that integrates his cognitive material and enables him to understand it; his only means of understanding is *conceptual.* A consciousness, like any other vital faculty, cannot accept its own impotence without protest. No matter how badly disorganized, a young person's mind still gropes for answers to fundamental questions, sensing that all of its content hangs precariously in a vacuum.

This is not a matter of "idealism," but of psycho-epistemological necessity. On the conscious level, the countless alternatives confronting him make a young person aware of the fact that he has to make choices and that he does not know what to choose or how to act. On the subconscious level, his psycho-epistemology has not yet automatized a lethargic resignation to a state of chronic suffering (which is the "solution" of most adults)—and the painful conflicts of his inner contradictions, of his self-doubt, of his impotent confusion, make him search frantically for some form of inner unity and mental order. His quest represents the last convulsions of his cognitive faculty at the approach of atrophy, like a last cry of protest.

For the few brief years of his adolescence, a young person's future is urgently, though dimly, real to him; he senses that *he* has to determine it in some unknown way.

A thinking youth has a vague glimmer of the nature of his need. It is expressed in his concern with broad philosophical questions, particularly with *moral* issues (i.e., with a code of values to guide his actions). An average youth merely feels helpless, and his erratic restlessness is a form of escape from the desperate feeling that "things ought to make sense."

By the time they are ready for college, both types of youths have been hurt, in and out of school, by countless clashes with the irrationality of their elders and of today's culture. The thinking youth has been frustrated in his longing to find people who take ideas seriously; but he believes that he will find them in college—in the alleged citadel of reason and wisdom. The average youth feels that things do not make sense to *him,* but they do to someone somewhere in the world, and someone will make the world intelligible to him someday.

For both of them, college is the last hope. They lose it in their freshman year.

It is generally known in academic circles that, according to surveys, the students' interest in their studies is greatest in their freshman year and diminishes progressively each year thereafter. The educators deplore it, but do not question the nature of the courses they are giving.

With rare exceptions, which are lost in the academic "mainstream," college courses in the humanities do not provide the students with knowledge, but with the conviction that it is wrong, naive or futile to seek knowledge. What they provide is not information, but rationalization—the rationalization of the students' concrete-bound, perceptual, emotion-oriented method of mental functioning. The courses are designed to protect the status quo—not the existential, political or social status quo, but the miserable status quo of the students' psycho-epistemology, as laid down in the Progressive nursery schools.

The Progressive nurseries pleaded for a delay of the process of education, asserting that cognitive training is premature for a young child—and conditioned his mind to an anti-cognitive method of functioning. The grade and high schools reinforced the conditioning: struggling helplessly with random snatches of knowledge, the student learned to associate a sense of dread, resentment and self-doubt with the process of learning. College completes the job, declaring explicitly—to a receptive audience—that there is nothing to learn, that reality is unknowable, certainty is unattainable, the mind is an instrument of self-deception, and the sole function of reason is to find conclusive proof of its own impotence.

Even though philosophy is held in a (today) well-earned contempt by the other college departments, it is philosophy that determines the nature and direction of all the other courses, because it is philosophy that formulates the principles of epistemology, i.e., the rules by which men are to acquire knowledge. The influence of the dominant philosophic theories permeates every other department, including the physical sciences—and becomes the more dangerous because accepted subconsciously. The philosophic theories of the past two hundred years, since Immanuel Kant, seem to justify the attitude of those who dismiss philosophy as empty, inconsequential verbiage. But *this* precisely is the danger: surrendering philosophy (i.e., the foundations of knowledge) to the purveyors of empty verbiage is far from inconsequential. It is particularly to philosophy that one must apply the advice of Ellsworth Toohey in *The Fountainhead:* "Don't bother to examine a folly, ask yourself only what it accomplishes."

Consider the progressive stages of modern philosophy, not from the aspect of its philosophic content, but of its psycho-epistemological goals.

When Pragmatism declares that reality is an indeterminate flux which can be anything people want it to be, nobody accepts it literally. But it strikes a note of emotional recognition in the mind of a Progressive nursery graduate, because it seems to justify a feeling he has not been able to explain: the omnipotence of the pack. So he accepts it as true in some indeterminate way—to be used when and as needed. When Pragmatism declares that truth is to be judged by consequences, it justifies his inability to project the future, to plan his course of action long-range, and sanctions his wish to act on the spur of the moment, to try anything once and then discover whether he can get away with it or not.

When Logical Positivism declares that "reality," "identity," "existence," "mind" are meaningless terms, that man can be certain of nothing but the sensory perceptions of the immediate moment—when it declares that the meaning of the proposition: "Napoleon lost the battle of Waterloo" is your walk to the library where you read it in a book—the Progressive nursery graduate recognizes it as an exact description of his inner state and as a justification of his concrete-bound, perceptual mentality.

When Linguistic Analysis declares that the ultimate reality is not even percepts, but words, and that words have no specific referents, but mean whatever people want them to mean, the Progressive graduate finds himself happily back at home, in the familiar world of his nursery school. He does not have to struggle to grasp an incomprehensible reality, all he has to do is focus on people and watch for the vibrations of how they use words—and compete with his fellow philosophers in how many different vibrations he is able to discover. And more: armed with the prestige of philosophy, he can now tell people what they mean when they speak, which they are unable to know without his assistance—i.e., he can appoint himself interpreter of the will of the pack. What had once been a little manipulator now grows to the full psycho-epistemological stature of a shyster lawyer.

And more: Linguistic Analysis is vehemently opposed to all the intellectual feats he is unable to perform. It is opposed to any kinds of principles or broad generalizations—i.e., to consistency. It is opposed to basic axioms (as "analytic" and "redundant")—i.e., to the necessity of any grounds for one's assertions. It is opposed to the hierarchical structure of concepts (i.e., to the process of abstraction) and regards any word as an isolated primary (i.e., as a perceptually given concrete). It is opposed to "system-building"—i.e., to the integration of knowledge.

The Progressive nursery graduate thus finds all his psycho-epistemological flaws transformed into virtues—and, instead of hiding them as a guilty secret, he can flaunt them as proof of his intellectual superiority. As to the students who did not attend a Progressive nursery, they are now worked over to make them equal his mental status.

It is the claim of Linguistic Analysis that its purpose is not the communication of any particular philosophic content, but the *training* of a student's mind. This is true—in the terrible, butchering sense of a comprachico operation. The detailed discussions of inconsequential minutiae—the discourses on trivia picked at random and in midstream, without base, context or conclusion—the shocks of self-doubt at the professor's sudden revelations of some such fact as the students' inability to define the word "but," which, he claims, proves that they do not understand their own statements—the countering of the question: "What is the meaning of philosophy?" with: "Which sense of 'meaning' do you mean?" followed by a discourse on twelve possible uses of the word "meaning," by which time the question is lost—and, above all, the necessity to shrink one's focus to the range of a flea's, and to keep it there—will cripple the best of minds, if it attempts to comply.

"Mind-training" pertains to psycho-epistemology; it consists in making a mind automatize certain processes, turning them into permanent habits. What habits does Linguistic Analysis inculcate? Context-dropping, "concept-stealing," disintegration, purposelessness, the inability to grasp, retain or deal with abstractions. Linguistic Analysis is not a philosophy, it is a method of eliminating the *capacity* for philosophical thought—it is a course in brain-destruction, a systematic attempt to turn a rational animal into an animal unable to reason.

Why? What is the comprachicos' motive?

To paraphrase Victor Hugo: "And what did they make of these children?

"Monsters.

"Why monsters?

"To rule."

Man's mind is his basic means of survival—and of self-protection. Reason is the most *selfish* human faculty: it has to be used in and by a man's own mind, and its product—truth—makes him inflexible, intransigent, impervious to the power of any pack or any ruler. Deprived of the ability to reason, man becomes a docile, pliant, impotent chunk of clay, to be shaped into any subhuman form and used for any purpose by anyone who wants to bother.

There has never been a philosophy, a theory or a doctrine that attacked (or "limited") reason, which did not also preach submission to the power of some authority. Philosophically, most men do not understand the issue to this day; but psycho-epistemologically, they have sensed it since prehistoric times. Observe the nature of mankind's earliest legends—such as the fall of Lucifer, "the light-bearer," for the sin of defying authority; or the story of Prometheus, who taught men the practical arts of survival. Power-seekers have always known that if men are to be made submissive, the obstacle is not their feelings, their wishes or their "instincts," but their minds; if men are to be ruled, then the enemy is reason.

Power-lust is a psycho-epistemological matter. It is not confined to potential dictators or aspiring politicians. It can be experienced, chronically or sporadically, by men in any profession, on any level of intellectual development. It is experienced by shriveled scholars, by noisy playboys, by shabby office managers, by pretentious millionaires, by droning teachers, by cocktail-chasing mothers—by anyone who, having uttered an assertion, confronts the direct glance of a man or a child and hears the words: "But that is not true." Those who, in such moments, feel the desire, not to persuade, but to *force* the mind behind the direct eyes, are the legions that make the comprachicos possible.

Not all of the modern teachers are consciously motivated by power-lust, though a great many of them are. Not all of them are consciously aware of the goal of obliterating reason by crippling the minds of their students. Some aspire to nothing but the mean little pleasure of fooling and defeating too intelligently, persistently inquiring a student. Some seek nothing but to hide and evade the holes and contradictions in their own intellectual equipment. Some had never sought anything but a safe, undemanding, respectable position—and would not dream of contradicting the majority of their colleagues or of their textbooks. Some are eaten by envy of the rich, the famous, the successful, the independent. Some believe (or try to believe) the thin veneer of humanitarian rationalizations coating the theories of Kant or John Dewey. And all of them are products of the same educational system in its earlier stages.

The system is self-perpetuating: it leads to many vicious circles. There are promising, intelligent teachers who are driven to despair by the obtuse, lethargic, invincibly unthinking mentalities of their students. The grade- and high-school teachers blame it on parental influences; the college professors blame it on the grade- and high-school teachers. Few, if any, question the content of the courses. After struggling for a few years, these better teachers give up and retire, or become convinced that reason is beyond the grasp of most men, and remain as bitterly indifferent camp followers of the comprachicos' advance.

But the comprachico leaders—past and present—are aware of

their own motives. It is impossible to be consumed by a single passion without knowing its nature, no matter what rationalizations one constructs to hide it from oneself. If you want to see hatred, do not look at wars or concentration camps—these are merely its consequences. Look at the writings of Kant, Dewey, Marcuse and their followers to see pure hatred—hatred of reason and of everything it implies: of intelligence, of ability, of achievement, of success, of self-confidence, of self-esteem, of every bright, happy, benevolent aspect of man. *This* is the atmosphere, the leitmotif, the sense of life permeating today's educational establishment.

(What brings a human being to the state of a comprachico? Self-loathing. The degree of a man's hatred for reason is the measure of his hatred for himself.)

A comprachico leader does not aspire to the role of political dictator. He leaves it to his heir: the mindless brute. The comprachicos are not concerned with establishing anything. The obliteration of reason is their single passion and goal. What comes afterward has no reality to them; dimly, they fancy themselves as the masters who will pull the strings behind the ruler's throne: the brute, they feel, will need them. (That they end up as terrorized bootlickers at the brute's court and at his mercy, as in Nazi Germany and Soviet Russia, is merely an instance of reality's justice.)

Power-lust requires guinea pigs, to develop the techniques of inculcating obedience—and cannon fodder that will obey the orders. College students fill both roles. Psycho-epistemological flattery is the most potent technique to use on a person with a damaged brain. The Progressive nursery graduate's last link to rationality—the feeling that there is something wrong with him—is cut off in college. There is nothing wrong with him, he is told, his is the healthy, natural state, he is merely unable to function in a "System" that ignores human nature; *he* is normal, the "System" is abnormal.

The term "System" is left undefined, at first; it may be the educational system, the cultural system, the private family system—anything that a student might blame for his inner misery. This induces a paranoid mood, the feeling that he is an innocent victim persecuted by some dark, mysterious powers—which builds up in him a blind, helpless rage. The theories of determinism—with which he is battered in most of his courses—intensify and justify his mood: if he is miserable, he cannot help it, they tell him, he cannot help anything he feels or does, he is a product of society and society has made a bad job of it. By the time he hears that all his troubles—from poor grades to sexual problems to chronic anxiety—are caused by the *political* system and that the enemy is capitalism, he accepts it as self-evident.

The methods of teaching are essentially the same as those used in high school, only more so. The curriculum is an embodiment of disintegration—a hodgepodge of random subjects, without continuity, context or purpose. It is like a series of Balkanized kingdoms, offering a survey course of floating abstractions or an overdetailed study of a professor's favorite minutiae, with the borders closed to the kingdom in the next classroom, with no connections, no bridges, no maps. Maps—i.e., systematization—are forbidden on principle. Cramming and memorizing are the students' only psycho-epistemological means of getting through. (There are graduates in philosophy who can recite the differences between the early and late Wittgenstein, but have never had a course on Aristotle. There are graduates in psychology who have puttered about with rats in mazes, with knee-jerking reflexes and with statistics, but never got to an actual study of human psychology.)

The "discussion" seminars are part of the technique of flattery: when an ignorant adolescent is asked to air his views on a subject he has not studied, he gets the message that the status of college student has transformed him from an ignoramus into an authority—and that the significance of any opinion lies in the fact that somebody holds it, with no reasons, knowledge or grounds necessary. (This helps to justify the importance of watching for the vibrations of the pack.)

Such "discussions" advance another purpose of the comprachico technique: the breeding of hostility—the encouragement of criticism rather than creativeness. In the absence of any reasoned views, the students develop the knack of blasting each other's nonsense (which is not difficult in the circumstances) and come to regard the demolition of a bad argument as the equivalent of the construction of a good one. (The example is set by the professors who, in their own publications and debates, are often brilliant at demolishing one another's irrational theories, but fall flat in attempting to present a new theory of their own.) In the absence of intellectual content, the students resort to personal attacks, practicing with impunity the old fallacy of *ad hominem,* substituting insults for arguments—with hooligan rudeness and four-letter words accepted as part of their freedom of speech. Thus malice is protected, ideas are not. The unimportance of ideas is further stressed by the demand that the nature of such "discussions" be ignored and the participants remain "good friends"—no matter what offensive exchanges took place—in the name of "intellectual tolerance."

An eloquent demonstration of today's general contempt for the power of ideas is offered by the fact that people did not expect an education of this kind to produce any consequences—and are now shocked by the spectacle of college students putting into practice what they have been taught. If, after such a training, the students demand the power to run the universities, why shouldn't they? They were given that power intellectually and decided to exercise it existentially. They were regarded as qualified arbiters of ideas, without knowledge, preparation or experience—and they decided that they were qualified administrators, without knowledge, preparation or experience.

The students' demand that their courses be "relevant" to their actual lives has a badly twisted element of validity. The only purpose of education *is* to teach a student how to live his life—by developing his mind and equipping him to deal with reality. The training he needs is theoretical, i.e., *conceptual.* He has to be taught to think, to understand, to integrate, to prove. He has to be taught the essentials of the knowledge discovered in the past—and he has to be equipped to acquire further knowledge by his own effort. All of this is what the colleges have renounced, failed in and defaulted on long ago. What they are teaching today has no relevance to anything—neither to theory nor practice nor reality nor human life.

But—in keeping with their concrete-bound psycho-epistemology—what the students regard as "relevant" are such things as courses in "community action," air pollution, rat-control and guerrilla warfare. Their criteria for determining a college curriculum are the newspaper headlines of the immediate moment, their hierarchy of concerns is established by tabloid editorials, their notion of reality does not extend beyond the latest TV talk-show.

Modern intellectuals used to denounce the influence of comic strips on children; the progress they achieved consists in pushing the children's interest to the front pages and freezing it there for life.

The conditioning phase of the comprachicos' task is completed. The students' development is arrested, their minds are set to respond to slogans, as animals respond to a trainer's whistle, their brains are embalmed in the syrup of altruism as an automatic substitute for self-esteem—they have nothing left but the terror of chronic anxiety, the blind urge to act, to strike out at whoever caused it, and a boiling hostility against the whole of the universe. They would obey anyone, they *need* a master, they need to be told what to do. They are ready now to be used as cannon fodder—to attack, to bomb, to burn, to murder, to fight in the streets and die in the gutters. They are a trained pack of miserably impotent freaks, ready to be unleashed against anyone. The comprachicos unleash them against the "System."

V

In the avalanche of commentaries on the campus riots, a great deal has been said about the students, as if those manifestations of savagery were spontaneous, and about the college administrators, as if their policies of abject appeasement were "repressive"—but very little is said about the faculties. Yet it is the faculty that causes, inspires, manipulates and often stage-manages the riots. In some cases, the majority of the faculty supports the rioters; in others, it is a small comprachico minority that overpowers the faculty majority by spitting in its face. (And if you want to see a negative demonstration of the power of ideas—i.e., a demonstration of what happens to men devoid of philosophical convictions—take a look at the cringing moral cowardice of allegedly civilized scholars in the presence of a handful of faculty hooligans. There have been notable exceptions to this attitude, but not many.)

For several generations, the destruction of reason was carried on under the cover and in the name of reason, which was the Kant-Hegel-James-Dewey method. When every girder of rationality had been undercut, a new philosophy made explicit what had been implicit, and took over the job of providing a rationalization of the students' psycho-epistemological state: Existentialism.

Existentialism elevates chronic anxiety into the realm of metaphysics. Fear, misery, nausea—it declares—are not an individual's fault, they are inherent in human nature, they are an intrinsic, predestined part of the "human condition." Action is the sole alleviation possible to man. What action? Any action. You do not know how to act? Don't be chicken, courage consists in acting without knowledge. You do not know what goals to choose? There are no standards of choice. Virtue consists in choosing a goal by whim and sticking to it ("committing yourself") to the grim death. It sounds unreasonable? Reason is man's enemy—your guts, muscles and blood know best.

For several generations, the destruction of freedom (i.e., of capitalism) was carried on under the cover and in the name of freedom. The genteel intellectual conformists, mass-produced in colleges, proclaimed every collectivist tenet, premise and slogan, while professing their abhorrence of dictatorship. When every girder of capitalism had been undercut, when it had been transformed into a crumbling mixed economy—i.e., a state of civil war among pressure groups fighting politely for the legalized privilege of using physical force—the road was cleared for a philosopher who scrapped the politeness and the legality, making explicit what had been implicit: Herbert Marcuse, the avowed enemy of reason and freedom, the advocate of dictatorship, of mystic "insight," of retrogression to savagery, of universal enslavement, of rule by brute force.

The student activists are the comprachicos' most successful products: they went obediently along every step of the way, never challenging the basic premises inculcated in the Progressive nursery schools. They act in packs, with the will of the pack as their only guide. The scramble for power among their pack leaders and among different packs does not make them question their premises: they are incapable of questioning anything. So they cling to the belief that mankind can be united into one happily, harmoniously unanimous pack—by force. Brute, physical force is, to them, a natural form of action. Philosophically, it is clear that when men abandon reason, physical force becomes their only means of dealing with one another and of settling disagreements. The activists are the living demonstration of this principle.

The activists' claim that they have no way of "attracting attention" to their demands and of getting what they want except by force—by violent demonstrations, obstruction and destruction—is a pure throwback to the Progressive nursery school, where a tantrum was the only thing required to achieve their wishes. Their hysterical screaming still carries a touch of pouting astonishment at a world that does not respond to an absolute such as: "I *want* it!" The three-year-old whim-worshiper becomes the twenty-year-old thug.

The activists are a small minority, but they are confronting a helpless, confused, demoralized majority consisting of those who were unable fully to accept the school conditioning or fully to reject it. Among them, a large group represents the activists' fellow travelers and prospective converts: the hippies. The hippies froze on the Progressive nursery school level and went no further. They took the Progressive nursery's metaphysics literally—and are now wandering in search of a world to fit it.

The hippies' "lifestyle" is an exact concretization of the nursery's ideal: no thought—no focus—no purpose—no work—no reality save the whim of the moment—the hypnotic monotony of primitive music, with the even beat that deadens the brain and the senses—the brotherhood of the pack, combined with pretensions at expressing individuality, at "doing one's thing" in the haze and stench of grimy coffeehouses, which "thing" consists in the monotonous repetition of the same jerking contortions with the same long whine of sounds that had been emitted by others for days on end—the inarticulate extolling of emotions above reason, of "spirituality" above matter, of "nature" above technology—and, above all, the quest for love, anyone's love, any kind of love as the key to finding someone who will take care of them.

Clinging to their nursery ideal, the hippies live down to its essential demand: non-effort. If they are not provided with brightly furnished rooms and toys, they live in dank basements, they sleep on floors, they eat what they find in garbage cans, they breed stomach ulcers and spread venereal diseases—anything rather than confront that implacable enemy of whims: reality.

And out of all those variants of Progressive education's results, out of that spectacle of human self-degradation, there rises a grim, factual, unanswerable proof of the place of reason in man's nature and existence, as a silent warning to all the comprachicos and their allies: You can destroy men's minds, but you will not find a substitute—you can condition men to irrationality, but you cannot make them bear it—you can deprive men of reason, but you cannot make them live with what is left. That proof and warning is: drugs.

The most damning refutation of the theories of all the hippie-activist-Marcusian hordes is the drug-glazed eyes of their members. Men who have found the right way of life do not seek to escape from awareness, to obliterate their consciousness and to drug themselves out of existence. Drug addiction is the confession of an unbearable inner state.

Drugs are not an escape from economic or political problems, they are not an escape from society, but from oneself. They are an escape from the unendurable state of a living being whose consciousness has been crippled, deformed, mutilated, but not eliminated, so that its mangled remnants are screaming that he cannot go on without it.

The phenomenon of an entire generation turning to drugs is such an indictment of today's culture—of its basic philosophy and its educational establishment—that no further evidence is necessary and no lesser causal explanation is possible.

If they had not been trained to believe that belonging to a pack is a moral and metaphysical necessity, would high-school children risk the physical destruction of their brains in order to belong to a pot-smoking "in-group"?

If they had not been trained to believe that reason is impotent, would college students take "mind-expanding" drugs to seek some "higher" means of cognition?

If they had not been trained to believe that reality is an illusion, would young persons take drugs to reach a "higher" reality that seems to obey their wishes, except that they are smashed on pavements in attempting to fly out of windows?

If a trained pack of commentators, sharing the same beliefs, did not glamorize the obscene epidemic of self-destruction—by means of such estimates as "idealistic," "revolutionary," "new life-style," "new morality," "drug *culture*"—would the young have any cover left to hide their own deep-down knowledge that drug addiction is nothing but a public confession of personal impotence?

It is the educational establishment that has created this national disaster. It is philosophy that has created the educational establishment. The anti-rational philosophic trend of the past two hundred years has run its course and reached its climax. To oppose it will require a *philosophical* revolution or, rather, a rebirth of philosophy. Appeals to "home, church, mother and tradition" will not do; they never did. Ideas can be fought only by means of ideas. The educational establishment has to be fought—from bottom to top, from cause to consequences, from nursery schools to universities, from basic philosophy to campus riots, from without *and from within.*

This last is addressed to the many intelligent youths who are aware of the state of higher education and refuse to go to college or, having gone, drop out in revulsion. They are playing into the comprachicos' hands. If the better minds desert the universities, this country will reach a situation in which the incompetent and the second-rate will carry the official badge of the intellect and there will be no place for the first-rate and independent to function or even to hide. To preserve one's mind intact through a modern college education is a test of courage and endurance, but the battle is worth it and the stakes are the highest possible to man: the survival of reason. The time spent in college is not wasted, if one knows how to use the comprachicos against themselves: one learns *in reverse*—by subjecting their theories to the most rigorously critical examination and discovering what is false and why, what is true, what are the answers.

As to the drugged contingents of hippies and activists, I should like to address the following to those among them who may still be redeemable, as well as to those who may be tempted to join their hordes.

The modern comprachicos have an advantage over their ancient predecessors: when a victim was mutilated physically, he retained the capacity to discover who had done it. But when a victim is mutilated mentally, he clings to his own destroyers as his masters and his only protectors against the horror of the state which *they* have created; he remains as their tool and their plaything—which is part of their racket.

If, in the chaos of your motives, some element is a genuine desire to crusade in a righteous cause and take part in a heroic battle, direct it against the proper enemy. Yes, the world is in a terrible state—but what caused it? Capitalism? Where do you see it, except for some battered remnants that still manage to keep us all alive? Yes, today's "Establishment" is a rotted structure of mindless hypocrisy—but who and what is the "Establishment"? Who directs it? Not the big businessmen, who mouth the same collectivist slogans as your professors and pour out millions of dollars to support them. Not the so-called "conservatives," who compete with your professors in attacking reason and in spreading the same collectivist-altruist-mystic notions. Not the Washington politicians, who are the eager dummies of your professorial ventriloquists. Not the communications media, who publicize your cause, praise your ideals and preach your professors' doctrines.

It is *ideas* that determine the actions of all those people, and it is the *Educational Establishment* that determines the ideas of a nation. It is your professors' ideas that have ruled the world for the past fifty years or longer, with a growing spread of devastation, not improvement—and today, in default of opposition, these ideas are destroying the world, as they destroyed your mind and self-esteem.

You are miserably helpless and want to rebel? Then rebel against the ideas of your teachers. You will never find a harder, nobler or more heroic form of rebellion. You have nothing to lose but your anxiety. You have your mind to win.

In conclusion, I should like to quote—for one of the guiltiest groups, the parents—a passage from *Atlas Shrugged*, which deals with Rearden's thoughts after the death of the Wet Nurse:

"He thought of all the living species that train their young in the art of survival, the cats who teach their kittens to hunt, the birds who spend such strident effort on teaching their fledglings to fly—yet man, whose tool of survival is the mind, does not merely fail to teach a child to think, but devotes the child's education to the purpose of destroying his brain, of convincing him that thought is futile and evil, before he has started to think. . . .

"Men would shudder, he thought, if they saw a mother bird plucking the feathers from the wings of her young, then pushing him out of the nest to struggle for survival—yet *that* was what they did to their children.

"Armed with nothing but meaningless phrases, this boy had been thrown to fight for existence, he had hobbled and groped through a brief, doomed effort, he had screamed his indignant, bewildered protest—and had perished in his first attempt to soar on his mangled wings."

(*August–December 1970*)

The Culture

Apollo and Dionysus

On July 16, 1969, one million people, from all over the country, converged on Cape Kennedy, Florida, to witness the launching of Apollo 11 that carried astronauts to the moon.

On August 15, 300,000 people, from all over the country, converged on Bethel, New York, near the town of Woodstock, to witness a rock music festival.

These two events were news, not philosophical theory. These were facts of our actual existence, the kinds of facts—according to both modern philosophers and practical businessmen—that philosophy has nothing to do with.

But if one cares to understand the meaning of these two events—to grasp their roots and their consequences—one will understand the power of philosophy and learn to recognize the specific forms in which philosophical abstractions appear in our actual existence.

The issue in this case is the alleged dichotomy of *reason versus emotion.*

This dichotomy has been presented in many variants in the history of philosophy, but its most colorfully eloquent statement was given by Friedrich Nietzsche. In *The Birth of Tragedy from the Spirit of Music,* Nietzsche claims that he observed two opposite elements in Greek tragedies, which he saw as metaphysical principles inherent in the nature of reality; he named them after two Greek gods: Apollo, the god of light, and Dionysus, the god of wine. Apollo, in Nietzsche's metaphysics, is the symbol of beauty, order, wisdom, efficacy (though Nietzsche equivocates about this last)—i.e., the symbol of reason. Dionysus is the symbol of drunkenness or, rather, Nietzsche cites drunkenness as his identification of what Dionysus stands for: wild, primeval feelings, orgiastic joy, the dark, the savage, the unintelligible element in man—i.e., the symbol of emotion.

Apollo, according to Nietzsche, is a necessary element, but an unreliable and thus inferior guide to existence, that gives man a superficial view of reality: the illusion of an orderly universe. Dionysus is the free, unfettered spirit that offers man—by means of a mysterious intuition induced by wine and drugs—a more profound vision of a different kind of reality, and is thus the superior. And—indicating that Nietzsche knew clearly what he was talking about, even though he chose to express it in a safely, drunkenly Dionysian manner—Apollo represents the principle of individuality, while Dionysus leads man "into complete self-forgetfulness" and into merging with the "Oneness" of nature. (Those who, at a superficial reading, take Nietzsche to be an advocate of individualism, please note.)

This much is true: reason *is* the faculty of an individual, to be exercised individually; and it is only dark, irrational emotions, obliterating his mind, that can enable a man to melt, merge and dissolve into a mob or a tribe. We may accept Nietzsche's symbols, but *not* his estimate of their respective values, nor the metaphysical necessity of a reason-emotion dichotomy.

It is *not* true that reason and emotion are irreconcilable antagonists or that emotions are a wild, unknowable, ineffable element in men. But this is what emotions become for those who do not care to know what they feel, and who attempt to subordinate reason to their emotions. For every variant of such attempts—as well as for their consequences—the image of Dionysus is an appropriate symbol.

Symbolic figures are a valuable adjunct to philosophy: they help men to integrate and bear in mind the essential meaning of complex issues. Apollo and Dionysus represent the fundamental conflict of our age. And for those who may regard them as floating abstractions, reality has offered two perfect, fiction-like dramatizations of these abstract symbols: at Cape Kennedy and at Woodstock. They were perfect in every respect demanded of serious fiction: they concretized the *essentials* of the two principles involved, in action, in a pure, extreme, isolated form. The fact that the spacecraft was called "Apollo" is merely a coincidence, but a helpful coincidence.

If you want to know fully what the conflict of reason versus irrational emotion means—in fact, in reality, on earth—keep these two events in mind: it means Apollo 11 versus the Woodstock festival. Remember also that you are asked to make a choice between these two—and that the whole weight of today's culture is being used to push you to the side of and into Woodstock's mud.

In my article "Apollo 11" (*The Objectivist,* September 1969), I discussed the meaning and the greatness of the moon landing. To quote: "No one could doubt that we had seen an achievement of man in his capacity as a rational being—an achievement of reason, of logic, of mathematics, of total dedication to the absolutism of reality. . . . The most confirmed evader in the worldwide audience could not escape the fact that . . . no feelings, wishes, urges, instincts or lucky 'conditioning' . . . could have achieved this incomparable feat—that we were watching the embodied concretization of a single faculty of man: his rationality."

This was the meaning and motive of the overwhelming worldwide response to Apollo 11, whether the cheering crowds knew it consciously or not—and most of them did not. It was the response of people starved for the sight of an achievement, for a vision of man the hero.

This was the motive that drew one million people to Cape Kennedy for the launching. Those people were not a stampeding herd nor a manipulated mob; they did not wreck the Florida communities, they did not devastate the countryside, they did not throw themselves, like whining thugs, at the mercy of their victims; they did not create any victims. They came as responsible individuals able to project the reality of two or three days ahead and to provide for their own needs. There were people of every age, creed, color, educational level and economic status. They lived and slept in tents or in their cars, some of them for several days, in great discomfort and unbearable heat; they did it gamely, cheerfully, gaily; they projected a general feeling of confident goodwill, the bond of a common enthusiasm; they created a public spectacle of responsible privacy—and they departed as they had come, without benefit of press agents.

The best account of the nature of that general feeling was given to me by an intelligent young woman of my acquaintance. She went to see the parade of the astronauts when they came to New York. For a few brief moments, she stood on a street corner and waved to them as they went by. "It was so wonderful," she told me. "People didn't want to leave after the parade had passed. They just stood there, talking about it—talking to strangers—smiling. It was so wonderful to feel, for once, that people aren't vicious, that one doesn't have to suspect them, that we have something good in common."

This is the essence of a genuine feeling of human brotherhood: the brotherhood of *values*. This is the only authentic form of unity among men—and only values can achieve it.

There was virtually no comment in the press on the meaning of the popular response to Apollo 11; the comments, for the most part, were superficial, perfunctory, mainly statistical. There was a brief flurry of nonsense about "unity"—as if it were some mysteriously causeless emotional primary—with suggestions about directing this unity to such inspiring goals as the crusades against poverty, air pollution, wilderness-desecration, even urban transportation. Then the subject was dropped, and the Apollo 11 story was dropped as of no further significance.

One of the paradoxes of our age is the fact that the intellectuals, the politicians and all the sundry voices that choke, like asthma, the throat of our communications media have never gasped and stuttered so loudly about their devotion to the public good and about the people's will as the supreme criterion of value—and never have they been so grossly indifferent to the people. The reason, obviously, is that collectivist slogans serve as a rationalization for those who intend, not to follow the people, but to rule it. There is, however, a deeper reason: the most profound breach in this country is not between the rich and the poor, but between the people and the intellectuals. In their view of life, the American people are predominantly Apollonian; the "mainstream" intellectuals are Dionysian.

This means: the people are reality-oriented, commonsense-oriented, technology-oriented (the intellectuals call this "materialistic" and "middle-class"); the intellectuals are emotion-oriented and seek, in panic, an escape from a reality they are unable to deal with, and from a technological civilization that ignores their feelings.

The flight of Apollo 11 brought this out into the open. With rare exceptions, the intellectuals resented its triumph. A two-page survey of their reactions, published by *The New York Times* on July 21, was an almost unanimous spread of denigrations and denunciations. (See my article "Apollo 11.") What they denounced was "technology"; what they resented was achievement and its source: reason. The same attitude—with rare exceptions—was displayed by the popular commentators, who are not the makers, but the products and the weather vanes of the prevailing intellectual trends.

Walter Cronkite of CBS was a notable exception. But Eric Sevareid of CBS was typical of the trend. On July 15, the eve of the launching, he broadcast from Cape Kennedy a commentary that was reprinted in *Variety* (July 23, 1969). "In Washington and elsewhere," he said, "the doubts concern future flights, their number, their cost and their benefits, as if the success of Apollo 11 were already assured. We are a people who hate failure. It's un-American. It is a fair guess that failure of Apollo 11 would not curtail future space programs but re-energize them."

Please consider these two sentences: "We are a people who hate failure. It's un-American." (In the context of the rest, this was not intended as a compliment, though it should have been; it was intended as sarcasm.) Who *doesn't* hate failure? Should one love it? Is there a nation on earth that doesn't hate it? Surely, one would have to say that failure is un-British or un-French or un-Chinese. I can think of only one nation to whom this would not apply: failure is *not* un-Russian (in a sense which is deeper than politics).

But what Mr. Sevareid had in mind was not failure. It was the American dedication to success that he was deriding. It is true that no other nation as a whole is as successful as America, which is America's greatest virtue. But success is never automatically immediate; passive resignation is not a typical American trait; Americans seldom give up. It is this precondition of success—the "try, try again" precept—that Mr. Sevareid was undercutting.

He went on to say that if Apollo 11 succeeded, "the pressure to divert these great sums of money to inner space, terra firma and inner man will steadily grow." He went on to discuss the views of men who believe "that this adventure, however majestic its drama, is only one more act of escape, that it is man once again running away from himself and his real needs, that we are approaching the bright side of the moon with the dark side of ourselves. . . . We know that the human brain will soon know more about the composition of the moon than it knows about the human brain . . . [and] why human beings do what they do."

This last sentence is true, and one would think that the inescapable conclusion is that man should use his brain to study human nature by the same *rational* methods he has used so successfully to study inanimate matter. But not according to Mr. Sevareid; he reached a different conclusion: "It is possible that the divine spark in man will consume him in flames, that the big brain will prove our ultimate flaw, like the dinosaur's big body, that the metal plaque Armstrong and Aldrin expect to place on the moon will become man's epitaph."

On July 20, while Apollo 11 was approaching the moon, and the world was waiting breathlessly, Mr. Sevareid found it appropriate to broadcast the following remark: no matter how great this event, he said, nothing much has changed, "man still puts his pants on, one leg at a time, he still argues with his wife," etc. Well, each to his own hierarchy of values and of importance.

On the same day, David Brinkley of NBC observed that since men can now see and hear everything directly on television, by sensory-perceptual means (as he stressed), commentators are no longer needed at all. This implies that perceived events will somehow provide men automatically with the appropriate conceptual conclusions. The truth is that the more men perceive, the more they need the help of commentators, but of commentators who are able to provide a *conceptual* analysis.

According to a fan letter I received from Canada, the U.S. TV-commentaries during Apollo 11's flight were mild compared to those on Canadian television. "We listened to an appalling panel of 'experts' disparage the project as a 'mere technological cleverness by a stupid, pretentious speck of dust in the cosmos.' . . . They were also very concerned about the 'inflated American ego' if the voyage succeeded. One almost got the impression that they would be greatly relieved if the mission failed!"

What is the actual motive behind this attitude—the unadmitted, subconscious motive? An intelligent American newsman, Harry Reasoner of CBS, named it inadvertently; I had the impression that he did not realize the importance of his own statement. Many voices, at the time, were declaring that the success of Apollo 11 would destroy the poetic-romantic glamor of the moon, its fascinating mystery, its appeal to lovers and to human imagination. Harry Reasoner summed it up by saying simply, quietly, a little sadly, that if the moon is found to be made of green cheese, it will be a blow to science; but if it isn't, it will be a blow to "those of us whose life is not so well organized."

And *this* is the whole shabby secret: to some men, the sight of an achievement is a reproach, a reminder that their own lives are irrational and that there is no loophole, no escape from reason and reality. Their resentment is the cornered Dionysian element baring its teeth.

What Harry Reasoner's statement implied was the fact that only the vanguard of the Dionysian cohorts is made up of wild, rampaging irrationalists, openly proclaiming their hatred of reason, dripping wine and blood. The bulk of Dionysus' strength, his grass-roots following, consists of sedate little souls who never commit any major crime against reason, who merely indulge their petty irrational whims once in a while, covertly—and, overtly, seek a "balance of power," a compromise between whims and reality. But reason is an absolute: in order to betray it, one does not have to dance naked in the streets with vine leaves in one's hair; one betrays it merely by sneaking down the back stairs. Then, someday, one finds oneself unable to grasp why one feels no joy at the scientific discoveries that prolong human life or why the naked dancers are prancing all over one's own body.

Such are the Dionysian followers. But who are the leaders? These are not always obvious or immediately identifiable. For instance, the greatest Dionysian in history was a shriveled little "square," well past thirty, who never drank or smoked pot, who took a daily walk with such precise, monotonous regularity that the townspeople set their clocks by him; his name was Immanuel Kant.

Kant was the first hippie in history.

But a generalissimo of that kind needs lieutenants and noncommissioned officers: Apollo cannot be defeated by buck privates who are merely the conditioned products of their officers. Nor can the buck privates unleash the Dionysian hordes on the world, out of the zoos, the coffeehouses and the colleges where they are bred. To do that job—and to blindfold the keepers—requires some men of stature, but men with a split face who have worn an Apollonian half-mask on the side turned to the world, thus convincing the unwary that a "compromise" is possible.

This brings us to one of Kant's noncommissioned officers (he is not the only one, but he is typical), a man who serves as a transmission belt to Dionysus and to Woodstock: Charles A. Lindbergh.

Forty-two years ago, Lindbergh was a hero. His great feat—the solo flight across the Atlantic—had required major virtues, including a significant degree of rationality. As a grim demonstration of the nature of man's volition—of the fact that neither rationality nor any other virtue is automatically permanent, but requires a constant, volitional practice—I offer in evidence a letter from Lindbergh, commenting on Apollo 11's coming flight, published in *Life* magazine, July 4, 1969. It demonstrates what is left of what had once been a hero.

Mr. Lindbergh confesses that he does not know all the motives that prompted him to fly the Atlantic (which proves nothing but a failure of introspection). "But I can say quite definitely that they sprang more from intuition than from rationality, and that the love of flying outweighed practical purposes—important as the latter often were."

Observe that the choice and love of one's profession are here regarded as having no connection with rationality or with practical purposes, whatever these might be.

"Then, as the art of flying transposed to a science, I found my interest in airplanes decreasing. Rationally I welcomed the advances that came with self-starters, closed cockpits, radio and automatic pilots. Intuitively I felt revolted by them, for they upset the balance between intellect and senses that had made my profession such a joy."

A great deal could be identified, in this sort of statement, about the nature of Mr. Lindbergh's "intuition" and about the motives he finds so mysterious. But I shall let him speak for himself and let you draw your own conclusions.

"And so, as intuition had led me into aviation in the first place, it led me back to an early boyhood interest, the contemplation of life."

He does not state by what means he intended to contemplate it, since he had rejected reason.

"I found the mechanics of life less interesting than the mystical qualities they manifest. With these conclusions, I began studying supersensory phenomena and, in 1937, flew to India in the hope of gaining insight to yogic practices."

Some years later, he states, he made expeditions into the

wildernesses of Africa, Eurasia and the American continents, which gave him a new perspective, "a perspective that drove into my bones, as well as into my mind, the fact that in instinct rather than in intellect is manifest the cosmic plan of life."

When he attended the launching of Apollo 8, he was momentarily impressed. "Talking to astronauts and engineers, I felt an almost overwhelming desire to reenter the fields of astronautics—with their scientific committees, laboratories, factories and blockhouses, possibly to voyage into space myself. But I know I will not return to them, despite limitless possibilities for invention, exploration and adventure.

"Why not? Decades spent in contact with science and its vehicles have directed my mind and senses to areas beyond their reach. I now see scientific accomplishment as a path, not an end; a path leading to and disappearing in mystery."

Observe the motive of placing one's own motives outside the power of reason: it permits one to regard an explanation of that kind as satisfactory, and an epistemological claim of that kind as requiring no further proof.

From the incoherent paragraphs that follow, one can gather only that what Mr. Lindbergh holds against science is the fact that science does not give us omniscience and omnipotence. "Scientific knowledge argues that space vehicles can never attain the speed of light, which makes a puny penetration of the universe within a human lifespan; and that, therefore, cosmic distances will confine our physical explorations to those planets which orbit the sun . . . scientifically established principles now seem to limit [man] to the space-territory of the minor star he orbits. We are blocked by lack of time as we were once blocked by lack of air."

But, he wonders, are we perhaps cracking open the entrance to another era, "one that will surpass the era of science as the era of science surpassed that of religious superstition? Following the paths of science, we become constantly more aware of mysteries beyond scientific reach. In these vaguely apprehended azimuths, I think the great adventures of the future lie—in voyages inconceivable by our 20th Century rationality—beyond the solar system, through distant galaxies, possibly through peripheries untouched by time and space."

If this does not make sense to you, the fault lies in your "20th

Century rationality." Mr. Lindbergh claims a different means of cognition. "We know that tens of thousands of years ago, man departed from both the hazards and the security of instinct's natural selection, and that his intellectual reactions have become too powerful to permit him ever to return. . . . We must find a way to blend with our present erratic tyranny of mind the countless, subtle and still-little-known elements that created the tangible shape of man and his intangible extensions."

There follows an incoherent paean to "wildness"—not "nature," but "*wildness.*" In "wildness"—as opposed to technological progress and civilization—Mr. Lindbergh has found "a direction . . . an awareness of values . . . and the means of our salvation."

To help you untangle this, I can only quote Ellsworth Toohey in *The Fountainhead:* "Don't bother to examine a folly—ask yourself only what it accomplishes." Mr. Lindbergh accomplishes the following:

"If we can combine our knowledge of science with the wisdom of wildness, if we can nurture civilization through roots in the primitive, man's potentialities appear to be unbounded . . . he can merge with the miraculous—to which we can attach what better name than 'God'? And in this merging, as long sensed by intuition but still only vaguely perceived by rationality, experience may travel without need for accompanying life.

"Will we then find life to be only a stage, though an essential one, in a cosmic evolution of which our evolving awareness is beginning to become aware? Will we discover that only *without* spaceships can we reach the galaxies; that only *without* cyclotrons can we know the interior of atoms? [Italics his.] To venture beyond the fantastic accomplishments of this physically fantastic age, sensory perception must combine with the extra-sensory, and I suspect that the two will prove to be different faces of each other."

What are the puny little compromises sought by today's politicians, compared to a quest for a compromise of *this* kind?

I have said, in *Atlas Shrugged,* that mysticism is anti-man, anti-mind, anti-life. I received violent protests from mystics, assuring me that this is not true. Observe that Mr. Lindbergh regards life, spaceships and cyclotrons as equally dispensable, that he talks of "experience" which travels "without need for accompanying life"—and that his intuition promises him achievements greater than those reached by the advocates of life, reason and civilization.

Well, reality has obliged him. He does not have to wait for tens of thousands of years, for evolution, for a reunion with wildness, for intergalactic travel. The goal, the ideal, the salvation and the ecstasy have been achieved—by 300,000 people wallowing in the mud on an excrement-strewn hillside near Woodstock. Their name for the experience of travel unaccompanied by life, to peripheries untouched by time and space, is "LSD trips."

The "Woodstock Music and Art Fair" did not take place in Woodstock; like everything else about that event, its title was a phony, an attempt to cash in on the artistic reputation of the Woodstock community. The fair took place on an empty thousand-acre pasture leased by the promoters from a local farmer. In response to $200,000 worth of publicity and advertising, 300,000 hippies showed up for the occasion. (These figures are from *The New York Times;* some sources place the attendance estimate higher.)

According to *Newsweek* (August 25): "The three-day Woodstock fair was different from the usual pop festival from the outset. It was not just a concert but a tribal gathering, expressing all the ideas of the new generation: communal living away from the cities, getting high, digging arts, clothes and craft exhibits, and listening to the songs of revolution." The article quotes one of the promoters as declaring: "People will all be going into their own thing. This is not just music, but a conglomeration of everything involved in the new culture."

So it was.

No living, eating or sanitary facilities were provided; the promoters claimed that they had not expected so large a crowd. *Newsweek* describes the conditions as follows: "Festival food supplies were almost immediately exhausted . . . and water coming from wells dug into the area stopped flowing or came up impure. A heavy rain Friday night turned the amphitheater into a quagmire and the concession area into a mudhole. . . . Throngs of wet, sick and wounded hippies trekked to impromptu hospital tents suffering from colds, sore throats, broken bones, barbed-wire cuts and nail-puncture wounds. Festival doctors called it a 'health emergency,' and 50 additional doctors were flown in from New York City to meet the crisis."

According to *The New York Times* (August 18), when the rainstorm came "at least 80,000 young people sat or stood in front of the stage and shouted obscenities at the darkened skies as trash rolled down the muddy hillside with the runoff of the rain. Others took shelter in dripping tents, lean-tos, cars and trucks. . . . Many boys and girls wandered through the storm nude, red mud clinging to their bodies."

Drugs were used, sold, shared or given away during the entire festival. Eyewitnesses claim that 99 percent of the crowd smoked marijuana; but heroin, hashish, LSD and other stronger drugs were peddled openly. The nightmare convulsions of so-called "bad trips" were a common occurrence. One young man died, apparently from an overdose of heroin.

The *Newsweek* report concludes with: "The promoters had hired members of the Hog Farm, a New Mexico hippie commune, to peacefully police the fair. At week's end near the Hog Farm campsite, a hard core of crazies barked like dogs and freaked out in a bizarre circle dance lit by flashing strobe lights. The songs seemed to sum up what the young Aquarians believed, despite all misadventures, the festival was all about: 'Now, now, now is all there is. Love is all there is. Love is. Love.' "

Who paid for this love-feast? Apparently, the unloved ones: those who know that there is more than the "now" for a human being—and that without it, even the "now" is not possible.

The citizens of Bethel, the nearest community, were the victims, abandoned by their law-enforcing agencies. These victims were neither bums nor millionaires; they were farmers and small businessmen, who worked hard to earn their living. Their stories, reported in *The New York Times* (August 20), sound like those of the survivors of a foreign invasion.

Richard C. Joyner, the operator of the local post office and general store on Route 17B, "said that the youngsters at the festival had virtually taken over his property—camping on his lawn, making fires on his patio and using the backyard as a latrine. . . .

"Clarence W. Townsend, who runs a 150-acre dairy farm . . . was shaken by the ordeal. 'We had thousands of cars all over our fields,' he said. 'There were kids all over the place. They made a human cesspool of our property and drove through the cornfields. There's not a fence left on the place. They just tore them up and used them for firewood.' . . .

" 'My pond is a swamp [said Royden Gabriele, another farmer]. I've got no fences and they used my field as a latrine. They picked corn and camped all over the place. They just landed wherever they could. . . . We pulled 30 of them out of the hay mow smoking pot. . , . If they come back next year I don't know what I'll do,' Mr. Gabriele said. 'If I can't sell, I'll just burn the place down.' "

No love—or thought—was given to these victims by the unsanitary apostles of love (and someday the world will discover that without thought there can be no love). Furthermore, the universal loving was not extended by the promoters of the festival even to one another. "In the aftermath of Woodstock," writes *The New York Times* (September 9), "as the euphoria of the 'three days of peace and music' dies out, the tales of the problems, the bickering, the power struggles and the diverse philosophies of the four young businessmen are coming out."

The promoters were four young men, all of them in their twenties; one of them, the heir to a drugstore products fortune, pledged his fortune to cover the festival's losses. Inasmuch as the Woodstock hordes broke down the ticket-selling procedure, and half the people got in without paying the $7 admission, the fair was "a financial disaster," according to the young heir who said (in an earlier story) that his debts might reach $2 million.

Now the four promoters are splitting up and fighting over control of the Woodstock Ventures Corporation.

One of them was described as "a hippie who keeps one foot in the financial world at all times" and as a boy "who eschews shoes, shirts and barbers (but who likes chauffeured Cadillacs and overseas jet travel and plunges in the stock market) . . ." All of them, apparently, have connections with "several large Establishment-oriented corporations and Wall Street investment firms [who] are interested in cashing in on the youth market . . ."

One of them stated openly: "Maybe the best way to define the Underground Industrial Complex . . . is materialistic people of the underground trying to make money off of a generation of underground kids who feel they aren't materialistic."

The problems that plagued these promoters "before, during and after the festival reflect the difficulties in merging the ideas of 'making money off the kids' and trying to let the kids believe that a rock festival, for example, is, as [one of them] likes to put it, 'a groovy meeting of the tribes, a part of the revolution.' "

If this is disgusting, there is something more disgusting still: the psychology of those hundreds of thousands of "underground kids"—who, in justice, deserve no better.

Under the title "Woodstock: Like It Was," *The New York Times* (August 25) published a lengthy interview with six young people who had attended the festival. The interview gives only their first names; five boys: Steve, Lindsey, Bill, Jimmy and Dan; and one girl: Judy. Most of them were college students; the youngest one was "a 16-year-old junior at one of the city's better private schools. . . . All were from comfortable middle-class backgrounds."

I shall quote some of this interview. It is a remarkable psychological document.

"Q. Why did you want to go [to the festival]?

"Lindsey. It was the music. I wanted to go because of the music. That was the only reason.

"Judy. They had the most fantastic line-up of stars that I've ever heard about, more than any place I've ever heard of, better than Newport.

"Q. Did you have any idea where you'd sleep or what there would be to eat?

"Judy. Well, we drove down in a caravan of two cars—there were four girls and two guys—but we were supposed to meet 20 or 30 other people who were driving down from New Hampshire and they were supposed to bring a tent, but we never met each other. We just scattered.

"Q. What about food?

"Judy. We brought a bag of carrots. And some soda.

"Q. Did you expect to be able to buy more there?

"Judy. We never really thought about it."

When they were asked what they felt at the scene, Judy answered: "I just had a feeling that, wow, there are so many of us, we really have power. I'd always felt like such a minority. But I thought, wow, we're a majority—it felt like that. I felt, here's the answer to anyone who calls us deviates.

"Q. Was that before you heard any music?

"Judy. I never made it to the concert. I never heard any music at all.

"Q. The whole weekend?

"Judy. Yeh. The whole weekend."

Further: "All the participants stressed a sense of what they called 'community.' . . .

"Steve. Everyone came there to be together—not that everyone would cease to be an individual—but everyone came there to be able to express their life style. . . .

"Q. Was there a lot of sharing?

"A voice. Everything was shared. . . .

"Bill. I was sitting in a group of people and it was hot and the sun was beating down. All of a sudden you'd have a box of Cocoa Puffs hit you in the side. They'd say, 'Take a handful and pass it on.' And like Saturday afternoon we were sitting there and this watermelon came by with three mouthfuls taken out of it. You were supposed to take a bite and pass it on. Because some guy three rows over said, 'Give those people some watermelon.' "

Further: "All the panel participants carried some kind of drug to the festival—mostly marijuana. . . . Not infrequently drugs were given away by young people eager to share. What couldn't be had free could be bought from dealers roaming freely through the crowd. . . . Most of the participants regarded the drugs as an essential part of the scene . . .

"Q. How much of the time were you people up there stoned [i.e., deeply drugged]?

"Lindsey. About 102 percent. . . .

"Q. Could you have had the festival without the drugs?

"Steve. I'm sure there were people there you would have had trouble with if there had not been drugs there."

One of the boys remarked that some of the older ones were using cocaine.

"Q. The older ones? How old?

"Judy. About 24 or 26."

When they were asked what they wanted to be in the future, they answered as follows:

"Jimmy. All my life I've had just about everything I want. And I have to have whatever I want for the rest of my life, except from now on I have to begin to think of how to provide it for myself. And I don't want to work because I can't have everything and do everything I want if I have to stay in the same place from 9 to 5.

"Judy. I'm going to try everything at least once. I lived on a communal farm for a month on the Cape. And, well, I liked it and

I really enjoyed staying there and I've always wanted to go back and try this thing again, grow tomatoes and things.

"Q. Do you want a family?

"Judy. One child. Just, you know, to procreate. But I don't want a family because I don't want to get into that much responsibility. I want to be able to move. I want to be able to leave at any time. I don't want that much restriction."

Further: "Q. Was sex an important part of the scene [at Woodstock]?

"Dan. It was just a part. I don't know if it was an important part or not.

"Steve. In any society of 500,000 people over the course of three days you're going to have sex—let's face it.

"Jimmy. . . . They were no more free or less free in Woodstock than they are any other place.

"Dan. There was some society to what people did. I mean, they waited until night.

"Q. You mean there were certain standards of decorum?

"Dan. I think there were, yes. People still have some reservations. Some. Not as many."

Had enough?

Has it ever occurred to you that it is not an accident, but the psychological mechanism of projection that has made people of this kind choose to call their opponents "pigs"?

These are the young people whom the press is hailing as a "new culture" and as a movement of great moral significance—the same press and the same intellectuals who dismissed or denounced Apollo 11 as "mere technology."

Of the publications I have read, *Newsweek* was the most fastidious in regard to Woodstock: it offered no praise. *The New York Times* started by denouncing the festival in an editorial entitled "Nightmare in the Catskills" (August 18), but reversed itself the next day and published an editorial with a softened tone.

Time magazine went whole hog: it published an essay under the title "The Message of History's Biggest Happening" (August 29). This included such statements as: "As the moment when the special culture of U.S. youth of the '60s openly displayed its strength, appeal and power, it may well rank as one of the significant political and sociological events of the age." And: "The spontaneous community of youth that was created at Bethel was the stuff of which legends are made . . ."

Life magazine straddled the fence. It published a special edition devoted to the Woodstock festival; the best skill that technology has created in the field of color photography was used to fill that issue with beautiful pictures of scummy young savages. And only toward the end of the two laudatory articles did the writer strike a note of alarm: "The great stoned rock show had worked a countermiracle, trading on the freedom to get stoned, transforming it into a force that tamed the crowd and extracted its compliance. Not that anyone minded, of course—the freedom to get stoned was all the freedom they wanted. . . . In the cold acid light, the spoiled field took on the aspect of an Orwellian concentration camp stocked with drugs and music and staffed with charming police. The [loud]speaker's coaxing voice only enriched the nightmare . . . I fear it will grow groovier in memory, when the market in madness leads on to shows we'd rather not see."

I found one brief letter to the editor of *The New York Times* (September 3), as a lone voice of cognitive and moral sanity. It said, in part: "Perhaps the most peculiar aspect of this event, if we are forced to regard the festival as symbolic, is the awful mindless conformity of external appearance and behavior, and the manifest desperation of this lonely herd of pilgrims doing what Dharma demands—the lack of personal will or spirit . . ."

These publications demonstrate that the hippies are right in one respect: the culture of today's Establishment is done for, it is rotted through and through—and rebelling against it is like rebelling against a dead horse.

The hippies are wrong, however, when they fancy themselves to be rebels. They are the distilled essence of the Establishment's culture, they are the embodiment of its soul, they are the personified ideal of generations of crypto-Dionysians now leaping into the open.

Among the various types of today's younger generation, the hippies are the most docile conformists. Unable to generate a thought of their own, they have accepted the philosophical beliefs of their elders as unchallengeable dogma—as, in earlier generations, the weakest among the young conformed to the fundamentalist view of the Bible.

The hippies were taught by their parents, their neighbors, their tabloids and their college professors that faith, instinct and emotion are superior to reason—and they obeyed. They were taught that material concerns are evil, that the State or the Lord will provide, that the Lilies of the Field do not toil—and they obeyed. They were taught that love, indiscriminate love, for one's fellowmen is the highest virtue—and they obeyed. They were taught that the merging of one's self with a herd, a tribe or a community is the noblest way for men to live—and they obeyed.

There isn't a single basic principle of the Establishment which they do not share—there isn't a belief which they have not accepted.

When they discovered that this philosophy did not work—because, in fact, it cannot work—the hippies had neither the wit nor the courage to challenge it; they found, instead, an outlet for their impotent frustration by accusing their elders of hypocrisy—as if hypocrisy were the only obstacle to the realization of their ideals. And—left blindly, helplessly lobotomized in the face of an inexplicable reality that is not amenable to their feelings—they have no recourse but to the shouting of obscenities at anything that frustrates their whims, at men or at a rainy sky, indiscriminately, with no concept of the difference.

It is typical of today's culture that these exponents of seething, raging hostility are taken as advocates of love.

Avowed anti-materialists whose only manifestation of rebellion and of individualism takes the material form of the clothes they choose to wear, are a pretty ridiculous spectacle. Of any type of nonconformity, this is the easiest to practice, and the safest.

But even in this issue, there is a special psychological component: observe the hippies' choice of clothing. It is not intended to make them look attractive, but to make them look grotesque. It is not intended to evoke admiration, but to evoke mockery and pity. One does not make oneself look like a caricature unless one intends one's appearance to plead: Please don't take me seriously.

And there is a kind of malicious wink, a contemptuous sneer, in the public voices acclaiming the hippies as heroes.

This is what I would call "the court-jester premise." The jester at the court of an absolute monarch was permitted to say anything and to insult anyone, even his master, because the jester had assumed the role of a fool, had abdicated any claim to personal dignity and was using self-abasement as his protection.

The hippies are a desperate herd looking for a master, to be taken over by anyone; anyone who would tell them how to live, without demanding the effort of thinking. Theirs is the mentality ready for a Führer.

The hippies are the living demonstration of what it means to give up reason and to rely on one's primeval "instincts," "urges," "intuitions"—and whims. With such tools, they are unable to grasp even what is needed to satisfy their wishes—for example, the wish to have a festival. Where would they be without the charity of the local "squares" who fed them? Where would they be without the fifty doctors, rushed from New York to save their lives—without the automobiles that brought them to the festival—without the soda pop and beer they substituted for water—without the helicopter that brought the entertainers—without all the achievements of the technological civilization they denounce? Left to their own devices, they literally didn't know enough to come in out of the rain.

Their hysterical incantations of worship of the "now" were sincere: the immediate moment is all that exists for the perceptual-level, concrete-bound, animal-like mentality; to grasp "tomorrow" is an enormous abstraction, an intellectual feat open only to the *conceptual* (i.e., the rational) level of consciousness.

Hence their state of stagnant, resigned passivity: if no one comes to help them, they will sit in the mud. If a box of Cocoa Puffs hits them in the side, they'll eat it; if a communally chewed watermelon comes by, they'll chew it; if a marijuana cigarette is stuck into their mouth, they'll smoke it. If not, not. How can one act, when the next day or hour is an impenetrable black hole in one's mind?

And how can one desire or feel? The obvious truth is that these Dionysian desire-worshipers do not really desire anything. The little parasite who declared: "I have to have whatever I want for the rest of my life," did not know what he wanted; observe the "whatever" in his statement. Neither did the girl who announced that she would "try everything at least once." All of them are looking desperately for somebody who will provide them with something they will be able to enjoy or to desire. Desires, too, are a product of the conceptual faculty.

But there is one emotion which the hippies do experience intensely: chronic fear. If you have seen any of them on television, you have seen it leaping at you from the screen. Fear is their brand, their hallmark; fear is the special vibration by which they claim to recognize one another.

I have mentioned the nature of the bond uniting the admirers of Apollo 11: the brotherhood of values. The hippies, too, have a brotherhood, but of a different kind: it is the brotherhood of fear.

It is fear that drives them to seek the warmth, the protection, the "safety" of a herd. When they speak of merging their selves into a "greater whole," it is their fear that they hope to drown in the undemanding waves of unfastidious human bodies. And what they hope to fish out of that pool is the momentary illusion of an unearned personal significance.

But all discussions or arguments about the hippies are almost superfluous in the face of one overwhelming fact: most of the hippies are drug addicts.

Is there any doubt that drug addiction is an escape from an unbearable inner state, from a reality one cannot deal with, from an atrophying mind one can never fully destroy? If Apollonian reason were unnatural to man, and Dionysian "intuition" brought him closer to nature and truth, the apostles of irrationality would not have to resort to drugs. Happy, self-confident men do not seek to get "stoned."

Drug addiction is the attempt to obliterate one's consciousness, the quest for a deliberately induced insanity. As such, it is so obscene an evil that any doubt about the moral character of its practitioners is itself an obscenity.

Such is the nature of the conflict of Apollo versus Dionysus.

You have all heard the old bromide to the effect that man has his eyes on the stars and his feet in the mud. It is usually taken to mean that man's reason and his physical senses are the element pulling him down to the mud, while his mystical, supra-rational emotions are the element that lifts him to the stars.

This is the grimmest inversion of many in the course of mankind's history. But, last summer, reality offered you a literal dramatization of the truth: it is man's irrational emotions that bring him down to the mud; it is man's reason that lifts him to the stars.

(*December 1969–January 1970*)

The "Inexplicable Personal Alchemy"

The following news story by Henry Kamm appeared in *The New York Times* on October 13, 1968, under the title "For Three Minutes I Felt Free."

MOSCOW—For three days last week, the "Prague spring" seemed to have come to one dingy street in Moscow. From morning into evening dissidents from the Soviet way of life openly put their radical views to milling, informal groups, while police blocked the streets to traffic.

The disaffected intellectuals spoke not only under the eyes of the K.G.B. (secret police), but they knew that many of those with whom they debated were either regular members of the security apparatus or were doing part time service for it.

If they had gathered for a similar protest at another time and place, they would have been arrested as surely as were the five dissidents for whom they had come to do vigil, in front of the courthouse on the dingy street.

Inside, the five—Larisa Daniel, Pavel Litvinov, Vadim Delone, Konstantin Babitsky, Vladimir Dremlyuga—were standing trial for having, for a few minutes around noon on Aug. 25 on Red Square, openly spoken their minds about the invasion of Czechoslovakia.

So did Natalya Gorbanevskaya, a poet, who was spared trial because she has two young children, and Viktor Fainberg, an art critic, who lost four teeth during the arrest and consequently appeared to be not presentable even to the limited public admitted to political trials. He was sent to a mental hospital instead.

But for three of the defendants the Government revived the old Czarist penalty for radical political agitators—exile. And the other two were sentenced to prison camps.

Litvinov, a 30-year-old physicist whose grandfather was Maxim Litvinov, Stalin's Foreign Minister, was sentenced to five years of exile in a remote area of Russia, as yet not announced. Mrs. Daniel, wife of Yuli Daniel, the imprisoned writer, was banished for four years to a similar spot. Babitsky, 40-year-old language scholar, received three years in exile.

Dremlyuga, 28, unemployed, was given the maximum jail term of three years. Delone, 23, a student and poet, got a two-and-a-half-year prison term and was ordered to serve four months of a previous suspended sentence.

The ironic circumstance that only when some dissidents are standing trial for having sought to awaken the conscience of this politically inert nation can other dissidents gather publicly, and that their audience is only those of proven immunity to radical thoughts, shows the hard limit to the infinitesimal scope of Soviet dissidence.

The average citizen had no idea that five men and two women had denounced their country's aggression and were being tried consequently on a charge of obstructing pedestrian traffic on the empty vastness of Red Square.

The only ones who knew were those who had been sent to the dingy street to pose as ordinary Communist youths or workers. Their mission was to observe and photograph the few who, through an inexplicable personal alchemy, have thrown off the leading conformity of the only society they have known and are condemned to be its outcasts.

But dissidents cannot change. As Larisa Daniel said outside another courthouse, during an earlier trial, "I cannot do otherwise."

They know that they are known only by those who hate them for raising their voices in protest and by those who love them because they are so few and draw together for company. Two of the principal figures in the street demonstrations—they have no leaders—only shrugged their shoulders when asked last week whether any but their own small number was aware of what they were doing.

But Vladimir Dremlyuga, denounced in court as a provincial Don Juan, replied to the judge who asked him Wednesday whether he thought what he had done on Red Square was right, "Would I go to jail for something I think is not right?"

The small band is becoming increasingly outspoken not because Soviet society has become more tolerant of dissent. What one senses in talking with them is an increasing sense of anguish that the small measure of liberty that appeared like a faint light at the end of the tunnel in the era of former Premier Nikita Khrushchev, earlier in the decade, is being snuffed out. Their courage is born of despair.

They are aware that among scientists particularly there may be chafing at the restrictiveness of life. But they say that most scientists are far removed from political thought and the passion that alone can create freedom.

They know that some poets enjoy a name for dissent outside this country, but if they really want to earn that name, why aren't they here, the radicals ask.

They are not politically naive, although a few have the other-worldly nobility of thought and passion of Don Quixote. Both share the earthly and real passion of Vadim Delone, who, without bravado, told the judge before sentencing:

"For three minutes on Red Square I felt free. I am glad to take your three years for that."*

This news story is such a remarkable example of journalism at its best that I wanted my readers to see it and to consider its wider implications.

It is written by a reporter who knew how to observe essentials and what questions to raise. It is a simple, straightforward, factual account, but its very simplicity and its heartbreaking perceptiveness give it the qualities, not of a news story, but of a work of art: beauty, grandeur, a desperate honesty and a quietly unstressed cry for help—a cry addressed to no one in particular, carried between the lines from the frozen cobblestones of Moscow's twilight to the universe at large.

In the many years since I left that country, this is the first news story about Russia that "got me." It made me feel the kind of personal identification and directly immediate, personal pain that I have not felt about events in Russia for a long time. It is an odd feeling: it is poignancy, wistfulness, helplessness and, above all, sadness—just pure, still sadness. The words in my mind, when I read that story, were: There, but for the grace of the United States of America, go I.

I do not mean that I would have been one of the accused in that Soviet courtroom: I knew enough, in my college days, to know that it was useless to attempt political protests in Soviet Russia. But that knowledge broke down, involuntarily, many times; so I would probably have been one of those protesters in the street who engaged in the terrible futility of debating with the secret police. I know how they felt and what would make them do it.

There is a fundamental conviction which some people never acquire, some hold only in their youth, and a few hold to the end of their days—the conviction that *ideas matter*. In one's youth that conviction is experienced as a self-evident absolute, and one is unable fully to believe that there are people who do not share it. That ideas matter means that knowledge matters, that truth matters, that one's mind matters. And the radiance of that certainty, in the process of growing up, is the best aspect of youth.

Its consequence is the inability to believe in the power or the triumph of evil. No matter what corruption one observes in one's immediate background, one is unable to accept it as normal, permanent or *metaphysically* right. One feels: "This injustice (or terror or falsehood or frustration or pain or agony) is the exception in life, not the rule." One feels certain that somewhere on earth—even if not anywhere in one's surroundings or within one's reach—a proper, human way of life is possible to human beings, and justice matters. It takes years, if ever, to accept the notion that one lives among the not-fully-human; it is impossible to accept that notion in one's youth. And if justice matters, then one fights for it: one speaks out—in the unnamed certainty that someone, somewhere will understand.

It is not the particular content of a young person's ideas that is of primary importance in this issue, but his attitude toward ideas as such. The best way to describe it would be to say that he takes ideas seriously—except that "serious" is too unserious a word in this context: he takes ideas with the most profound, solemn and passionate earnestness. (Granted this attitude, his mind is always open to correct his ideas, if they are wrong or false; but nothing on earth can take precedence for him over the truth of an idea.)

This is the "inexplicable personal alchemy" that puzzled Henry Kamm: an independent mind dedicated to the supremacy of ideas, i.e., of truth.

Young persons who hold that conviction, do not have to "throw off the leading conformity of the only society they have known." They do not conform in the first place: they judge and evaluate; if they accept any part of the prevalent social trends, it is through intellectual agreement (which may be mistaken), not through conformity. They do not need to know different types of society in order to discover the evils, falsehoods or contradictions of the one in which they live: intellectual honesty is the only tool required.

Men who possess this "personal alchemy" are exceedingly rare; they are a small minority in any country or culture. In Soviet Russia, they are tragic martyrs.

It is very likely that many of those young protesters were socialists or "idealistic communists"—like the doomed Czechoslovakian rebels whose subjugation they were protesting. (This was not true in my case and time, I had never been attracted to or fooled by any form of collectivism, but it is likely to be the case of young people some forty years later.) It is likely that those young protesters took Soviet propaganda seriously: brought up on slogans extolling (undefined) freedom, justice, brotherhood and condemning military aggression, they were able to observe the absence of all those social values in Russia and to recognize the invasion of Czechoslovakia as the most brutal type of military aggression. Thus, if they took ideas seriously, they rebelled in the name of the very ideas they had been taught.

(This, incidentally, is the ultimate penalty of all dictators [and all liars]: their nemesis is those who believe them. A dictatorship has to promulgate some sort of distant goals and moral ideals in order to justify its rule and the people's immolation; the extent to which it succeeds in convincing its victims, is the extent of its own danger; sooner or later, its contradictions are thrown in its face by the best of its subjects: the ablest, the most intelligent, the *most honest.* Thus a dictatorship is forced to destroy and to keep on destroying the best of its "human resources." And be it fifty years or five centuries later, ambitious thugs and lethargic drones are all a dictatorship will have left to exploit and rule; the rest will die young, physically or spiritually.)

The dedication to ideas leads, in practice, to an almost involuntary goodwill toward men—or rather to something deeper and more important, which is the root of goodwill: *respect.* It leads to the attitude, in individual encounters, of treating men as rational beings, on the unstated premise that a man is innocent until proved guilty, that he is not evil until he has proved himself to be; "evil," in terms of this attitude, means closed to the power of ideas, i.e., of reason.

This is what would make the young dissenters debate political issues with the agents of the secret police. Wordlessly, the unnamed, unidentified feeling "These are human beings" would take precedence over the knowledge that these are human monsters. If named, the driving motive of the dissenters would be an appeal which, to them, is irresistible: "But don't you see? It's *true!*"—and they would speak, regardless of circumstances, regardless of danger, regardless of their audience, so long as the audience had a human form, they would speak in desperate innocence, knowing that a life-or-death imperative compels them to speak, not knowing fully why.

And, facing a firing squad, if necessary, they would still feel it, with no time to learn why and to discover that they are moved by the noblest form of *metaphysical* self-preservation: the refusal to commit spiritual suicide by abnegating one's own mind and to survive as a lobotomized automaton.

While her husband was being tried and sentenced to a prison camp, Larisa Daniel said, supporting him: "I cannot do otherwise." As a human being, she could not.

Replying to a judge "who asked him whether he thought what he had done on Red Square was right," Vladimir Dremlyuga said: "Would I go to jail for something I think is not right?" Observe that this is an appeal to reason, an answer that springs spontaneously from the implicit premise that the "right" matters, that a logically and morally incontrovertible answer would matter to a judge who is a human being. I doubt that, at the age of 28, Dremlyuga would be able to conceive of the psychological depravity he was dealing with—of the fact that the very purity and rightness of his answer would evoke in the judge's mind, not a sense of justice, but a response of guilty, vindictive hatred.

Now consider the words of Vadim Delone when he said quietly ("without bravado") to a judge about to sentence him to three years in prison: "For three minutes on Red Square I felt free. I am glad to take your three years for that."

This, I submit, is one of the noblest and most revealing statements ever recorded. It is revealing psycho-epistemologically, as an indication of the kind of soul that would make it.

Delone seemed to be aware of the nature of his judges and of the social system they represented. Whom, then, was he addressing?

Observe, in this connection, that these young dissenters had "sought to awaken the conscience of this politically inert nation"—a nation resigned to slavery, indifferent to good or evil—yet they were not "politically naive" and two of their supporters in the street demonstrations "only shrugged their shoulders when asked . . . whether any but their own small number was aware of what they were doing."

Consciously or not, in the mind of any rebel in Soviet Russia, particularly of the young, there is only one court of final appeal against the injustice, the brutality, the sadistic horror of the inhuman social system in which they are trapped: *abroad.*

The meaning of that word for a Soviet citizen is incommunicable to anyone who has not lived in that country: if you project what you would feel for a combination of Atlantis, the Promised Land and the most glorious civilization on another planet, as imagined by a benevolent kind of science fiction, you will have a pale approximation. "Abroad," to a Soviet Russian, is as distant, shining and unattainable as these; yet to any Russian who lifts his head for a moment from the Soviet muck, the concept "abroad" is a psychological necessity, a lifeline and soul preserver.

That concept is made of brilliant bits sneaked, smuggled or floating in through the dense gray fog of the country's physical and spiritual barbed-wire walls: in foreign movies, magazines, radio broadcasts, or even the clothing and the confident posture of foreign visitors. These bits are so un-Soviet and so alive that they blend in one's mind into a vision of freedom, abundance, unimaginable technological efficacy, inconceivable achievements and, above all, a sense of joyous, fearless, benevolent gaiety. And if European countries, in this vision, are shining planets, America is the sun.

It is not that one hopes for material help or liberation to come from "abroad"; it is that such a place *exists.* The mere knowledge that a nobler way of life is possible somewhere, redeems the human race in one's mind. And when, in moments of despair or final extremity, one cries out in protest, that cry is not consciously addressed to anyone, only to whatever justice might exist in the universe at large; but, subconsciously, the universe at large is "abroad."

And what *is* "abroad," in fact? What is America today?

According to the dominant voices of her press, America, too, has a vanguard of young rebels, dissenters and fighters for freedom. Marching down the aisle of a theater, they shout their protest to the world: "I cannot travel without a passport! . . . I am not allowed to smoke marijuana! . . . I am not allowed to take my clothes off!" (*The New York Times,* October 15, 1968.)

These self-made puppets in search of a master, dangling and jerking hysterically at the end of strings no one wants to pick up, begging and demanding to be taken care of—these exhibitionists who have nothing to exhibit, who combine the methods of a thug with the candied platitudes of a small-town evangelist, whose "creative self-expression" is as stale as their unwashed bodies, with drugs eating away their brains, obscenities as the (appropriate) voice of their souls, and an all-consuming hatred as their only visible emotion—are the embodied symbols and protégés of the Establishment they are going through the motions of defying. There is a level of cowardice lower than that of a conformist: the "fashionable non-conformist."

Akin, in spirit, to any other product of decomposition, these are the products of a decadent culture, who crawl out of the wreckage left on college campuses by generations practicing the cult of irrationality. With one eye on the gallery of their applauding teachers, they rebel against the "System" of their groggy elders in the name of such controversial issues as "Love" and "Poverty," they demand the freedom to batter down doors and chase speakers away from university lecterns, the freedom to burn the manuscripts of professors, the freedom to bash in the skulls of their opponents—and, openly proclaiming their intention to kill, they win the apologies of judges, college presidents and newspaper editors, who call them "youthful idealists," they are tailed by television crews, they fight on the barricades of coffeehouses and discotheques, they lay siege to Hollywood and storm the Bastille of the jet set's cocktail parties.

While, under dictatorships, young men are giving their lives for the freedom of the mind, it is against the mind—against the "tyranny" of reason and reality—that young thugs are rebelling in America. It is the mind—the power of ideas—that Western culture is now rigged to destroy, offering the power of dope, guns and gangs as a substitute.

There is a level of intellectual corruption lower than that of adolescent hoodlums: their aging, sanctimonious apologists who gush that the hoodlums are moved by *compassion*. "Compassion?" "Justice?" "Brotherhood?" "Concern for suffering?" "The liberation of the oppressed?" If any of these were their actual motives, where were those crusaders in October of last year? Why aren't they staging a demonstration in front of the Soviet Embassy?

If anyone wonders at the *moral* credibility gap of today—at the heavy, gray dullness of our cultural atmosphere, with its sickening mixture of boredom and blood, at the lethargic cynicism, the skeptical indifference, the moral limpness, and the contempt of the country at large for all those prostituted slogans (as well as its desperately blind quest and need of morality)—this Grand Guignol of altruism is the reason.

Who can take any values seriously if he is offered, for moral inspiration, a choice between two images of youth: an unshaved, barefooted Harvard graduate, throwing bottles and bombs at policemen—or a prim, sun-helmeted, frustrated little autocrat of the Peace Corps, spoon-feeding babies in a jungle clinic?

No, these are not representative of America's youth—they are, in fact, a very small minority with a very loud group of unpaid p.r. [agents] on university faculties and among the press—but where are its representatives? Where are America's young fighters for ideas, the rebels against conformity to the gutter—the young men of "inexplicable personal alchemy," the independent minds dedicated to the supremacy of truth?

With very rare exceptions, they are perishing in silence, unknown and unnoticed. Consciously or subconsciously, philosophically and psychologically, it is against them that the cult of irrationality—i.e., our entire academic and cultural Establishment—is directed.

They perish gradually, giving up, extinguishing their minds before they have a chance to grasp the nature of the evil they are facing. In lonely agony, they go from confident eagerness to bewilderment to indignation to resignation—to obscurity. And while their elders putter about, conserving redwood forests and building sanctuaries for mallard ducks, nobody notices those youths as they drop out of sight one by one, like sparks vanishing in limitless black space; nobody builds sanctuaries for the best of the human species.

So will the young Russian rebels perish spiritually—if they survive their jail terms physically. How long can a man preserve his sacred fire if he knows that jail is the reward for loyalty to reason? No longer than he can preserve it if he is taught that that loyalty is irrelevant—as he is taught both in the East and in the West. There are exceptions who will hold out, no matter what the circumstances. But these are exceptions that mankind has no right to expect.

When I read that news story about the Russian rebels, I thought of what I would have felt, in my youth and in their place: if I knew that someone had escaped from the Soviet hell, it is him (or her) that I would have expected to speak for me. Today, since I did escape and have acquired a public voice, I felt that I had to speak for them—in the name of justice—even if few will hear me in the empty vastness of a decadent culture.

I do not know what effect my one voice can have in a matter of this kind. But I am addressing myself to the best within any man, Objectivist or not, who has preserved some sense of humanity, justice and *compassion,* and is still able to *care* and to *give a damn.*

There is only one form of protest open to the men of goodwill in the semi-free world: *do not sanction the Soviet jailers of those young people*—do not help them to pretend that they are the morally acceptable leaders of a civilized country. Do not patronize or support the evil pretense of the so-called "cultural exchanges"—any Soviet-government-sponsored scientists, professors, writers, artists, musicians, dancers (who are either vicious bootlickers or doomed, tortured victims). Do not patronize, support or deal with any Soviet supporters and apologists in this country: *they* are the guiltiest men of all. Speak out on any scale open to you, public or private, in protest and in defense of those young victims.

In a somewhat inadequate editorial (October 13, 1968), *The New York Times* said that the sentences of the young rebels "could have been—and probably would have been—much harsher had there not been such widespread admiration for these Soviet opponents of Soviet aggression, and so much world concern about their fate."

If the protest of the men of goodwill were wide enough and sustained enough, it might possibly save the condemned.

And one can never tell in what way or form some feedback from such a protest might reach the loncly children in Red Square.

(*January 1969*)

The Age of Envy

A culture, like an individual, has a sense of life or, rather, the equivalent of a sense of life—an emotional atmosphere created by its dominant philosophy, by its view of man and of existence. This emotional atmosphere represents a culture's dominant values and serves as the leitmotif of a given age, setting its trends and its style.

Thus Western civilization had an Age of Reason and an Age of Enlightenment. In those periods, the quest for reason and enlightenment was the dominant intellectual drive and created a corresponding emotional atmosphere that fostered these values.

Today, we live in the Age of Envy.

"Envy" is not the emotion I have in mind, but it is the clearest manifestation of an emotion that has remained nameless; it is the only element of a complex emotional sum that men have permitted themselves to identify.

Envy is regarded by most people as a petty, superficial emotion and, therefore, it serves as a semihuman cover for so inhuman an emotion that those who feel it seldom dare admit it even to themselves. Mankind has lived with it, has observed its manifestations and, to various extents, has been ravaged by it for countless centuries, yet has failed to grasp its meaning and to rebel against its exponents.

Today, that emotion is the leitmotif, the sense of life of our culture. It is all around us, we are drowning in it, it is almost explicitly confessed by its more brazen exponents—yet men continue to evade its existence and are peculiarly afraid to name it, as primitive people were once afraid to pronounce the name of the devil.

That emotion is: *hatred of the good for being the good.*

This hatred is not resentment against some prescribed view of the good with which one does not agree. For instance, if a child resents some conventional type of obedient boy who is constantly held up to him as an ideal to emulate, this is not hatred of the good: the child does *not* regard that boy as *good,* and his resentment is the product of a clash between his values and those of his elders (though he is too young to grasp the issue in such terms). Similarly, if an adult does not regard altruism as good and resents the adulation bestowed upon some "humanitarian," this is a clash between his values and those of others, not hatred of the good.

Hatred of the good for being the good means hatred of that which one regards as good by one's own (conscious or subconscious) judgment. It means hatred of a person for possessing a value or virtue one regards as desirable.

If a child wants to get good grades in school, but is unable or unwilling to achieve them and begins to hate the children who do, *that* is hatred of the good. If a man regards intelligence as a value, but is troubled by self-doubt and begins to hate the men *he* judges to be intelligent, *that* is hatred of the good.

The nature of the particular values a man chooses to hold is not the primary factor in this issue (although irrational values may contribute a great deal to the formation of that emotion). The primary factor and distinguishing characteristic is an emotional mechanism set in reverse: a response of hatred, not toward human vices, but toward human virtues.

To be exact, the emotional mechanism is not set in reverse, but is set one way: its exponents do not experience love for evil men; their emotional range is limited to hatred or indifference. It is impossible to experience love, which is a response to values, when one's automatized response to values is hatred.

In any specific instance, this type of hatred is heavily enmeshed in rationalizations. The most common one is: "I don't hate him for his intelligence, but for his conceit!" More often than not, if one asks the speaker to name the evidence of the victim's conceit, he exhausts such generalities as: "He's insolent . . . he's stubborn . . . he's selfish," and ends up with some indeterminate accusation which amounts to: "He's intelligent and he knows it." Well, why shouldn't he know it? Blank out. Should he hide it? Blank out. From whom should he hide it? The implicit, but never stated, answer is: "From people like me."

Yet such haters accept and even seem to admire the spectacle of conceit put on for their benefit by a man who shows off, boasting about his own alleged virtues or achievements, blatantly confessing a lack of self-confidence. This, of course, is a clue to the nature of the hatred. The haters seem unable to differentiate conceptually between "conceit" and a deserved *pride,* yet they seem to know the difference "instinctively," i.e., by means of their automatized sense of life.

Since very few men have fully consistent characters, it is often hard to tell, in a specific instance, whether a given man is hated for his virtues or for his actual flaws. In regard to one's own feelings, only a rigorously conscientious habit of introspection can enable one to be certain of the nature and causes of one's emotional responses. But introspection is the mental process most fiercely avoided by the haters, which permits them a virtually unlimited choice of rationalizations. In regard to judging the emotional responses of others, it is extremely difficult to tell their reasons in a specific case, particularly if it involves complex personal relationships. It is, therefore, in the broad, impersonal field of responses to strangers, to casual acquaintances, to public figures or to events that have no direct bearing on the haters' own lives that one can observe the hatred of the good in a pure, unmistakable form.

Its clearest manifestation is the attitude of a person who characteristically resents someone's success, happiness, achievement or good fortune—and experiences pleasure at someone's failure, unhappiness or misfortune. This is pure, "nonvenal" hatred of the good for being the good: the hater has nothing to lose or gain in such instances, no practical value at stake, no existential motive, no knowledge except the fact that a human being has succeeded or failed. The expressions of this response are brief, casual, as a rule involuntary. But if you have seen it, you have seen the naked face of evil.

Do not confuse this response with that of a person who resents someone's unearned success, or feels pleased by someone's deserved failure. These responses are caused by a sense of justice, which is an entirely different phenomenon, and its emotional manifestations are different: in such cases, a person expresses indignation, not hatred—or relief, not malicious gloating.

Superficially, the motive of those who hate the good is taken to be envy. A dictionary definition of envy is: "1. a sense of discontent or jealousy with regard to another's advantages, success, possessions, etc. 2. desire for an advantage possessed by another." (*The Random House Dictionary,* 1968.) The same dictionary adds the following elucidation: "To *envy* is to feel resentful because someone else possesses or has achieved what one wishes oneself to possess or to have achieved."

This covers a great many emotional responses, which come from different motives. In a certain sense, the second definition is the opposite of the first, and the more innocent of the two.

For example, if a poor man experiences a moment's envy of another man's wealth, the feeling may mean nothing more than a momentary concretization of his desire for wealth; the feeling is not directed against that particular rich person and is concerned with the wealth, not the person. The feeling, in effect, may amount to: "I wish I had an income (or a house, or a car, or an overcoat) like his." The result of this feeling may be an added incentive for the man to improve his financial condition.

The feeling is less innocent, if it involves personal resentment and amounts to: "I want to put on a front, like this man." The result is a second-hander who lives beyond his means, struggling to "keep up with the Joneses."

The feeling is still less innocent, if it amounts to: "I want *this man's* car (or overcoat, or diamond shirt studs, or industrial establishment)." The result is a criminal.

But these are still human beings, in various stages of immorality, compared to the inhuman object whose feeling is: "I *hate* this man because he is wealthy and I am not."

Envy is part of this creature's feeling, but only the superficial, semirespectable part; it is like the tip of an iceberg showing nothing worse than ice, but with the submerged part consisting of a compost of rotting living matter. The envy, in this case, is semirespectable because it seems to imply a desire for material possessions, which is a human being's desire. But, deep down, the creature has no such desire: it does not want to be rich, it wants the human being to be poor.

This is particularly clear in the much more virulent cases of hatred, masked as envy, for those who possess personal values or virtues: hatred for a man (or a woman) because he (or she) is beautiful or intelligent or successful or honest or happy. In these cases, the creature has no desire and makes no effort to improve its appearance, to develop or to use its intelligence, to struggle for success, to practice honesty, to be happy (nothing can make it happy). It knows that the disfigurement or the mental collapse or the failure or the immorality or the misery of its victim would not endow it with his or her value. *It does not desire the value: it desires the value's destruction.*

"They do not want to own your fortune, they want you to lose it; they do not want to succeed, they want you to fail; they do not want to live, they want you to die; they desire nothing, they hate existence . . ." (*Atlas Shrugged.*)

What endows such a creature with a quality of abysmal evil is the fact that it has an awareness of values and is able to recognize them in people. If it were merely amoral, it would be indifferent; it would be unable to distinguish virtues from flaws. But it does distinguish them—and the essential characteristic of its corruption is the fact that its mind's recognition of a *value* is transmitted to its emotional mechanism as *hatred,* not as love, desire or admiration.

Consider the full meaning of this attitude. Values are that which one acts to gain and/or keep. Values are a necessity of man's survival, and wider: of any living organism's survival. Life is a process of self-sustaining and self-generated action, and the successful pursuit of values is a precondition of remaining alive. Since nature does not provide man with an automatic knowledge of the code of values he requires, there are differences in the codes which men accept and the goals they pursue. But consider the abstraction "value," apart from the particular content of any given code, and ask yourself: What is the nature of a creature in which the sight of a value arouses hatred and the desire to destroy? In the most profound sense of the term, such a creature is a killer, not a physical, but a metaphysical one—it is not an enemy of *your* values, but of *all* values, it is an enemy of anything that enables men to survive, it is an enemy of life as such and of everything living.

A community of values—of some sort of values—is a necessity of any successful relationship among living beings. If you were training an animal, you would not hurt it every time it obeyed you. If you were bringing up a child, you would not punish him whenever he acted properly. What relationship can you have with the hating creatures, and what element do they introduce into social relationships? If you struggle for existence and find that your success brings you, not approval and appreciation, but hatred, if you strive to be moral and find that your virtue brings you, not the love, but the hatred of your fellow-men, what becomes of your own benevolence? Will you be able to generate or to maintain a feeling of good will toward your fellow-men?

The greatest danger in this issue is men's inability—or worse: unwillingness—fully to identify it.

Evil as the hating creatures are, there is something still more evil: those who try to appease them.

It is understandable that men might seek to hide their vices from the eyes of people whose judgment they respect. But there are men who hide their virtues from the eyes of monsters. There are men who apologize for their own achievements, deride their own values, debase their own character—for the sake of pleasing those they know to be stupid, corrupt, malicious, evil. An obsequious pandering to the vanity of some alleged superior, such as a king, for the sake of some practical advantage, is bad enough. But pandering to the vanity of one's inferiors—inferior specifically in regard to the value involved—is so shameful an act of treason to one's values that nothing can be left thereafter of the person who commits it, neither intellectually nor morally, and nothing ever is.

If men attempt to play up to those they admire, and fake virtues they do not possess, it is futile, but understandable, if not justifiable. But to fake vices, weaknesses, flaws, disabilities? To shrink one's soul and stature? To play down—or write down, or speak down, or think down?

Observe just one social consequence of this policy: such appeasers do not hesitate to join some cause or other appealing for mercy; they never raise their voices in the name of justice.

Cowardice is so ignoble an inner state that men struggle to overcome it, in the face of real dangers. The appeaser chooses a state of cowardice where no danger exists. To live in fear is so unworthy a condition that men have died on barricades, defying the tyranny of the mighty. The appeaser chooses to live in chronic fear of the impotent. Men have died in torture chambers, on the stake, in concentration camps, in front of firing squads, rather than renounce their convictions. The appeaser renounces his under the pressure of a frown on any vacant face. Men have refused to sell their souls in exchange for fame, fortune, power, even their own lives. The appeaser does not sell his soul: he gives it away for free, getting nothing in return.

The appeaser's usual rationalization is: "I don't want to be disliked." By whom? By people he dislikes, despises and condemns.

Let me give you some examples. An intellectual who was recruiting members for Mensa—an international society allegedly restricted to intelligent men, which selects members on the dubious basis of I.Q. tests—was quoted in an interview as follows: "Intelligence is not especially admired by people. Outside Mensa you had to be very careful not to win an argument and lose a friend. Inside Mensa we can be ourselves and that is a great relief." (*The New York Times,* September 11, 1966.) A friend, therefore, is more important than the truth. What kind of friend? The kind that resents you for being right.

A professor, the head of a department in a large university, had a favorite graduate student who wanted to be a teacher. The professor had tested him as an instructor and regarded him as exceptionally intelligent. In a private conversation with the young man's parents, the professor praised him highly and declared: "There is only one danger in his future: he is such a good teacher that the rest of the faculty will resent him." When the young man got his Ph.D., the professor did not offer him a job, even though he had the power to do so.

The notion that an intelligent girl should hide her intelligence in order to be popular with men and find a husband, is widespread and well-known. Of what value would such a husband be to her? Blank out.

In an old movie dealing with college life, a boy asks a girl to help him get good grades by means of an actually criminal scheme (it involves the theft of a test from the professor's office). When she refuses, the boy asks scornfully: "Are you some sort of moralist?" "Oh, no, no," she answers hastily and *apologetically,* "it's just my small-town upbringing, I guess."

Do not confuse appeasement with tactfulness or generosity. Appeasement is not consideration for the feelings of others, it is *consideration for and compliance with the unjust, irrational and evil feelings of others.* It is a policy of exempting the emotions of others from moral judgment, and of willingness to sacrifice innocent, virtuous victims to the evil malice of such emotions.

Tactfulness is consideration extended only to rational feelings. A tactful man does not stress his success or happiness in the presence of those who have suffered failure, loss or unhappiness; not because he suspects them of envy, but because he realizes that the contrast can revive and sharpen their pain. He does not stress his virtues in anyone's presence: he takes for granted that they are recognized. As a rule, a man of achievement does not flaunt his achievements, neither among equals nor inferiors nor superiors; he does not evaluate himself—or others—by a comparative standard. His attitude is not: "I am better than you," but: "I am good."

If, however, he encounters an envious hater who gets huffy, trying to ignore, deny or insult his achievements, he asserts them proudly. In answer to the hater's stock question: "Who do you think you are?"—he tells him.

It is the pretentious mediocrity—the show-off, the boaster, the snooty posturer—who seeks, not virtue or value, but *superiority*. A comparative standard is his only guide, which means that he has no standards and that he has a vested interest in reducing others to inferiority. Decent people, properly, resent a show-off, but the haters and enviers do not: they recognize him as a soul mate.

Offensive boasting or self-abasing appeasement is a false alternative. As in all human relationships, the guidelines of proper conduct are: objectivity and justice. But this is not what men are taught or were taught in the past.

"Use your head—but don't let anyone know it. Set your goals high—but don't admit it. Be honest—but don't uphold it. Be successful—but hide it. Be great—but act small. Be happy—but God help you if you are!" Such are the moral injunctions we gather from the cultural atmosphere in which we grow up—as men did in the past, throughout history.

The appeasement of evil—of an unknowable, undefinable, inexplicable evil—has been the undertow of mankind's cultural stream all through the ages. In primitive cultures (and even in ancient Greece) the appeasement took the form of the belief that the gods resent human happiness or success, because these are the prerogatives of the gods to which men must not aspire. Hence the superstitious fear of acknowledging one's good fortune—as, for instance, the ritual of parents wailing that their newborn son is puny, ugly, worthless, for fear that a demon would harm him if they admitted their happy pride in his health and looks. Observe the contradiction: Why attempt to deceive an omnipotent demon who would be able to judge the infant's value for himself? The intention of the ritual, therefore, is not: "Don't let him know that the infant is good," but: "Don't let him know that *you* know it and that you're happy!"

Men create gods—and demons—in their own likeness; mystic fantasies, as a rule, are invented to explain some phenomenon for which men find no explanation. The notion of gods who are so malicious that they wish men to live in chronic misery, would not be conceived or believed unless men sensed all around them the presence of some inexplicable malevolence directed specifically at their personal happiness.

Are the haters of the good that numerous? No. The actual haters are a small, depraved minority in any age or culture. The spread and perpetuation of this evil are accomplished by those who profiteer on it.

The profiteers are men with a vested interest in mankind's psychological devastation, who burrow their way into positions of moral-intellectual leadership. They provide the haters with unlimited means of rationalization, dissimulation, excuse and camouflage, including ways of passing vices off as virtues. They slander, confuse and disarm the victims. Their vested interest is power-lust. Their stock-in-trade is any system of thought or of belief aimed at keeping men *small.*

Observe the nature of some of mankind's oldest legends.

Why were the men of Babel punished? Because they attempted to build a tower to the sky.

Why did Phaëthon perish? Because he attempted to drive the chariot of the sun.

Why was Icarus smashed? Because he attempted to fly.

Why was Arachne transformed into a spider? Because she challenged a goddess to a competition in the art of weaving—and won it.

"Do not aspire—do not venture—do not rise—ambition is self-destruction," drones this ancient chorus through the ages—through all the ages, changing its lyrics, but not its tune—all the way to the Hollywood movies in which the boy who goes to seek a career in the big city becomes a wealthy, but miserable scoundrel, while the small-town boy who stays put wins the girl next door, who wins over the glamorous temptress.

There is and was abundant evidence to show that the curse of an overwhelming majority of men is passivity, lethargy and fear, not ambition and audacity. But men's well-being is not the motive of that chorus.

Toward the end of World War II, newspapers reported the following: when Russian troops moved west and occupied foreign towns, the Soviet authorities automatically executed any person who had a bank account of $100 or a high-school education; the rest of the inhabitants submitted. This is a physical dramatization of the spiritual policy of mankind's moral-intellectual leaders: destroy the tops, the rest will give up and obey.

Just as a political dictator needs specially indoctrinated thugs to enforce his orders, so his intellectual road-pavers need them to maintain their power. Their thugs are the haters of the good; the special indoctrination is the morality of altruism.

It is obvious—historically, philosophically and psychologically—that altruism is an inexhaustible source of rationalizations for the most evil motives, the most inhuman actions, the most loathsome emotions. It is not difficult to grasp the meaning of the tenet that *the good is an object of sacrifice*—and to understand what a blanket damnation of anything living is represented by an undefined accusation of "selfishness."

But here is a significant phenomenon to observe: the haters and enviers—who are the most vociferous shock troops of altruism—seem to be subconsciously impervious to the altruist criterion of the good. The touchy vanity of these haters—which flares up at any suggestion of their inferiority to a man of virtue—is not aroused by any saint or hero of altruism, whose moral superiority they profess to acknowledge. Nobody envies Albert Schweitzer. Whom do they envy? The man of intelligence, of ability, of achievement, of independence.

If anyone ever believed (or tried to believe) that the motive of altruism is compassion, that its goal is the relief of human suffering and the elimination of poverty, the state of today's culture now deprives him of any foothold on self-deception. Today, altruism is running amuck, shedding its tattered rationalizations and displaying its soul.

Altruists are no longer concerned with material wealth, not

even with its "redistribution," only with its destruction—but even this is merely a means to an end. Their savage fury is aimed at the destruction of intelligence—of ability, ambition, thought, purpose, justice; the destruction of morality, any sort of morality; the destruction of values qua values.

The last fig leaf of academic pretentiousness is the tag used to disguise this movement: *egalitarianism.* It does not disguise, but reveals.

Egalitarianism means the belief in the equality of all men. If the word "equality" is to be taken in any serious or rational sense, the crusade for this belief is dated by about a century or more: the United States of America has made it an anachronism—by establishing a system based on the principle of individual rights. "Equality," in a human context, is a political term: it means equality before the law, the equality of fundamental, inalienable rights which every man possesses by virtue of his birth as a human being, and which may not be infringed or abrogated by man-made institutions, such as titles of nobility or the division of men into castes established by law, with special privileges granted to some and denied to others. The rise of capitalism swept away all castes, including the institutions of aristocracy and of slavery or serfdom.

But this is not the meaning that the altruists ascribe to the word "equality."

They turn the word into an anti-concept: they use it to mean, not *political,* but *metaphysical* equality—the equality of personal attributes and virtues, regardless of natural endowment or individual choice, performance and character. It is not man-made institutions, but nature, i.e., *reality,* that they propose to fight—by means of man-made institutions.

Since nature does not endow all men with equal beauty or equal intelligence, and the faculty of volition leads men to make different choices, the egalitarians propose to abolish the "unfairness" of nature and of volition, and to establish universal equality *in fact*—in defiance of facts. Since the Law of Identity is impervious to human manipulation, it is the Law of Causality that they struggle to abrogate. Since personal attributes or virtues cannot be "redistributed," they seek to deprive men of their consequences—of the rewards, the benefits, the achievements created by personal attributes and virtues.

It is not equality before the law that they seek, but *inequality:*

the establishment of an inverted social pyramid, with a new aristocracy on top—*the aristocracy of non-value.*

Observe the nature of the various methods used to accomplish this goal.

Since equal pay for unequal performance is too obvious an injustice, the egalitarians solve the problem by forbidding unequal performance. (See the policy of many labor unions.)

Since some men are able to rise faster than others, the egalitarians forbid the concept of "merit" and substitute the concept of "seniority" as the basis of promotions. (See the state of modern railroads.)

Since the expropriation of wealth is a somewhat discredited policy, the egalitarians place limits on the use of wealth and keep shrinking them, thus making wealth inoperative. It is "unfair," they cry, that only the rich can obtain the best medical care—or the best education—or the best housing—or any commodity in short supply, which should be rationed, not competed for—etc., etc. (See any newspaper editorial.)

Since some women are beautiful and others are not, the egalitarians are fighting to forbid beauty contests and television commercials using glamorous models. (See Women's Lib.)

Since some students are more intelligent and study more conscientiously than others, the egalitarians abolish the system of grades based on the objective value of a student's scholastic achievement, and substitute for it a system of grading "on a curve" based on a *comparative* standard: a set number of grades, ranging from A's to failures, is given to each class, regardless of the students' individual performances, with the "distribution" of grades calculated on the relative basis of the collective performance of the class as a whole. Thus a student may get an A or an F for the same work, according to whether he happens to be in a class of morons or of child prodigies. No better way could be devised to endow a young man with a vested interest in the inferiority of others and with fear and hatred of their superiority. (See the state of modern education.)

Observe the fact that all these methods do not provide the inferiors with any part of the virtues of their superiors, but merely frustrate and paralyze the virtues. What, then, is the common denominator and basic premise of these methods? Hatred of the good for being the good.

But most of these examples are merely the older and quieter manifestations of a premise which, once introduced into a culture, grows geometrically, pushing the haters forward and creating new haters where none had existed before. Look at today's stampede.

Pressure-group warfare is an inexorable result of a mixed economy and follows the course of its philosophical progression: it starts with economic groups and leads to an explosion of anti-intellectual, anti-ideological gang warfare. Anything and everything may serve as a rallying point for a new pressure group today, provided it is someone's *weakness.*

Weakness of any sort—intellectual, moral, financial or numerical—is today's standard of value, criterion of rights and claim to privileges. The demand for an institutionalized inequality is voiced openly and belligerently, and the right to a double standard is proclaimed self-righteously.

Since numerical superiority has a certain value, at least in practical politics, the same collectivists who once upheld the vicious doctrine of unlimited majority rule, now deny to the majority—in any given issue—the special privileges they grant to any group that claims to be a minority.

Racism is an evil and primitive form of collectivism. Today, racism is regarded as a crime if practiced by a majority—but as an inalienable right if practiced by a minority. The notion that one's culture is superior to all others solely because it represents the traditions of one's ancestors, is regarded as chauvinism if claimed by a majority—but as "ethnic" pride if claimed by a minority. Resistance to change and progress is regarded as reactionary if demonstrated by a majority—but retrogression to a Balkan village, to an Indian tepee or to the jungle is hailed if demonstrated by a minority.

"Tolerance" and "understanding" are regarded as unilateral virtues. In relation to any given minority, we are told, it is the duty of all others, i.e., of the majority, to tolerate and understand the minority's values and customs—while the minority proclaims that its soul is beyond the outsiders' comprehension, that no common ties or bridges exist, that it does not propose to grasp one syllable of the majority's values, customs or culture, and will continue hurling racist epithets (or worse) at the majority's faces.

Nobody can pretend any longer that the goal of such policies is the elimination of racism—particularly when one observes that the real victims are the better members of these privileged minorities. The self-respecting small home owners and shop owners are the unprotected and undefended victims of every race riot. The minority's members are expected by their egalitarian leaders to remain a passive herd crying for help (which is a precondition of the power to control a pressure group). Those who ignore the threats and struggle to rise through individual effort and achievement are denounced as traitors. Traitors—to what? To a physiological (racial) collective—to the incompetence or unwillingness or lethargy or malingering of others. If the exceptional men are black, they are attacked as "Uncle Toms." But the status of privileged minority is not confined to the blacks, it extends to all racial minorities—on one condition—and some of the most offensive herds are white.

That condition—the deeper issue involved, of greater importance to the egalitarians than mere numerical weakness—is the *primitive* nature of a given minority's traditions, i.e., its *cultural* weakness.

It is primitive cultures that we are asked to study, to appreciate and to respect—any sort of culture except our own. A piece of pottery copied from generation to generation is held up to us as an achievement—a plastic cup is not. A bearskin is an achievement—synthetic fiber is not. An oxcart is an achievement—an airplane is not. A potion of herbs and snake oil is an achievement—open-heart surgery is not. Stonehenge is an achievement—the Empire State Building is not. Black magic is an achievement—Aristotle's *Organon* is not. And if there is a more repulsive spectacle than a television broadcast presenting, as news, any two-bit group of pretentious, self-conscious adolescents, out of old vaudeville, performing some Slavonic folk dance on a street corner, in the shadow of New York's skyscrapers—I have not discovered it yet.

Why is Western civilization admonished to admire primitive cultures? Because they are *not* admirable. Why is a primitive man exhorted to ignore Western achievements? Because they *are.* Why is the self-expression of a retarded adolescent to be nurtured and acclaimed? Because he has nothing to express. Why is the self-expression of a genius to be impeded and ignored? Because he *has.*

"It is to the Mohammedans, the Buddhists, and the cannibals—to the underdeveloped, the undeveloped, and the not-to-be-developed cultures—that the Capitalist United States of America is asked to apologize for her skyscrapers, her automobiles, her plumbing, and her smiling, confident, untortured, un-skinned-alive, un-eaten young men! . . . It is not for her flaws that the United States of America is hated, but *for her virtues*—not for her weaknesses, but *for her achievements*—not for her failures, but *for her success*—her magnificent, shining, life-giving success." ("The Obliteration of Capitalism," *The Objectivist Newsletter,* October 1965.)

If there were such a thing as a passion for equality (not equality *de jure,* but *de facto*), it would be obvious to its exponents that there are only two ways to achieve it: either by raising all men to the mountaintop—or by razing the mountains. The first method is impossible because it is the faculty of volition that determines a man's stature and actions; but the nearest approach to it was demonstrated by the United States and capitalism, which protected the freedom, the rewards and the incentives for every individual's achievement, each to the extent of his ability and ambition, thus raising the intellectual, moral and economic state of the whole society. The second method is impossible because, if mankind were leveled down to the common denominator of its least competent members, it would not be able to survive (and its best would not choose to survive on such terms). Yet it is the second method that the altruist-egalitarians are pursuing. The greater the evidence of their policy's consequences, i.e., the greater the spread of misery, of injustice, of vicious inequality throughout the world, the more frantic their pursuit—which is one demonstration of the fact that there is no such thing as a benevolent passion for equality and that the claim to it is only a rationalization to cover a passionate hatred of the good for being the good.

To understand the meaning and motives of egalitarianism, project it into the field of medicine. Suppose a doctor is called to help a man with a broken leg and, instead of setting it, proceeds to break the legs of ten other men, explaining that this would make the patient feel better; when all these men become crippled for life, the doctor advocates the passage of a law compelling everyone to walk on crutches—in order to make the cripples feel better and equalize the "unfairness" of nature.

If this is unspeakable, how does it acquire an aura of morality—or even the benefit of a moral doubt—when practiced in regard to man's mind? Yet this kind of motivation—hatred of the healthy for being healthy, i.e., of the good for being the good—is the ruling spirit of today's culture.

Observe some random symptoms cracking open all around us, like the skin lesions of a hidden disease.

Egalitarian educators defeated a plan to establish a Montessori day-care center for disadvantaged children, because they "feared that the Montessori-trained disadvantaged children would enter public kindergarten or the first grade with an advantage over the other children." What was these educators' motive: the desire to lift the children of the poor—or to bring everyonc down?

A noted economist proposed the establishment of *a tax on personal ability,* suggesting that "a modest first step might be a special tax on persons with high academic scores." What would this do to the talented, purposeful young people who are barely able to make a living while working their way through school? Would they be able to pay a tax for the privilege of using their intelligence? Who—rich or poor—would want to use his intelligence in such conditions? Is it love that would condemn the best of men to a lifetime of hiding their intelligence as a guilty secret?

Was compassion the motive of the noted social worker who, years ago, wrote about her visit to Soviet Russia: "It was wonderful to see that everybody in the streets was equally shabby"? Is compassion the motive of those who denounce the United States for the existence of slums in cities—yet keep silent about or sympathize with the Soviet system, which has turned an entire country into a gigantic slum, with the exception of a small elite of rulers on top, and a vast, bloody sewer of forced labor camps below?

Ask yourself what were the motives in the following example. A professor asked his class which of two projected systems they would prefer: a system of unequal salaries—or a system paying everyone the same salary, but which would be lower than the lowest one paid under the unequal system. With the exception of one student, the entire class voted for the system of equal salaries (which was also the professor's preference).

In politics, observe the sanctimonious smugness of any ward heeler who recites the ritualistic formula about defending the interests of "the poor, the black and the young." Why these? Because they are (presumably) weak. Who are the other kinds of citizens and what about their interests? Blank out. The implication he conveys is not that the opposite kinds are "the rich, the white and the old" (the "hard-hats" are not rich, the "Uncle Toms" are black, and the old are the heroes of Medicare). The implication is that there is only one kind of opposite, regardless of age, sex, creed, color or economic status: *the competent.*

At the turn of the century, when the notions of socialism were gaining adherents, it was believed that the competent should be enslaved in order to raise the rest of mankind to their level and equalize material benefits. Even though such a belief is evil, its adherents were better than today's egalitarians—as a man who kills for the sake of robbery is better than a man who kills for kicks. Today, socialism's record has demonstrated the impracticality of enslaving man's mind—and has brought deeply buried motives out into the open. Today's advocates of "equality" do not pretend that they wish to improve the lot of the poor; they do not wish to exploit the competent, but to destroy them.

If anyone doubted the possibility of such motives, the ecological crusade should remove all doubts.

When men's greatest benefactor, technology, is denounced as an enemy of mankind—when the U.S. is damned, not for the alleged exploitation of the masses, but explicitly for their material prosperity—when the villain is no longer the Wall Street tycoon, but the American worker—when his crime is held to be his paycheck, and his greed consists in owning a television set—when the current pejorative is not "the rich," but "the middle class" (which means the best, the most competent, the most ambitious, the most productive group in any society, the group of self-made men)—when the plight of the poor is held to be, not poverty, but *relative* poverty (i.e., envy)—when the great emancipator, the automobile, is attacked as a public menace, and highways are decried as a violation of the wilderness—when bleary-eyed, limp-limbed young hobos of both sexes chant about the evil of labor-saving devices, and demand that human life be devoted to the grubby hand-planting of truck gardens, and to garbage disposal—when alleged scientists stretch, fake or suppress scientific evidence in order to panic the ignorant about the interplanetary perils augured by some such omen as the presence of mercury in tuna fish—when their leading philosopher proclaims that work is an outdated prejudice, that fornication should replace ambition, and that mankind's standard of living should be *brought down*—when sundry hordes block the construction of electric generators and are about to plunge New York City into the catastrophe of an overloaded power system's failure—it is time to grasp that we are not dealing with man-lovers, but with killers.

A cultural movement often produces caricatures of itself that emphasize its essence. The hippies are one such caricature. These ecological crusaders—who would pollute any stream by stepping into it—are the physical embodiments of the spirit of today's culture. Much more can be said about their motives, but for the moment observe the intention of the physical appearance they choose to assume. The purpose of flaunting deliberate ugliness and bodily dirt is to offend others (while simultaneously playing for pity)—to defy, to affront, to bait those who hold values, any values.

But the hippies were not enough. They were surpassed by the caricature to end all caricatures: Women's Lib.

Just as the egalitarians ride on the historical prestige of those who fought for political equality, and struggle to achieve the opposite—so their special sorority, Women's Lib, rides on the historical prestige of women who fought for individual rights against government power, and struggles to get special privileges by means of government power.

Screaming that it is out to fight prejudice against women, this movement is providing evidence on a grand public scale—on any street corner and television screen—to support the worst prejudices of the bitterest misogynist.

As a group, American women are the most privileged females on earth: they control the wealth of the United States—through inheritance from fathers and husbands who work themselves into an early grave, struggling to provide every comfort and luxury for the bridge-playing, cocktail-party-chasing cohorts, who give them very little in return. Women's Lib proclaims that they should give still less, and exhorts its members to refuse to cook their husbands' meals—with its placards commanding: "Starve a rat today!" (Where would the cat's food come from, after the rat is starved? Blank out.)

The notion that a woman's place is in the home—the *Kinder-Küche-Kirche* axis—is an ancient, primitive evil, supported and perpetuated by women as much as, or more than, by men. The aggressive, embittered, self-righteous and envious housewife is the greatest enemy of the career woman. Women's Lib pounces upon this aggressiveness, bitterness, self-righteousness, envy—and directs it toward men. (It gives the lie, however, to one masculine prejudice: women are thought to be catty, but no cat and very few men could experience the degree of malicious hostility that these women are now displaying.)

There is no place on earth where so many opportunities are open to career women as in the United States, or where so many women have achieved successful careers. Women's Lib proclaims that success should not have to be achieved, but should be guaranteed as a right. Women, it claims, should be pushed by law into any job, club, saloon or executive position they choose—and let the employer prove in court that he failed to promote a woman because she is a slob and *not* because she is a woman.

There *are* men who fear and resent intelligent, ambitious women. Women's Lib proposes to eliminate such feelings by asserting that intelligence and ability do not matter, only gender does.

Some men believe that women are irrational, illogical, incompetent, emotion-driven and unreliable. Women's Lib sets out to disprove it by the spectacle of sloppy, bedraggled, unfocused females stomping down the streets and chanting brief slogans, over and over again, with the stuporous monotony of a jungle ritual and the sulkiness of a badly spoiled child.

Denouncing masculine oppression, Women's Lib screams protests against the policy of regarding women as "sex objects"—through speakers who, too obviously, are in no such danger.

Proclaiming women's independence from and equality with men, Women's Lib demands liberation from the consequences of whatever sex life a woman might choose, such consequences to be borne by others: it demands free abortions and free day-nurseries. To be paid for—by whom? By men.

The sex views professed by Women's Lib are so hideous that they cannot be discussed—at least, not by me. To regard man as an enemy—to regard woman as a combination matriarch and stevedore—to surpass the futile sordidness of a class war by instituting a sex war—to drag sex into politics and around the floor of smoke-filled back rooms, as a tool of the pressure-group jockeying for power—to proclaim spiritual sisterhood with lesbians, and to swear eternal hostility to men—is so repulsive a set of premises from so loathsome a sense of life that an accurate commentary would require the kind of language I do not like to see in print.

(I regard myself as surpassed by Women's Lib in one respect: I did not know that it was possible to blow up the character of Comrade Sonia to such gigantic proportions.)

Is there something worse than the women of the Lib movement? Yes. The men who support it. The fact that there are such men is a clue to that grotesque phenomenon.

Every other pressure group has some semi-plausible complaint or pretense at a complaint, as an excuse for existing. Women's Lib has none. But it has a common denominator with the others, the indispensable element of a modern pressure group: a claim based on *weakness*. It is because men are metaphysically the dominant sex and are regarded (though for the wrong reasons) as the stronger that a thing such as Women's Lib could gain plausibility and sympathy among today's intellectuals. It represents a rebellion against masculine strength, against strength as such, by those who neither attempt nor intend to develop it—and thus it is the clearest giveaway of what all the other rebellions are after.

To the credit of the majority of American women, the Lib movement did not go over too well. But neither did the college activists nor the hippies nor the nature-lovers. Yet these are the loudest voices we hear in public and these are the snarling figures we see on television screens, displaying their sores and brandishing their fists. These are the commandos of the haters' army, who crawl out of the sewer of centuries and shake themselves in public, splattering muck over the passers-by, over the streets, the plate-glass windows and the clean white sheets of newspapers, where the drippings are scrambled into a long, steady whine that strives to induce guilt and to receive "compassion" in return.

The passers-by are the rest of us, who have to live, breathe and work in this atmosphere.

No, the majority of people are not haters of the good. The majority are disgusted by all those pathological manifestations. But a chronic experience of disgust in looking at the state of one's society is not conducive to respect, mutual confidence or good will among men. A chronic spectacle of grotesque posturing, unintelligible proclamations, incomprehensible demands, inexplicable contradictions, sordid ugliness, unopposed brutality, cynical injustice—the spectacle of aggressive malice being answered by maudlin, sentimental appeasement—will erode the morale and the morality of all but the most exceptional men.

The process of erosion starts with bewilderment and goes on to discouragement, to frustration, to bitterness, to fear, inwardly to withdrawal into a fog of subjectivity, outwardly to mistrust of all men—then to the gradual paralysis of the quest for values, to hopelessness, and to a blind hatred of everything and everyone, resembling the behavior of the actual haters who manipulated it all.

The manipulators are the intellectuals, i.e., those who disseminate ideas and whose professional work lies in the field of the humanities. The majority of people, guided by nothing but common sense and naive, unidentified feelings, are still groping blindly for the guidance of reason. They do not know that their guides, the intellectuals, have long since abandoned reason in favor of feelings which they, the victims, can neither grasp nor believe. The clearest example of the psychological abyss between the people and the intellectuals was their respective reactions to Apollo 11.

The intellectuals themselves are part-victims, part-killers. Who, then, are the killers? The small—frighteningly small—minority who, by the grace of default, have monopolized the field of philosophy and, by the grace of Immanuel Kant, have dedicated it to the propagation of hatred of the good for being the good.

But this type of hatred is ancient. Modern philosophy is merely its munitions-maker and rationalizer, not its cause. What is the cause? The answer lies in the nature of man's consciousness.

Man cannot deal with reality on the merely perceptual level of awareness; his survival requires a conceptual method of mental functioning—but the conceptual level of awareness is *volitional.* Man may choose to function conceptually or not. Most men stumble through the transition from the predominantly perceptual functioning of childhood to the conceptual functioning of adulthood with various degrees of success, and settle on some precarious mixture of both methods. The hater of the good is the man who did not make this transition. He is a case of arrested psycho-epistemological development.

The hater's mental functioning remains on the level of childhood. Nothing is fully real to him except the concrete, the perceptually given, i.e., the immediate moment without past or future. He has learned to speak, but has never grasped the process of conceptualization. Concepts, to him, are merely some sort of code signals employed by other people for some inexplicable reason, signals that have no relation to reality or to himself. He treats concepts as if they were percepts, and their meaning changes with any change of circumstances. Whatever he learns or happens to retain is treated, in his mind, as if it had always been there, as if it were an item of direct awareness, with no memory of how he acquired it—as a random store of unprocessed material that comes and goes at the mercy of chance.

This is the crucial difference between his mentality and that of a child: a normal child is intensely active in seeking knowledge. The hater stands still; he does not seek knowledge—he "exposes himself" to "experience," hoping, in effect, that it will push something into his mind; if nothing happens, he feels with self-righteous rancor that there is nothing he can do about it. Mental action, i.e., mental *effort*—any sort of processing, identifying, organizing, integrating, critical evaluation or control of his mental content—is an alien realm which he spends his twisted lifetime struggling to escape. His is as stagnant a mentality as a human being can sustain on the edge of the borderline separating passivity from psychosis.

A mind that seeks to escape effort and to function automatically, is left at the mercy of the inner phenomenon over which it has no direct control: emotions. Psycho-epistemologically (any conscious assertions to the contrary notwithstanding), a hater regards his emotions as irreducible and irresistible, as a power he cannot question or disobey. But emotions come from automatized value-judgments, which come from abstract, metaphysical premises. The hater has no lasting value-judgments, only the random urges of a given moment. His emotions, therefore, are not great passions to which he sacrifices his intellect, they are not overpowering demons, but smutty little imps, transient, superficial and incredibly banal. He is moved, not by desires, but by *whims.*

How does a human being descend to such a state? There are different psychological reasons, but—in pattern—the process of self-stultification is initiated by the child who lies too often and gets away with it. In his early, formative years, when he needs to learn the mental processes required to grasp the great unknown surrounding him, reality, he learns the opposite. He learns, in effect, that he can get whatever he wants not by observing facts, but by inventing them and by cheating, begging, threatening (throwing tantrums), i.e., by *manipulating* the adults. He concludes implicitly that reality is his enemy, since he has to fake it—to lie—in order to obtain what he wants, that the truth would defeat him and that he'd better not be concerned with it. Reality does not obey him, it frustrates his wishes, it is impervious to his feelings, it does not respond to him as the adults do; but, he feels, it is a negligible enemy, since *he* has the power to defeat it by means of nothing but his own *imagination,* which commands the mysteriously omnipotent adults who can do what he is unable to do: circumvent reality somehow and satisfy his whims.

Gradually, these subconscious conclusions are automatized in his mind, in the form of a habitual, ambivalent feeling: a sneaky sense of triumph—and a sense of inferiority, since he is helpless when left on his own. He counteracts it by telling himself that he is superior, since he can deceive anyone; and, seeking reassurance, he multiplies the practice of deception. Wordlessly, as an implicit premise, he acquires the belief that his means of survival is his ability to manipulate others. At a certain stage of his development, he acquires the only authentic and permanent emotion he will ever be able to experience: *fear.*

As he grows up, the fear grows proportionately. He becomes aware of his impotence in the face of a reality as unknown to him as it was in his childhood, only now it is a dark, menacing, demanding unknown that confronts him with problems he cannot handle (but others, somehow, can). He is able to grasp the given, the immediately present, but that is not enough: he is unable to integrate it to anything. He is trapped between two gaping black holes he has never learned to consider: yesterday and tomorrow. He has no way of knowing what (deserved) dangers will spring at him suddenly from behind or are lying in wait for him ahead (he senses only that they *are* deserved). He senses that there is something wrong with him, with his mind, some terrible defect which must be hidden from everyone, above all from himself, at any price. He is torn by the conflict of two contradictory desires which he dares not identify: the retarded child's desire to be led, protected, told what to do—and the manipulator's desire to seek reassurance by reasserting his power of command over others.

At this stage, two different roads are open to such persons. Most of them seek the safety of stagnation and vanish into some venomous obscurity where—as slatternly housewives or incompetent clerks—they contribute to the misery of anyone they deal with, curse existence, damn mankind, and chortle with glee when they hear of someone's failure or misfortune.

But those of a more ambitious and pretentious kind take a different road. A man of this type decides to brazen it out—and cashes in on his childhood scorn of conceptualization. Language, to him, is merely some arbitrary code of signals which he can manipulate without having to confront reality. It was by means of language that he used to control others—it is by means of language that he will now attempt to control them. Such, in pattern, is the birth of the intellectual who believes that *ideas are tools of deception.*

Psychologists have observed a phenomenon called "the idiot-savant," a man who has the mentality of a moron, but, for some as yet undiscovered reason, is able to perform a prodigy's feats of arithmetical calculation. The hater of the good becomes a similar phenomenon: "the idiot-philosopher," a man who is unable to grasp the relation of ideas to reality, but devotes his life to the manufacture, propagation and manipulation of ideas—as a means of sustaining his pseudo-self-esteem.

The ideas of such philosophers (and of their followers) are singularly, startlingly unrelated to reality—like a structure of playing cards made of fog, to be dissolved by the breath of a single fact. Whatever their coiling complexity and variations, these ideas have a single, immutable goal: to dig an abyss between man's mind and reality, and thus to invalidate reality's agent in human affairs, man's reason—and a single method: the playing on human weaknesses, doubts and fears, as the fledgling hater played on them in his childhood.

On the basis of his works, I offer Immanuel Kant in evidence, as the archetype of this species: a system as consistently evil as his cannot be constructed innocently.

If one wonders about the paradox presented by this type of intellectual—a man who seeks a shortcut to escape mental effort, then devotes his life to excruciating mental contortions—one may observe a similar paradox on the material level of existence. It is the case of a man who believes that "only suckers work" and seeks a shortcut to wealth by becoming a bank robber, then spends his life in and out of jails, devoting his brief snatches of freedom to the excruciating work of devising ingenious schemes for his next bank robbery.

The explanation lies in the fact that the mental contexts required to produce wealth or to stage a robbery are different, and so are the mental processes involved. The production of wealth requires the personal responsibility of dealing with reality; robbery requires only the outwitting of a few guards or policemen. The formulation of philosophical ideas requires the personal responsibility of observing, judging and integrating the facts of reality on an enormous scale; the faking of ideas requires only the outwitting of careless, frightened or ignorant men. Both the bank robber and the "idiot-philosopher" are psychological parasites. The basic cause in both cases is the same: a mental development arrested by a concrete-bound quest for the unearned. The basic motivation is the same: an overwhelming terror of reality and the desire to escape it.

Man's need of self-esteem is the hater's nemesis. Self-esteem is reliance on one's power to think. It cannot be replaced by one's power to deceive. The self-confidence of a scientist and the self-confidence of a con man are not interchangeable states, and do not come from the same psychological universe. The success of a man who deals with reality augments his self-confidence. The success of a con man augments his panic.

The intellectual con man has only one defense against panic: the momentary relief he finds by succeeding at further and further frauds. To preserve his illusion of superiority becomes his overriding obsession. Superiority—in what? He does not know. He does not function conceptually. He judges people, events and actions "instinctively," i.e., not by what they *are,* but by what they make him *feel.* Putting something over on people makes him feel superior—he has long since forgotten (and has never fully known) why.

He has developed a special kind of "instinct" for appraising people: he can "smell" the presence of weaknesses in people, of pretentiousness, uncertainty, self-doubt and fear—particularly fear (not fear of him, but of their common enemy: reality). Such people make him feel like "a big shot," and his act is successful among them. But when he meets the better type of man, he goes to pieces: what he feels is terror. It is by means of his own terror that he recognizes authentic self-confidence.

The man of authentic self-confidence is the man who relies on the judgment of his own mind. Such a man is not malleable; he may be mistaken, he may be fooled in a given instance, but he is *inflexible* in regard to the absolutism of reality, i.e., in seeking and demanding truth. The manipulator feels impotent and in mortal danger; his terror of the man is not personal, but metaphysical: he feels stripped of his means of survival.

There is only one source of authentic self-confidence: reason. Hence the intellectual con man's impassioned hatred of reason and of all its manifestations and consequences: of intelligence, of certainty, of ambition, of success, of achievement, of virtue, of happiness, of pride. All these are phenomena from a universe that would destroy him. Like a creature from the ooze at the bottom of the ocean, he senses a breath of air, which he cannot breathe.

Such is the cause and such is the pattern of development whose end product is hatred of the good for being the good.

At this final stage, moved by nothing but his feelings, the hater cannot tell what makes him act, he is aware only of the hatred and of an overwhelming compulsion to destroy. He does not know what long-since-forgotten whims he is paying for now, he does not know what goal he is trying to achieve—he has no goals, no desires, no whims any longer, his quest for pleasure has petered out—he has nothing to gain or to seek, his hatred is aimless and wholly nonvenal, all he knows is that he must destroy—destroy the bright, the sparkling, the smiling, the clean, destroy "the light bulb look" on a child's face—destroy, in order to preserve in the universe the *possibility* that some *potential* whim will succeed, even when he has no whim in sight and none to pursue any longer.

To explain the nature of his feeling, he snatches rationalizations at random, as he had snatched them all his life. "This man," he cries, "is arrogant and selfish! . . . He defies the gods or the will of God! . . . He is intransigent, intractable, inflexible! . . . He defies the will of the people! He endangers the common good! He is a threat to his fellow-men, whom he robs, despoils and exploits! . . . He is cold, unfeeling, unloving! . . . He is immoral: he does not forgive! . . . He has invented morality to make us feel guilty! . . . He is the cause of all the misery on earth! . . . We are poor, because he's rich . . . we are weak, because he's strong . . . we suffer, because he's happy . . . We couldn't help it, couldn't help it, couldn't help it! No one can blame us, all men are equal! Who does he think he is?" The frenzy deflects the knowledge of the answer: he is a *man.*

The desire to escape that answer is the motive that attracts so many haters to the intellectual professions today—as they were attracted to philosophy or to its primitive precursor, religion, through all the ages. There have always been men of arrested mental development who, dreading reality, found psychological protection in the art of incapacitating the minds of others.

It takes many years for a man (and many, many centuries for mankind) to grasp the fact that, in order to live, man needs a comprehensive view of existence, which he relies on, consciously or not. But the formulation of such a view is the most difficult of human endeavors—and (with a few exceptions, to whom mankind owes its lives) rats rushed in where lions feared to tread. While other men were busy struggling to live, the haters were busy undercutting their means of survival—in the primitive jungle, in ancient Greece or in the United States of America.

Today, while America's best minds go into the physical professions—where reality is harder (but not impossible) to fake—the realm of philosophy, abandoned like a vacant lot, has become overgrown with Kantian weeds and overrun with Kantian squatters. Weeds, if unchecked, will grow faster than other plants and will consume the nourishment of flowers, of trees, of orchards, of farms, then will sprout through the cracks of the cement at the foundation of impregnable skyscrapers—which is the spectacle we are seeing today.

The haters are in control of our culture and in the open. They have dropped the pretense of such covers as God, The People, The Future or even Love. They proclaim pure hatred of the good—of man, of reason, of values, of existence—in classrooms, in drawing rooms, in public halls, in theaters, in books, in paintings, in the streets, by land, by sea, by air and through the gutter.

Their G.H.Q. is in the field of education, which they control. "Progressive" schools are manufacturing haters wholesale. The hordes they have produced are roaming the land, proclaiming the rule of the "*Now*"—which is the confession of an arrested, perceptual mentality that cannot project the future, cannot hold a theory, a purpose or a value, can do nothing but hate and destroy. This is the invasion of Western civilization by psycho-epistemological barbarians. They howl and brandish the tag of "Liberation." According to their philosophical chieftain, what they demand is *liberation from reality.* It is as simple and open as that.

What does this do to normal men? At a time when they need it most, they are left without a remnant of philosophical guidance. If they struggle to make sense out of what they see, they encounter so much irrationality, such a chaos of inexplicable evil, that they begin to believe that reality *in fact* is the nightmare constructed by the hater's imagination. Some of them give up, some join the hordes, some take the blame for their failure to understand, some continue to struggle day by day with no thought of past or future. One cannot fight when one does not understand—and when the voices of craven appeasers keep striving to whitewash the nature of the enemy.

As long as men believe that they are facing "misguided idealists"—or "rebellious youth"—or "a counter-culture"—or "a new morality"—or the transition period of a changing world, or an irresistible historical process, or even an invincibly powerful monster—confusion undercuts their will to resist, and intellectual self-defense is impossible. It is imperative to grasp that this is not the time for temporizing, compromising and self-deception. It is necessary fully to understand the nature of the enemy and his mentality.

There is no giant behind the devastation of the world—only a shriveled creature with the wizened face of a child who is out to blow up the kitchen because he cannot steal his cookies and eat them, too. "Take a look at [him] now, when you face your last choice—and if you choose to perish, do so with full knowledge of how cheaply how small an enemy has claimed your life." (*Atlas Shrugged.*)

What is the weapon one needs to fight such an enemy? For once, it is I who will say that *love* is the answer—love in the actual meaning of the word, which is the opposite of the meaning they give it—love as a response to values, love of the good for being the good. If you hold on to the vision of any value you love—your mind, your work, your wife or husband, or your child—and remember that *that* is what the enemy is after, your shudder of rebellion will give you the moral fire, the courage and the *intransigence* needed in this battle. What fuel can support one's fire? Love for man at his highest potential.

(*July–August 1971*)

THE POLITICS

The Left: Old and New

If you happened to see *Sign of the Pagan,* a very bad movie recently shown on television, dealing with Attila's invasion of Europe, you may have noticed that Attila kept an astrologer by his side, as his only adviser, and consulted him before undertaking every bloody new campaign. You may have felt a touch of superiority (which Western man took fifteen centuries to earn), best expressed by the sentence: "It can't happen now." You may have regarded the reliance on astrology as crude, primitive or amusing, but quite appropriate to Attila; besides, he had nothing but clubs and swords to devastate the world with.

Would you find it amusing if you saw the same Attila balancing a nuclear bomb in the palm of his hand and consulting the astrologer on whether to toss it?

Well, you can see it or, rather, you can hear it being announced in advance and welcomed, not in the scriptures of the Huns, but in a magazine regarded as safely reputable, read by respectable commuters of the somewhat conservative type—not in A.D. 450, but in *Time* magazine on December 19, 1969.

A piece entitled "The Next Decade: A Search for Goals" begins by invoking the sanction of astrology, as justification for its prophecies about the coming decade. The present motion of the planet Neptune, it seems, is a "sign of idealism and spiritual values," which will work "a profound change" in people's ways of thinking and acting.

"Just possibly," declares—no, not Attila's adviser, but *Time* magazine, "the astrologers may be proved right. . . . In the long run, this decade and the next may well constitute an historical era of transition, like that which followed the Middle Ages and preceded the Renaissance.

"The veneration of rationality was the special myth of modern man. The world view created by the enthronement of reason included a universal belief in individualism and competition; now that myth is dying. Faith in science and technology has given way to fear of their consequences . . . The cultural revolution of the '60s that emphasized Dionysian rather than Apollonian virtues will continue into the '70s."

Nothing but astrology could justify a statement of this kind. It is embarrassing to have to comment on it. But for the benefit of the very young, I will point out a few things that should be almost self-evident.

The Middle Ages were an era of mysticism, ruled by blind faith and blind obedience to the dogma that faith is superior to reason. The Renaissance was specifically the *rebirth of reason,* the liberation of man's mind, the triumph of *rationality* over mysticism—a faltering, incomplete, but impassioned triumph that led to the birth of science, of individualism, of freedom.

I have no way of knowing whether *Time*'s statement came from ignorance or worse. I know only that when I advocate the supremacy of reason, I do not equate it with a historical period exemplifying its opposite. But this is an Apollonian, not a Dionysian, virtue.

There is one element of truth in that quotation and it is interesting to find such an admission in such a context: the fact that reason leads to (and is the foundation of) individualism and competition, i.e., capitalism. Capitalism's enemies know it. Its alleged friends are still twisting themselves into double-jointed pretzels in the struggle to evade that knowledge.

Let me also remind you that reason is the faculty that identifies and integrates the material provided by man's senses—i.e., that reason is man's only means of grasping reality and of acquiring knowledge—and, therefore, the rejection of reason means that men should act regardless of and/or in contradiction to the facts of reality.

One of these facts is the existence of nuclear weapons. If men discard "the myth of rationality," by what means will they decide whether to use these weapons, when, where and against whom? They will have nothing but their Dionysian "instincts" and their astrologers to guide them. Attila was a piker compared to a prospect of this kind.

This does not seem to deter the *Time* prophet, who speaks of the fear engendered by the "consequences" of "science and technology." Nuclear weapons are his ideological brothers' main reproach against science and their main instrument of intellectual terrorization. But if this, in fact, were their fear and their motive, they would have become passionate advocates of reason overnight: they would have known that a hydrogen bomb cannot descend on a city of its own volition—and they would have known that for this reason, among many others, mankind cannot afford irrationality any longer. But that is not their fear or their motive.

"It is possible," *Time* goes on, "that the hippie may have pioneered—in spirit, at least—the way men will live and think [?] in the next decade. . . . Individualism may continue to wane as men seek personal identity in group identity. . . . Marshall McLuhan predicts confidently: 'We are going through a tribal cycle once again, but this time we are wide awake.' "

How one manages to be "wide awake" when one has rejected reason, and how one can describe as "wide awake" the specifically out-of-focus, zombie-like state of trance characteristic of and necessitated by a tribal mentality, *Time* does not explain. It is only Apollonians, not Dionysians, that require explanations.

"While industrial technology will provide a dazzling variety of innovative gadgets, from phonovision to computers for the home, possession will be less of an ideal. When goods are needed, says Buckminster Fuller [a bright young man of 75], more and more will be rented rather than bought. 'Ownership,' says Fuller, 'is obsolete.' "

Another youthful authority, the Harvard sociologist Pitirim Sorokin, predicted, according to *Time,* that "the U.S. will become a 'late sensate society' . . . By this he meant the glorification of pleasure over Puritan duty, of leisure over work." Mr. Sorokin, a thoroughly Russian mystic-altruist, was born in 1889. The youngest of these rebels and trend-setters for youth is Marshall McLuhan, aged 59. I suppose when one writes under the aegis of astrology, one cannot be too choosy about the sort of authorities one quotes. But the hippies should observe who molded their docile minds and plastic souls, and how much novelty or originality is contained in the moth-eaten notions they spout.

"Education for enrichment or amusement," *Time* marches on,

"rather than for professional skills will become a lifetime process . . . In fact, says Marshall McLuhan, older people will have to go back to school to learn basic skills. The young, he says, are not interested in the mundane knowledge it takes to run a technological civilization; the old will have to learn it if they are to keep their world running." Why should they want to? What if they shrug? No answer is given.

Time is not indifferent, however, to the continuation of that world. "All this [the Dionysian Utopia of the future]," the article declares, "will depend on the continued expansion of the U.S. economy, which virtually all experts agree will take place. . . . Business will be operating in a new, probably tougher atmosphere. While profit will still be the prime mover, some of the money once considered the stockholders' will have to be sacrificed to the needs of society and to pollution control."

Further on, a faint note of apprehension creeps into the euphoric prophecy: "It may be that the early '70s will see a period of repressive reaction against the Dionysian tendencies of the young. . . . It is possible, too, that a decline in the work ethic or a weakening of demand for material goods may disrupt the foundation of a hedonist civilization—the economy."

After considering this possibility for two paragraphs, *Time* concludes: "Possible—but not likely, for at least the greater part of the decade." Observe the length and range of concern of these supposedly responsible social commentators. What is to happen *after* a decade of that kind? It is only Apollonians who look that far; Dionysians do not and cannot.

As for other predictions: "The most significant trend of the '70s may well be a religious revival. . . . In reaction against the trend toward secularization [i.e., toward rationality], there may well be a sweeping revival of fundamentalism, particularly in its fervent, Pentecostal variety. . . . Many people will reject traditional Western religions, finding inspiration and solace in the mystery cults of the East or in eclectic spiritual systems of their own devising. . . . For many, astrology, numerology and phrenology will become no longer fads but ways of life."

As to art: "The changed atmosphere will affect the arts as well, which may become ephemeral, instant, faddish and ultimately disposable." Here the prophet is confessing his estimate of the arts of the present by projecting it into the future. Except for the wrong tense, the estimate is right. "Ephemeral, instant, faddish and ultimately disposable" is a euphemism for: junk that cannot last overnight, is not needed by anyone, has no value but that of clique-press-agentry, and ultimately belongs in the trash can.

In the ugliest form, this is a confirmation of the metaphysical nature of art: Dionysian brutes who reject reason and live on the sensations of the immediate moment have no capacity for a metaphysical view of life and no need of art, beyond the Halloween masks or New Year's Eve hats that the charwomen of history will sweep up wearily the next morning.

Under the subtitle "Man and Environment," a lengthy section of the *Time* article is devoted to the subject of pollution. "Government and business will be forced to spend ever increasing sums—possibly $10 billion to $20 billion a year, in Herman Kahn's estimate—to control pollution of air and water and *to prevent the destruction of natural beauty.*" (Italics mine.) And: "In the next few years . . . it will be widely recognized that like most forms of pollution, defiling of the landscape, whether it be with shopping centers or expressways, is hard to reverse."

The word "pollution" implies health hazards, such as smog or dirty waters. But these are not the article's main concern; observe that they are lumped together into one package dealing with such matters as "natural beauty" and that the pollutants threatening us are *shopping centers* and *expressways.*

Young men who live under the nightmare threat of the military draft should also observe that the people who propose to spend $10 to $20 billion a year on the preservation of "natural beauty" regard $4 billion a year as too high a price to pay for a volunteer army.

The real motive behind the anti-pollution campaign is stated all but explicitly: "As the decade advances, it will become clear that if the ecological effort is to succeed, much of today's existing technology will have to be scrapped and something new developed in its place. ["You'll do something, Mr. Rearden!"] . . . Increasingly, it will be seen that any kind of mass transportation, however powered, is more efficient than the family car. [Such as the New York subway, for instance?] . . . Planning will have to be a much greater concern."

And here is the motive behind the motive: "The attitude, central to the modern mind, that all technology is good technology will have to be changed radically. 'Our society is trained to accept all new technology as progress, or to look upon it as an aspect of fate,' says George Wald, Harvard's Nobel-laureate biologist. 'Should one do everything one can? The usual answer is "Of course"; but the right answer is "Of course not." ' . . .

"Bertrand de Jouvenal adds: 'Western man has not lived with his natural environment. He has merely conquered it.' "

By the grace of Aristotle, of Galileo, of Pasteur, of Edison and of a long, thin line of often-martyred men stretching back through millennia, Western man has not lived with his natural environment, in the sense intended by that quotation. But the rest of mankind has and does.

An Asian peasant who labors through all of his waking hours, with tools created in Biblical times—a South American aborigine who is devoured by piranha in a jungle stream—an African who is bitten by the tsetse fly—an Arab whose teeth are green with decay in his mouth—these do live with their "natural environment," but are scarcely able to appreciate its beauty. Try to tell a Chinese mother, whose child is dying of cholera: "Should one do everything one can? Of course not." Try to tell a Russian housewife, who trudges miles on foot in sub-zero weather in order to spend hours standing in line at a state store dispensing food rations, that America is defiled by shopping centers, expressways and family cars.

It is not possible that the "anti-pollution"—i.e., *anti-technology*—crusaders are ignorant of man's condition in the midst of an *unconquered* nature. It does not seem possible that, knowing it, they would advocate its return. But there it is, out of their own mouth.

The thing that permits men to utter public statements which, if believed, would cause people to run from them as from lepers, is the fact that no one believes it. Most people have been conditioned to regard broad generalizations, abstract ideas, fundamental principles and logical consequences as impotent, irrelevant, invalid or non-existent. "Aw, they don't mean it," is the general attitude toward the anti-technologists, "they don't want to go that far. They just want to clean up the smog and the sewage." Well, Hitler, too, announced his abstract principles and goals in advance, and evoked a similar reaction from the pragmatists of the time. The Soviets have openly preached world conquest for fifty years and have conquered one-third of the globe's population—yet some people still do not believe that they mean it.

(As far as the issue of actual pollution is concerned, it is primarily a scientific, not a political, problem. In regard to the political principle involved: if a man creates a physical danger or harm to others, which extends beyond the line of his own property, such as unsanitary conditions or even loud noise, and if this is *proved,* the law can and does hold him responsible. If the condition is collective, such as in an overcrowded city, appropriate and *objective* laws can be defined, protecting the rights of all those involved—as was done in the case of oil rights, air-space rights, etc. But such laws cannot demand the impossible, must not be aimed at a single scapegoat, i.e., the industrialists, and must take into consideration the whole context of the problem, i.e., the absolute necessity of the continued existence of industry—if the preservation of human life is the standard.)

It has been reported in the press many times that the issue of pollution is to be the next big crusade of the New Left activists, after the war in Vietnam peters out. And just as peace was not their goal or motive in that crusade, so clean air is not their goal or motive in this one.

There is a significant change in the leftist-liberal ideology of today, a difference between the old left and the new—not in essential goals or fundamental motives, but in their forms—and the *Time* article is an unusually eloquent demonstration of it.

In a certain sense, the line of the New Left is cruder and more honest—not honest in an honorable sense of the word, but in the sense of a combination of brazenness and despair, prompted by the belief or the hope that one can get away with it, as a drunk (or a drug addict) will blurt out some part of a truth he has spent years evading and repressing. The social veneer of the collectivists is cracking and their psychological motivation is showing through.

The old left had spent years of effort, tons of print, billions of dollars and rivers of blood to maintain an Apollonian mask. Old-line Marxists claimed that they were champions of *reason,* that socialism or communism was a *scientific* social system, that an advanced technology could not function in a capitalist society, but required a scientifically planned and organized human community to bring its maximum benefits to every man, in the form of material comforts and a higher standard of living. They predicted that the progress of Soviet technology would surpass that of the United States. They accused capitalist societies of deluding the masses by means of the policy known as "pie in the sky," i.e., by means of promising spiritual rewards to those suffering from material poverty. Communist propagandists even accused some governments—notably, the old rulers of China and the British in India—of deliberately fostering the drug traffic in order to keep the masses passive, dazed, docile and impotent.

That mask crumbled in the aftermath of World War II.

In full view of the fate of industry and the standard of living in Soviet Russia, in socialist Britain, in the communist countries of Europe, no one can claim very loudly or very effectively the technological superiority of socialism over capitalism. The old line to the effect that capitalism was necessary to create an industrial civilization, but not to maintain it, is not heard too often these days. The promises of socialist abundance are not very convincing in a world where most of the working youth worship American products and gadgets, and would swim the ocean, if they could, to come to America—and the promises of socialism's liberation of man's mind ring hollow in a world made progressively more anxious by the drain of its best brains.

There was a time when the necessity of industrialization was the crusading slogan of Western liberals, which justified anything and whitewashed any atrocity, including the wholesale slaughter in Soviet Russia. We do not hear that slogan any longer. Confronted with the choice of an industrial civilization or collectivism, it is an industrial civilization that the liberals discarded. Confronted with the choice of technology or dictatorship, it is technology that they discarded. Confronted with the choice of reason or whims, it is reason that they discarded.

And so today we see the spectacle of old Marxists blessing, aiding and abetting the young hoodlums (who are their products and heirs) who proclaim the superiority of feelings over reason, of faith over knowledge, of leisure over production, of spiritual concerns over material comforts, of primitive nature over technology, of astrology over science, of drugs over consciousness.

The old-line Marxists used to claim that a single modern factory could produce enough shoes to provide for the whole population of the world and that nothing but capitalism prevented it.

When they discovered the facts of reality involved, they declared that going barefoot is superior to wearing shoes.

So much for their concern with poverty and with the improvement of human life on earth.

At a superficial (a *very* superficial) glance, there might have been, for the morally undiscriminating, some plausibility in the notion of enslaving and sacrificing generations of men for the sake of establishing a permanent state of material abundance for all. But to do it for the sake of preserving "natural beauty"? To replace the union of bloody thugs and ivory-tower intellectuals, which was gruesome enough, with a union of bloody thugs and ladies' garden clubs?

In form, if not in essence, the old-line Marxists were cleaner.

But the essence—the fundamental principles, the psychological motivation, the ultimate goal—of the leftist-liberals has not changed. The essence is hatred of reason—whether it takes the cover of "the mystics of muscle" or drops the mask and opts for the "spirituality" of the jungle, whether it preaches dialectic materialism or replaces it with doctrines of equal scientific validity: astrology, numerology, phrenology.

The forms may vary, the slogans may change, everything may be dispensable in the Heraclitean-Hegelian-Dionysian flux, but three fundamentals remain untouched: mysticism-altruism-collectivism. And so does their psychological manifestation: the lust for power, i.e., the lust to destroy.

The activists of the New Left are closer to revealing the truth of their motives: they do not seek to take over industrial plants, they seek to destroy technology.

Commentators such as the *Time* prophet(s) are not necessarily aware of the full philosophical meaning and consequences of their statements: they have been inoculated against ideas by the same Pragmatism in the same colleges as their victims. A typical modern intellectual is not consciously eager to destroy a technological society or the last remnants of capitalism in a mixed economy. He merely swims with the "mainstream" and seeks to create "a tougher atmosphere" for businessmen, never doubting that they will always deliver the goods or anything demanded of them. He slings ideas for a living, as others sling hash.

But that the victims stand for it, that the advocacy of raw nature and astrology is voiced without any noticeable protest—*that* is the culturally ominous and significant aspect of the *Time* article. It is an indication of the degree of today's contempt for the intellect. It is a demonstration of the bankruptcy of the left—and of the vacuum in a culture whose respect for the mind has been destroyed by generations of Kantian-pragmatist-linguistic philosophizing.

As far as the left is concerned, its new line is a grotesque caricature of the old and, therefore, revealing, as caricatures often are. Hatred of reason leads to fear of reality; since fear has always been the intense motivational emotion of the leftists, it is fear that they have always used as their chief psychological tool of propaganda, apparently in the belief that it has as irresistible a power in the consciousness of others as in their own.

With the destruction of capitalism as their unalterable goal, they tried, at first, to engender economic fear—by spreading the notion that capitalism leads to general impoverishment and the concentration of wealth in fewer and fewer hands. This line was somewhat successful in Europe, but not in this country, where the factual evidence to the contrary was too obviously clear.

The next leftist line was fear of the atom bomb, accompanied by the suggestion that we should surrender to communism without a fight, in order to avoid universal destruction. Do you remember the slogan: "Better Red than dead"? This did not go over, either—not in *this* country, nor among any men or animals with a vestige of self-esteem.

If, after the failure of such accusations as: "Capitalism leads you to the poorhouse" and "Capitalism leads you to war," the New Left is left with nothing better than: "Capitalism defiles the beauty of your countryside," one may justifiably conclude that, as an intellectual power, the collectivist movement is through.

But the leftists may still have a chance—by default. A society cannot exist for long in an intellectual vacuum. Culturally, we are approaching the stage where anyone can take over, provided his doctrines are sufficiently irrational. A cultural vacuum produces its own variants of fishers in muddy waters—and, on such terms, whoever is the muddiest, wins.

In "The Cashing-In: The Student 'Rebellion' " (*The Objectivist Newsletter,* July–September 1965), dealing with the rebellion at Berkeley, I wrote: "For its motley leftist leadership, the student rebellion is a trial balloon, a kind of cultural temperature-taking.

It is a test of how much they can get away with and what sort of opposition they will encounter." I wrote also that the main ideological purpose of the rebellion's leaders was "to condition the country to accept force as the means of settling political controversies."

Observe the extent of the spread of violence since that time, and the condoning, excusing, endorsement and/or advocacy of violence by the public voices of today.

An article such as the *Time* prophecy is one of the trial balloons of a similar kind, as are all the hooligan tactics of the New Left: it is part of a test to find out how much they can get away with philosophically, i.e., how far the destruction of reason has gone.

I asked an intelligent young friend of mine how college students could read such an article without protesting. "But they don't read it," she answered. "They read only the news sections. At most, they skim through the editorial stuff, barely getting some fuzzy approximation." This, of course, applies to businessmen as well.

And *this* is the real danger in articles of that kind: not that the readers will agree—they are not expected to agree—but that their indifference to ideas, to intellectual issues and to long-range thinking will be reaffirmed, reinforced and ultimately turned into mental atrophy.

If Ellsworth Toohey were speaking today, he would say to Peter Keating: "We get them coming and going. Those who believe in astrology will flock to us: we'll be the only defenders of their guilty weakness. Those who don't believe in it will be so disgusted, indignant and frustrated that they'll give up the realm of ideas—and of reason—anyway. Intellectual paralysis, Peter. Whether caused by drugs, or by bitter skepticism, or by unbearable disgust, doesn't make any difference—so long as they stop thinking and give up, give up, give up . . ."

If businessmen are willing to ignore the proclamations of the New Left and to serve as milch cows for brazen, nature-loving hoodlums—they deserve what they will get.

But the young do not deserve it—not those among the young who are suffocating in today's atmosphere and are groping blindly for some glimmer of rationality. It is they who should fight for their precarious foothold on reason, which is now being systematically undercut.

The first step of the battle is to realize that their enemy is not the screeching Dionysian hippie-puppets, but those exponents of middle-of-the-road respectability who tell them gently, in their classrooms, that words, ideas and philosophy do not matter and that the Attilas do not mean it.

(*February 1970*)

From a Symposium

The New Left does not portend a revolution, as its press agents claim, but a *Putsch*. A revolution is the climax of a long philosophical development and expresses a nation's profound discontent; a *Putsch* is a minority's seizure of power. The goal of a revolution is to overthrow tyranny; the goal of a *Putsch* is to establish it.

Tyranny is any political system (whether absolute monarchy or fascism or communism) that does not recognize individual rights (which necessarily include property rights). The overthrow of a political system by force is justified only when it is directed against tyranny: it is an act of self-defense against those who rule by force. For example, the American Revolution. The resort to force, not in defense, but in violation, of individual rights, can have no moral justification; it is not a revolution, but gang warfare.

No revolution was ever spearheaded by wriggling, chanting drug addicts who are boastfully anti-rational, who have no program to offer, yet propose to take over a nation of 200 million, and who spend their time manufacturing grievances, since they cannot tap any authentic source of popular discontent.

Physically, America is not in a desperate state, but intellectually and culturally she is. The New Left is the product of cultural disintegration; it is bred not in the slums, but in the universities; it is not the vanguard of the future, but the terminal stage of the past.

This article was published in *The New York Times Magazine,* May 17, 1970, as part of a symposium on the question: "Are We in the Middle of the 'Second American Revolution'?"

Intellectually, the activists of the New Left are the most docile conformists. They have accepted as dogma all the philosophical beliefs of their elders for generations: the notions that faith and feeling are superior to reason, that material concerns are evil, that love is the solution to all problems, that the merging of one's self with a tribe or a community is the noblest way to live. There is not a single basic principle of today's Establishment which they do not share. Far from being rebels, they embody the philosophic trend of the past 200 years (or longer): the mysticism-altruism-collectivism axis, which has dominated Western philosophy from Kant to Hegel to James and on down.

But this philosophic tradition is bankrupt. It crumbled in the aftermath of World War II. Disillusioned in their collectivist ideals, America's intellectuals gave up the intellect. Their legacy is our present political system, which is not capitalism, but a mixed economy, a precarious mixture of freedom and controls. Injustice, insecurity, confusion, the pressure-group warfare of all against all, the amorality and futility of random, pragmatist, range-of-the-moment policies are the joint products of a mixed economy and of a philosophical vacuum.

There *is* a profound discontent, but the New Left is not its voice; there is a sense of bitterness, bewilderment and frustrated indignation, a profound anxiety about the intellectual-moral state of this country, a desperate need of philosophical guidance, which the church-and-tradition-bound conservatives were never able to provide and the liberals have given up.

Without opposition, the hoodlums of the New Left are crawling from under the intellectual wreckage. Theirs is the Anti-Industrial Revolution, the revolt of the primordial brute—no, not against capitalism, but against capitalism's roots—against reason, progress, technology, achievement, reality.

What are the activists after? Nothing. They are not pulled by a goal, but pushed by the panic of mindless terror. Hostility, hatred, destruction for the sake of destruction are their momentary forms of escape. They are a desperate herd looking for a Führer.

They are not seeking any specific political system, since they cannot look beyond the "now." But the sundry little Führers who manipulate them as cannon-fodder do have a mongrel system in mind: a statist dictatorship with communist slogans and fascist policies. It is their last, frantic attempt to cash in on the intellectual vacuum.

Do they have a chance to succeed? No. But they might plunge the country into a blind, hopeless civil war, with nothing but some other product of anti-rationality, such as George C. Wallace, to oppose them.

Can this be averted? Yes. The most destructive influence on the nation's morale is not the young thugs, but the cynicism of respectable publications that hail them as "idealists." Irrationality is not idealistic; drug addiction is not idealistic; the bombing of public places is not idealistic.

What this country needs is a *philosophical* revolution—a rebellion against the Kantian tradition—in the name of the first of our Founding Fathers: Aristotle. This means a reassertion of the supremacy of reason, with its consequences: individualism, freedom, progress, civilization. What political system would it lead to? An untried one: full, laissez-faire capitalism. But this will take more than a beard and a guitar.

"Political" Crimes

A very dangerous notion is now being smuggled into our cultural atmosphere. It is being introduced in reverse, in a form that looks like the opposite of its actual meaning and logical consequences. The form is sympathy for criminals who claim to be motivated by political goals; the notion is the legal category of "political crimes."

There can be no such thing as a *political* crime under the American system of law. Since an individual has the right to hold and to propagate any ideas he chooses (obviously including political ideas), the government may not infringe his right; it may neither penalize nor reward him for his ideas; it may not take any judicial cognizance whatever of his ideology.

By the same principle, the government may not give special leniency to the perpetrator of a crime, on the grounds of the nature of his ideas.

A crime is a violation of the right(s) of other men by force (or fraud). It is only the initiation of physical force against others—i.e., the recourse to violence—that can be classified as a crime in a free society (as distinguished from a civil wrong). Ideas, in a free society, are not a crime—and neither can they serve as the justification of a crime.

If one keeps clearly in mind the moral-legal context (and hierarchical derivation) of any given political principle, one will not find any difficulty or contradiction in applying it to specific cases. For instance, American citizens possess the right to freedom of religion; but if some sect adopted primitive beliefs and began to practice human sacrifices, it would be prosecuted for murder. Clearly, this is not an infringement of the sect's religious freedom; it is the proper application of the principle that all rights are derived from the right to life and that those who violate it cannot claim its protection, i.e., cannot claim the right to violate a right.

In exactly the same way, for the same reasons, the unspeakable little drugged monstrosities who resort to violence—and who have progressed, without significant opposition, from campus sit-ins to arson to such an atrocity as mass terrorization and the bombing of public places—should be treated as the criminals they are, and *not* as political "dissenters."

Morally, they are worse than the plain criminal: he, at least, does not subvert the realm of ideas; he does not posture as a champion of rights, justice and freedom. Legally, both kinds should be given the same treatment. Ideas end where a gun begins.

The moral bankruptcy of today's liberal Establishment (including its concomitant: the erosion of the concept of individual rights) is the basic cause of the young thugs' activities. The granting to these thugs of such titles as "political dissenters" and "idealists" is the major reason of their accelerating growth. The alleged economic justification of their violence—the notion that it is caused by poverty—would be inexcusably evil, if the notion were true; but it becomes grotesque in the light of the mounting evidence that the young thugs are predominantly children of the well-to-do.

There is only one doctrine that can permit this to go on: the morality of altruism. I have said that altruism is, in fact, the negation of morality. "Your code hands out, as its version of the absolute, the following rule of moral conduct: . . . if the motive of your action is *your* welfare, don't do it; if the motive is the welfare of others, then anything goes." (*Atlas Shrugged.*) You can now see it demonstrated in practice. If such monstrous actions as bombings are regarded as "idealistic" because the actors profess to be motivated by the "welfare of others"—and the liberal journalists who proclaim this are not hooted out of their profession—then the last vestige of and pretense at morality are gone from today's culture.

The actual motive of whoever manipulates the opinions of the dazed, scared liberals is fairly obvious: by arousing sympathy for "political" criminals, by staging protests and demanding leniency from the courts—allegedly in the name of political freedom—the statists are establishing the precedent of *political trials.* Once the issue of ideology is made part of a court's consideration, the principle is established: the government is brought into the courtroom as an arbiter of ideas. If the government assumes the power to exonerate a man on the grounds of his political ideas, it has assumed the power to prosecute and condemn him on the same grounds.

It is in Europe, under the despotism of absolute monarchies, that a legal distinction was made between political and non-political crimes. The first category consisted predominantly, not of acts of violence, but of such acts as uttering or publishing ideas that displeased the government. And, in the growing trend toward political freedom, public opinion was on the side of such offenders: they were fighting for individual rights, against the rule of force.

If and when the public opinion of a free country accepts a distinction between political and non-political criminals, it accepts the notion of political crimes, it supports the use of force in violation of rights—and the historical process takes place in reverse: the country crosses the borderline into political despotism.

(*May 1970*)

Racism

Racism is the lowest, most crudely primitive form of collectivism. It is the notion of ascribing moral, social or political significance to a man's genetic lineage—the notion that a man's intellectual and characterological traits are produced and transmitted by his internal body chemistry. Which means, in practice, that a man is to be judged, not by his own character and actions, but by the characters and actions of a collective of ancestors.

Racism claims that the content of a man's mind (not his cognitive apparatus, but its *content*) is inherited; that a man's convictions, values and character are determined before he is born, by physical factors beyond his control. This is the caveman's version of the doctrine of innate ideas—or of inherited knowledge—which has been thoroughly refuted by philosophy and science. Racism is a doctrine of, by and for brutes. It is a barnyard or stock-farm version of collectivism, appropriate to a mentality that differentiates between various breeds of animals, but not between animals and men.

Like every form of determinism, racism invalidates the specific attribute which distinguishes man from all other living species: his rational faculty. Racism negates two aspects of man's life: reason and choice, or mind and morality, replacing them with chemical predestination.

The respectable family that supports worthless relatives or covers up their crimes in order to "protect the family name" (as if the moral stature of one man could be damaged by the actions of another)—the bum who boasts that his great-grandfather was an empire-builder, or the small-town spinster who boasts that her maternal great-uncle was a state senator and her third cousin gave a concert at Carnegie Hall (as if the achievements of one man could rub off on the mediocrity of another)—the parents who search genealogical trees in order to evaluate their prospective sons-in-law—the celebrity who starts his autobiography with a detailed account of his family history—all these are samples of racism, the atavistic manifestations of a doctrine whose full expression is the tribal warfare of prehistorical savages, the wholesale slaughter of Nazi Germany, the atrocities of today's so-called "newly emerging nations."

The theory that holds "good blood" or "bad blood" as a moral-intellectual criterion, can lead to nothing but torrents of blood in practice. Brute force is the only avenue of action open to men who regard themselves as mindless aggregates of chemicals.

Modern racists attempt to prove the superiority or inferiority of a given race by the historical achievements of some of its members. The frequent historical spectacle of a great innovator who, in his lifetime, is jeered, denounced, obstructed, persecuted by his countrymen, and then, a few years after his death, is enshrined in a national monument and hailed as a proof of the greatness of the German (or French or Italian or Cambodian) race—is as revolting a spectacle of collectivist expropriation, perpetrated by racists, as any expropriation of material wealth perpetrated by communists.

Just as there is no such thing as a collective or racial mind, so there is no such thing as a collective or racial achievement. There are only individual minds and individual achievements—and a *culture* is not the anonymous product of undifferentiated masses, but the sum of the intellectual achievements of individual men.

Even if it were proved—which it is not—that the incidence of men of potentially superior brain power is greater among the members of certain races than among the members of others, it would still tell us nothing about any given individual and it would be irrelevant to one's judgment of him. A genius is a genius, regardless of the number of morons who belong to the same race—and a moron is a moron, regardless of the number of geniuses who share his racial origin. It is hard to say which is the more outrageous injustice: the claim of Southern racists that a Negro genius should be treated as an inferior because his race has "produced" some brutes—or the claim of a German brute to the status of a superior because his race has "produced" Goethe, Schiller and Brahms.

These are not two different claims, of course, but two applications of the same basic premise. The question of whether one alleges the superiority or the inferiority of any given race is irrelevant; racism has only one psychological root: the racist's sense of his own inferiority.

Like every other form of collectivism, racism is a quest for the unearned. It is a quest for automatic knowledge—for an automatic evaluation of men's characters that bypasses the responsibility of exercising rational or moral judgment—and, above all, a quest for *an automatic self-esteem* (or pseudo-self-esteem).

To ascribe one's virtues to one's racial origin, is to confess that one has no knowledge of the process by which virtues are acquired and, most often, that one has failed to acquire them. The overwhelming majority of racists are men who have earned no sense of personal identity, who can claim no individual achievement or distinction, and who seek the illusion of a "tribal self-esteem" by alleging the inferiority of some other tribe. Observe the hysterical intensity of the Southern racists; observe also that racism is much more prevalent among the poor white trash than among their intellectual betters.

Historically, racism has always risen or fallen with the rise or fall of collectivism. Collectivism holds that the individual has no rights, that his life and work belong to the group (to "society," to the tribe, the state, the nation) and that the group may sacrifice him at its own whim to its own interests. The only way to implement a doctrine of that kind is by means of brute force—and *statism* has always been the political corollary of collectivism.

The absolute state is merely an institutionalized form of gang-rule, regardless of which particular gang seizes power. And—since there is no rational justification for such rule, since none has ever been or can ever be offered—the mystique of racism is a crucial element in every variant of the absolute state. The relationship is reciprocal: statism rises out of prehistorical tribal warfare, out of the notion that the men of one tribe are the natural prey for the men of another—and establishes its own internal subcategories of racism, a system of castes determined by a man's birth, such as inherited titles of nobility or inherited serfdom.

The racism of Nazi Germany—where men had to fill questionnaires about their ancestry for generations back, in order to prove their *Aryan* descent—has its counterpart in Soviet Russia, where men had to fill similar questionnaires to show that their ancestors had owned no property and thus to prove their *proletarian* descent. The Soviet ideology rests on the notion that men can be conditioned to communism *genetically*—that is, that a few generations conditioned by dictatorship will transmit communist ideology to their descendants, who will be communists *at birth.* The persecution of racial minorities in Soviet Russia, according to the racial descent and whim of any given commissar, is a matter of record; anti-Semitism is particularly prevalent—only the official pogroms are now called "political purges."

There is only one antidote to racism: the philosophy of individualism and its politico-economic corollary, laissez-faire capitalism.

Individualism regards man—every man—as an independent, sovereign entity who possesses an inalienable right to his own life, a right derived from his nature as a rational being. Individualism holds that a civilized society, or any form of association, cooperation or peaceful coexistence among men, can be achieved only on the basis of the recognition of individual rights—and that a group, as such, has no rights other than the individual rights of its members.

It is not a man's ancestors or relatives or genes or body chemistry that count in a free market, but only one human attribute: productive ability. It is by his own individual ability and ambition that capitalism judges a man and rewards him accordingly.

No political system can establish universal rationality by law (or by force). But capitalism is the only system that functions in a way which rewards rationality and penalizes all forms of irrationality, including racism.

A fully free, capitalist system has not yet existed anywhere. But what is enormously significant is the correlation of racism and political controls in the semifree economies of the nineteenth century. Racial and/or religious persecutions of minorities stood in inverse ratio to the degree of a country's freedom. Racism was strongest in the more controlled economies, such as Russia and Germany—and weakest in England, the then freest country of Europe.

It is capitalism that gave mankind its first steps toward freedom and a rational way of life. It is capitalism that broke through national and racial barriers, by means of free trade. It is capitalism that abolished serfdom and slavery in all the civilized countries of the world. It is the capitalist North that destroyed the slavery of the agrarian-feudal South in the United States.

Such was the trend of mankind for the brief span of some hundred and fifty years. The spectacular results and achievements of that trend need no restatement here.

The rise of collectivism reversed that trend.

When men began to be indoctrinated once more with the notion that the individual possesses no rights, that supremacy, moral authority and unlimited power belong to the group, and that a man has no significance outside his group—the inevitable consequence was that men began to gravitate toward some group or another, in self-protection, in bewilderment and in subconscious terror. The simplest collective to join, the easiest one to identify—particularly for people of limited intelligence—the least demanding form of "belonging" and of "togetherness" is: *race.*

It is thus that the theoreticians of collectivism, the "humanitarian" advocates of a "benevolent" absolute state, have led to the rebirth and the new, virulent growth of racism in the twentieth century.

In its great era of capitalism, the United States was the freest country on earth—and the best refutation of racist theories. Men of all races came here, some from obscure, culturally undistinguished countries, and accomplished feats of productive ability which would have remained stillborn in their control-ridden native lands. Men of racial groups that had been slaughtering one another for centuries, learned to live together in harmony and peaceful cooperation. America had been called "the melting pot," with good reason. But few people realized that America did not melt men into the gray conformity of a collective: she united them by means of protecting their right to individuality.

The major victims of such race prejudice as did exist in America were the Negroes. It was a problem originated and perpetuated by the noncapitalist South, though not confined to its boundaries. The persecution of Negroes in the South was and is truly disgraceful. But in the rest of the country, so long as men were free, even that problem was slowly giving way under the pressure of enlightenment and of the white men's own economic interests.

Today, that problem is growing worse—and so is every other form of racism. America has become race-conscious in a manner reminiscent of the worst days in the most backward countries of nineteenth-century Europe. The cause is the same: the growth of collectivism and statism.

In spite of the clamor for racial equality, propagated by the "liberals" in the past few decades, the Census Bureau reported recently that "[the Negro's] economic status relative to whites has not improved for nearly 20 years." It had been improving in the freer years of our "mixed economy"; it deteriorated with the progressive enlargement of the "liberals' " Welfare State.

The growth of racism in a "mixed economy" keeps step with the growth of government controls. A "mixed economy" disintegrates a country into an institutionalized civil war of pressure groups, each fighting for legislative favors and special privileges at the expense of one another.

The existence of such pressure groups and of their political lobbies is openly and cynically acknowledged today. The pretense at any political philosophy, any principles, ideals or long-range goals is fast disappearing from our scene—and it is all but admitted that this country is now floating without direction, at the mercy of a blind, short-range power game played by various statist gangs, each intent on getting hold of a legislative gun for any special advantage of the immediate moment.

In the absence of any coherent political philosophy, every economic group has been acting as its own destroyer, selling out its future for some momentary privilege. The policy of the businessmen has, for some time, been the most suicidal one in this respect. But it has been surpassed by the current policy of the Negro leaders.

So long as the Negro leaders were fighting against government-enforced discrimination—right, justice and morality were on their side. But that is not what they are fighting any longer. The confusions and contradictions surrounding the issue of racism have now reached an incredible climax.

It is time to clarify the principles involved.

The policy of the Southern states toward Negroes was and is a shameful contradiction of this country's basic principles. Racial discrimination, imposed and enforced by law, is so blatantly inexcusable an infringement of individual rights that the racist statutes of the South should have been declared unconstitutional long ago.

The Southern racists' claim of "states' rights" is a contradiction in terms: there can be no such thing as the "right" of some men to violate the rights of others. The constitutional concept of "states' rights" pertains to the division of power between local and national authorities, and serves to protect the states from the Federal government; it does not grant to a state government an unlimited, arbitrary power over its citizens or the privilege of abrogating the citizens' individual rights.

It is true that the Federal government has used the racial issue to enlarge its own power and to set a precedent of encroachment upon the legitimate rights of the states, in an unnecessary and unconstitutional manner. But this merely means that both governments are wrong; it does not excuse the policy of the Southern racists.

One of the worst contradictions, in this context, is the stand of many so-called "conservatives" (not confined exclusively to the South) who claim to be defenders of freedom, of capitalism, of property rights, of the Constitution, yet who advocate racism at the same time. They do not seem to possess enough concern with principles to realize that they are cutting the ground from under their own feet. Men who deny individual rights cannot claim, defend or uphold any rights whatsoever. It is such alleged champions of capitalism who are helping to discredit and destroy it.

The "liberals" are guilty of the same contradiction, but in a different form. They advocate the sacrifice of all individual rights to unlimited majority rule—yet posture as defenders of the rights of minorities. But the smallest minority on earth is the individual. Those who deny individual rights, cannot claim to be defenders of minorities.

This accumulation of contradictions, of shortsighted pragmatism, of cynical contempt for principles, of outrageous irrationality, has now reached its climax in the new demands of the Negro leaders.

Instead of fighting against racial discrimination, they are demanding that racial discrimination be legalized and enforced. Instead of fighting against racism, they are demanding the establishment of racial quotas. Instead of fighting for "color-blindness" in social and economic issues, they are proclaiming that "color-blindness" is evil and that "color" should be made a primary consideration. Instead of fighting for equal rights, they are demanding special race privileges.

They are demanding that racial quotas be established in regard to employment and that jobs be distributed on a racial basis, in proportion to the percentage of a given race among the local population. For instance, since Negroes constitute 25 percent of the population of New York City, they demand 25 percent of the jobs in a given establishment.

Racial quotas have been one of the worst evils of racist regimes. There were racial quotas in the universities of Czarist Russia, in the population of Russia's major cities, etc. One of the accusations against the racists in this country is that some schools practice a secret system of racial quotas. It was regarded as a victory for justice when employment questionnaires ceased to inquire about an applicant's race or religion.

Today, it is not an oppressor, but an oppressed minority group that is demanding the establishment of racial quotas. (!)

This particular demand was too much even for the "liberals." Many of them denounced it—properly—with shocked indignation.

Wrote *The New York Times* (July 23, 1963): "The demonstrators are following a truly vicious principle in playing the 'numbers game.' A demand that 25 percent (or any other percentage) of jobs be given to Negroes (or any other group) is wrong for one basic reason: it calls for a 'quota system,' which is in itself discriminatory. . . . This newspaper has long fought a religious quota in respect to judgeships; we equally oppose a racial quota in respect to jobs from the most elevated to the most menial."

As if the blatant racism of such a demand were not enough, some Negro leaders went still farther. Whitney M. Young Jr., executive director of the National Urban League, made the following statement (*New York Times,* August 1):

"The white leadership must be honest enough to grant that throughout our history there has existed a special privileged class of citizens who received preferred treatment. That class was white. Now we're saying this: If two men, one Negro and one white, are equally qualified for a job, hire the Negro."

Consider the implications of that statement. It does not merely demand special privileges on racial grounds—it demands that white men be penalized *for the sins of their ancestors.* It demands that a white laborer be refused a job because his grandfather may have practiced racial discrimination. But perhaps his grandfather had *not* practiced it. Or perhaps his grandfather had not even lived in this country. Since these questions are not to be considered, it means that that white laborer is to be charged with *collective racial guilt,* the guilt consisting merely of the color of his skin.

But *that* is the principle of the worst Southern racist who charges all Negroes with collective racial guilt for any crime committed by an individual Negro, and who treats them all as inferiors on the ground that their ancestors were savages.

The only comment one can make about demands of that kind, is: "By what right?—By what code?—By what standard?"

That absurdly evil policy is destroying the moral base of the Negroes' fight. Their case rested on the principle of individual rights. If they demand the violation of the rights of others, they negate and forfeit their own. Then the same answer applies to them as to the Southern racists: there can be no such thing as the "right" of some men to violate the rights of others.

Yet the entire policy of the Negro leaders is now moving in that direction. For instance, the demand for racial quotas in schools, with the proposal that hundreds of children, white and Negro, be forced to attend school in distant neighborhoods—for the purpose of "racial balance." Again, this is pure racism. As opponents of this demand have pointed out, to assign children to certain schools by reason of their race, is equally evil whether one does it for purposes of segregation or integration. And the mere idea of using children as pawns in a political game should outrage all parents, of any race, creed or color.

The "civil rights" bill, now under consideration in Congress, is another example of a gross infringement of individual rights. It is proper to forbid all discrimination in government-owned facilities and establishments: the government has no right to discriminate against any citizens. And by the very same principle, the government has no right to discriminate *for* some citizens at the expense of others. It has no right to violate the right of private property by forbidding discrimination in privately owned establishments.

No man, neither Negro nor white, has any claim to the property of another man. A man's rights are not violated by a private individual's refusal to deal with him. Racism is an evil, irrational and morally contemptible doctrine—but doctrines cannot be forbidden or prescribed by law. Just as we have to protect a communist's freedom of speech, even though his doctrines are evil, so we have to protect a racist's right to the use and disposal of his own property. Private racism is not a legal, but a moral issue—and can be fought only by private means, such as economic boycott or social ostracism.

Needless to say, if that "civil rights" bill is passed, it will be the worst breach of property rights in the sorry record of American history in respect to that subject.*

It is an ironic demonstration of the philosophical insanity and the consequently suicidal trend of our age, that the men who need the protection of individual rights most urgently—the Negroes—are now in the vanguard of the destruction of these rights.

A word of warning: do not become victims of the same racists by succumbing to racism; do not hold against all Negroes the disgraceful irrationality of some of their leaders. No group has any proper intellectual leadership today or any proper representation.

In conclusion, I shall quote from an astonishing editorial in *The New York Times* of August 4—astonishing because ideas of this nature are not typical of our age:

"But the question must be not whether a group recognizable in color, features or culture has its rights as a group. No, the question is whether any American individual, regardless of color, features or culture, is deprived of his rights as an American. If the individual has all the rights and privileges due him under the laws and the Constitution, we need not worry about groups and masses—those do not, in fact, exist, except as figures of speech."

(*September 1963*)

*The bill was passed in 1964, including the sections that violate property rights.

Global Balkanization

Have you ever wondered about the process of the collapse of a civilization? Not the *cause* of the collapse—the ultimate cause is always philosophical—but the *process,* the specific means by which the accumulated knowledge and achievements of centuries vanish from the earth?

The possibility of the collapse of Western civilization is not easy to imagine or to believe. Most people do not quite believe it—in spite of all the horror movies about the end of the world in a nuclear blast. But of course the world has never been destroyed by a sudden catastrophe. Man-made catastrophes of that size are not sudden; they are the result of a long, slow, gradual process, which can be observed in advance.

Let me remind you—as I have said many times before—that there is no such thing as historical determinism. The world does not have to continue moving toward disaster. But unless men change their philosophical direction—which they still have time to do—the collapse will come. And if you want to know the specific process that will bring it about, that process—the beginning of the end—is visible today.

In *The New York Times* of January 18, 1976, under the title "Europe's Restive Tribes," columnist C. L. Sulzberger is crying out in anxious bewilderment against a phenomenon he cannot understand: "It is distressing to return from Africa and find the cultivated old continent of Europe subsiding into its own form of tribalism just as new African governments make concerted efforts

This lecture was delivered at the Ford Hall Forum on April 10, 1977.

to curb the power of tribes and subordinate them to the greater concept of the nation-state."

By "tribalism," Mr. Sulzberger means the separatist movements spreading throughout Europe. "Indeed," he declares,

> it is a peculiar phenomenon of contemporary times that so many lands which had formerly been powerful and important seem obsessed with reducing the remnants of their own strength. . . . *There is no logical reason* that a Scotland which was proud to be considered part of the British Empire's heart when the sun never set on it, from Calcutta to Capetown, is now increasingly eager to disengage from what is left of that grand tradition on an offshore European island. [Emphasis added.]

Oh yes, there *is* a very logical reason why Great Britain is falling apart, but Mr. Sulzberger does not see it—just as he does not see what was grand about that old tradition. He is the *Times'* columnist specializing in European affairs, and, like a conscientious reporter, he is disturbed by something which he senses to be profoundly wrong—but, tending to be a liberal, he is unable to explain it.

He keeps coming back to the subject again and again. On July 3, 1976, in a column entitled "The Split Nationality Syndrome," he writes: "The present era's most paradoxical feature is the conflict between movements seeking to unify great geographical blocs into federations or confederations, and movements seeking to disintegrate into still smaller pieces the component nations trying to get together."

He offers an impressive list of examples. In France there is a Corsican autonomy movement, and similar movements of French Basques, of French Bretons, and of French inhabitants of the Jura belt west of Switzerland. "Britain is now obsessed with what is awkwardly called 'devolution.' This means watered-down autonomy and is designed to satisfy Welsh, but above all Scottish, nationalists." Belgium remains split "by an apparently insoluble language dispute between French-speaking Walloons and Dutch-speaking Flemish." Spain is facing demands for local independence "in Catalonia and the northern Basque country. . . . German-speaking inhabitants of Italy's Alto Adige yearn to leave

Rome and submit to Vienna. There is a tiny British-Danish argument . . . over the status of the Faroe Islanders. . . . In Yugoslavia there are continuing disputes between Serbs and Croats . . . There is also unresolved ferment among Macedonians . . . some of whom, on occasion, revive old dreams of their own state including Greek Salonika and part of Bulgaria."

Please remember that these tribes and subtribes, which most of the world has never heard of—since they have achieved no distinction to hear about—are struggling to secede from whatever country they are in and to form their own separate, sovereign, independent nations on their two-by-four stretches of the earth's crust.

I must make one correction. These tribes did achieve a certain kind of distinction: a history of endless, bloody warfare.

Coming back to Mr. Sulzberger: Africa, he points out, is torn apart by tribalism (in spite of the local governments' efforts), and most of Africa's recent wars were derived "from tribal causes." He concludes by observing: "The schizophrenic impulses splitting Europe threaten actually to atomize Africa—and all in the name of progress and unity."

In a column entitled "Western Schizophrenia" (December 22, 1976), Mr. Sulzberger cries: "The West is not drawing closer together; it is coming apart. This is less complicated but perhaps more distressing in North America than in Europe." For myself, I will add: and more disgusting.

Mr. Sulzberger continues: "Canada is apparently getting ready to tear itself asunder for emotional if illogical reasons which, on a massive scale, resemble the language dispute that continually splits Belgium . . ." He predicts the possibility of a formal separation between French-speaking Quebec and the rest of Canada, and comments sadly and helplessly: "Whatever happens, it is hard to foresee much good for the West ensuing." Which is certainly true.

Now what are the nature and the causes of modern tribalism?

Philosophically, tribalism is the product of irrationalism and collectivism. It is a logical consequence of modern philosophy. If men accept the notion that reason is not valid, what is to guide them and how are they to live? Obviously, they will seek to join some group—any group—which claims the ability to lead them and to provide some sort of knowledge acquired by some sort of unspecified means. If men accept the notion that the individual is helpless, intellectually and morally, that he has no mind and no rights, that he is nothing, but the group is all, and his only moral significance lies in selfless service to the group—they will be pulled obediently to join a group. But which group? Well, if you believe that you have no mind and no moral value, you cannot have the confidence to make choices—so the only thing for you to do is to join an *unchosen* group, the group into which you were born, the group to which you were predestined to belong by the sovereign, omnipotent, omniscient power of your body chemistry.

This, of course, is racism. But if your group is small enough, it will not be called "racism": it will be called "*ethnicity*."

For over half a century, modern liberals have been observing the fact that their ideas are achieving the opposite of their professed goals: instead of "liberation," communism has brought the blood-drenched dictatorship of Soviet Russia—instead of "prosperity," socialism has brought starvation to China, and Cuba, and India (and Russia)—instead of "brotherhood," the welfare state has brought the crumbling stagnation and the fierce, "elitist" power struggle of Great Britain, and Sweden, and many other, less obvious victims—instead of "peace," the spread of international altruism has brought about two world wars, an unceasing procession of local wars, and the suspending of a nuclear bomb over the heads of mankind. Yet this record does not prompt the liberals to check their premises or to glance, for contrast, at the record of the social system the last remnants of which they are so ferociously destroying.

Now we are seeing another demonstration of the fact that their professed goals are *not* the motive of today's liberals. We are seeing a special kind of intellectual cover-up—a cover-up so dirty and so low that it makes Watergate look like a childish caper.

Observe that ever since World War II, racism has been regarded as a vicious falsehood and a great evil, which it certainly is. It is not the root of all social evils—the root is collectivism—but, as I have written before (in *The Virtue of Selfishness*), "Racism is the lowest, most crudely primitive form of collectivism." One would think that Hitler had given a sufficient demonstration of racism's evil. Yet today's intellectuals, particularly the liberals, are supporting and propagating the most virulent form of racism on earth: tribalism.

The cover-up that makes it possible lies in a single word: *ethnicity.*

"Ethnicity" is an anti-concept, used as a disguise for the word "racism"—and it has no clearly definable meaning. But you can get a lead to its meaning if you hunt through a dictionary. The following are the results of my hunt through *The Random House College Dictionary* (1960), a book intended for young people.

I found no such term as "ethnicity." But I found "ethnic," which is defined as follows: "pertaining or peculiar to a population, esp. to a speech group, loosely also to a race." Under "ethnic group," the definition given as sociological usage reads: "a group of people, racially or historically related, having a common and distinctive culture, as an Italian or Chinese colony in a large American city."

I looked up the word "culture." The definition given as sociological usage reads: "the sum total of ways of living built up by a group of human beings, which is transmitted from one generation to another." I looked up also the word "tribe." The definition reads: "1. any aggregate of people united by ties of descent from a common ancestor, community of customs, and traditions, adherence to the same leaders, etc. 2. a local division of a primitive or barbarous people."

The meaning of the sum of these definitions is fairly clear: the term "ethnicity" stresses the traditional, rather than the physiological characteristics of a group, such as language—but physiology, i.e., *race,* is involved and mentioned in all but one of these definitions. So the advocacy of "ethnicity," means *racism plus tradition*—i.e., racism plus conformity—i.e., racism plus staleness.

The acceptance of the achievements of an individual by other individuals does not represent "ethnicity": it represents a cultural division of labor in a free market; it represents a conscious, individual choice on the part of all the men involved; the achievements may be scientific or technological or industrial or intellectual or esthetic—and the sum of such accepted achievements constitutes a free, civilized nation's *culture.* Tradition has nothing to do with it; tradition is being challenged and blasted daily in a free, civilized society: its citizens accept ideas and products because they are true and/or good—*not* because they are old *or* because their ancestors accepted them. In such a society, concretes change, but what remains immutable—by individual conviction, not by tradition—are those philosophical principles which correspond to reality, i.e., which are true.

The "old" and the "ancestral" are the standards of *tradition,* which supersedes reality, the standards of value of those who accept and practice "ethnicity." Culture, in the modern sociologists' view, is not a sum of achievements, but of "ways of living . . . transmitted from one generation to another." This means: concrete, specific ways of living. Can you—who are still the children of the United States of America—imagine the utter horror of a way of living that does not change from generation to generation? Yet this is what the advocates of ethnicity are advocating.

Is such a way of living compatible with reason? It is not. Is it compatible with independence or individuality? It is not. Is it compatible with progress? Obviously not. Is it compatible with capitalism? Don't be funny. What century are we talking about? We are dealing with a phenomenon that is rising out of prehistorical ages.

Atavistic remnants and echoes of those ages have always existed in the backwaters of civilized countries, particularly in Europe, among the old, the tired, the timid, and those who gave up before they started. Such people are the carriers of "ethnicity." The "ways of living" they transmit from generation to generation consist in: folk songs, folk dances, special ways of cooking food, traditional costumes, and folk festivals. Although the professional "ethnics" would (and did) fight wars over the differences between *their* songs and those of their neighbors, there are no significant differences between them; all folk art is essentially similar and excruciatingly boring: if you've seen one set of people clapping their hands while jumping up and down, you've seen them all.

Now observe the nature of those traditional ethnic "achievements": all of them belong to the *perceptual level of man's consciousness.* All of them are ways of dealing with or manipulating the concrete, the immediately given, the directly perceivable. All of them are manifestations of the *preconceptual* stage of human development.

I quote from one of my articles: "The concrete-bound, anticonceptual mentality can cope only with men who are bound by the same concretes—by the same kind of 'finite' world. To this mentality, it means a world in which men do not have to deal with abstract principles: principles are replaced by memorized rules of behavior, which are accepted uncritically as the given. What is 'finite' in such a world is not its extension, but the degree of mental effort required of its inhabitants. When they say 'finite,' they mean 'perceptual.' " (This is from "The Missing Link" in [*Philosophy: Who Needs It*]. That article deals with the psycho-epistemological roots of modern tribalism.)

In the same article I said: "John Dewey's theory of Progressive education (which has dominated the schools for close to half a century), established a method of crippling a child's conceptual faculty and replacing cognition with 'social adjustment.' It was and is a systematic attempt to manufacture tribal mentalities."

A symptom of the tribal mentality's self-arrested, perceptual level of development may be observed in the tribalists' position on *language*.

Language is a conceptual tool—a code of visual-auditory symbols that denote concepts. To a person who understands the function of language, it makes no difference what sounds are chosen to name things, provided these sounds refer to clearly defined aspects of reality. But to a tribalist, language is a mystic heritage, a string of sounds handed down from his ancestors and memorized, not understood. To him the importance lies in the perceptual concrete, the *sound* of a word, not its meaning. He would kill and die for the privilege of printing on every postage stamp the word "postage" for the English-speaking and the word "postes" for the French-speaking citizens of his bilingual Canada. Since most of the ethnic languages are not full languages, but merely dialects or local corruptions of a country's language, the distinctions which the tribalists fight for are not even as big as that.

But, of course, it is not for their language that the tribalists are fighting: they are fighting to protect their level of awareness, their mental passivity, their obedience to the tribe, and their desire to ignore the existence of outsiders.

The learning of another language expands one's abstract capacity and vision. Personally, I speak four—or rather three-and-a-half—languages: English, French, Russian, and the half is German, which I can read but not speak. I found this knowledge extremely helpful when I began writing: it gave me a wider range and choice of concepts; it showed me four different styles of expression; it made me grasp the nature of languages as such, apart from any set of concretes.

(Speaking of concretes, I would say that every civilized language has its own inimitable power and beauty, but the one I love is English—the language of my choice, not of my birth. English is the most eloquent, the most precise, the most economical, and, therefore, the most powerful. English fits me best—but I would be able to express *my* identity in any Western language.)

The tribalists clamor that their language preserves their "ethnic identity." But there is no such thing. Conformity to a racist tradition does not constitute a human identity. Just as racism provides a pseudo-self-esteem for men who have not earned an authentic one, so their hysterical loyalty to their own dialect serves a similar function: it provides a pretense at "collective self-esteem," an illusion of safety for the confused, frightened, precarious state of a tribalist's stagnant consciousness.

The proclaimed desire to preserve one's language and/or its literary works, if any, is a cover-up. In a free, or even semi-free country, no one is forbidden to speak any language he chooses with those who wish to speak it. But he cannot *force* it on others. A country has to have only *one* official language if men are to understand one another—and it makes no difference which language it is, since men live by the *meaning,* not the sound, of words. It is eminently fair that a country's official language should be the language of the majority. As to literary works, their survival does not depend on political enforcement.

But to the tribalists, language is not a tool of thought and communication. Language to them is a symbol of tribal status and power—the power to *force* their dialect on all outsiders. This appeals not even to the tribal leaders, but to the sick, touchy vanity of the tribal rank and file.

In this connection, I want to mention a hypothesis of mine, which is only a hypothesis because I have given no special study to the subject of bilingual countries, i.e., countries that have *two* official languages. But I have observed the fact that bilingual countries tend to be culturally impoverished by comparison to the major countries whose language they share in part. Bilingual countries do not produce many great, first-rate achievements in any intellectual line of endeavor, whether in science, philosophy, literature, or art. Consider the record of Belgium (which is French-speaking in part) as against the record of France—or the record of Switzerland (a trilingual country) as against the record of France, of Germany, of Italy—or the record of Canada as against the record of the United States.

The cause of the poor records may lie in the comparative territorial smallness of those countries—but this does not apply to Canada versus the United States. The cause may lie in the fact that the best, most talented citizens of the bilingual countries tend to emigrate to the major countries—but this still leaves the question: Why do they?

My hypothesis is as follows: the policy of bilingual rule (which spares some citizens the necessity to learn another language) is a concession to, and a perpetuation of, a strong ethnic-tribalist element within a country. It is an element of anti-intellectuality, conformity, and stagnation. The best minds would run from such countries: they would sense, if not know it consciously, that tribalism leaves them no chance.

But quite apart from this particular hypothesis, there can be no doubt that the spread of tribalism is an enormously anti-intellectual evil. If, as I said, some elements of "ethnicity" did remain in the backyards of civilized countries and stayed harmless for centuries, why the sudden epidemic of their rebirth? Irrationalism and collectivism—the philosophical notions of the prehistorical eras—had to be implemented in practice, in *political* action, before they could engulf the greatest scientific-technological achievements mankind had ever reached. The political cause of tribalism's rebirth is the *mixed economy*—the transitional stage of the formerly civilized countries of the West on their way to the political level from which the rest of the world has never emerged: the level of permanent tribal warfare.

As I wrote in my article on "Racism" (in *The Virtue of Selfishness*): "The growth of racism in a 'mixed economy' keeps step with the growth of government controls. A 'mixed economy' disintegrates a country into an institutionalized civil war of pressure groups, each fighting for legislative favors and special privileges at the expense of one another."

When a country begins to use such expressions as "seeking a bigger share of the pie," it is accepting a tenet of pure collectivism: the notion that the goods produced in a country do not belong to the producers, but belong to everybody, and that the government is the distributor. If so, what chance does an individual have of getting a slice of that pie? No chance at all, not even a few crumbs. An individual becomes "fair game" for every sort of organized predator. Thus people are pushed to surrender their independence in exchange for tribal protection.

The government of a mixed economy *manufactures* pressure groups—and, specifically, *manufactures* "ethnicity." The profiteers are those group leaders who discover suddenly that they can exploit the helplessness, the fear, the frustration of their "ethnic" brothers, organize them into a group, present demands to the government—and deliver the vote. The result is political jobs, subsidies, influence, and prestige for the *leaders* of the ethnic groups.

This does not improve the lot of the group's rank and file. It makes no difference to the hard-pressed unemployed of any race or color what quota of jobs, college admissions, and Washington appointments were handed out to the political manipulators from their particular race or color. But the ugly farce goes on, with the help and approval of the intellectuals, who write about "minority victories."

Here is a sample of the goal of such victories. In *The New York Times* of January 17, 1977, a news story was headlined as follows: "Hispanic Groups Say They Are Inequitably Treated in Support for Arts." At a hearing on the subject, New York State Senator Robert Garcia declared: "What we are really talking about is dollars and whether we are receiving a fair share of the revenues generated in this state." The purpose of the demands for state dollars was "to assure the growth of 'non-mainstream art forms.' " This means: art forms which people do not care to see or to support. The recommendations reached at the hearing included the demand that "at least twenty-five percent of the money goes to Hispanic arts."

This, ladies and gentlemen, is what your tax money is being spent on: the new profiteers of altruism are not the poor, the sick, or the unemployed, but ethnic females swishing their skirts in old Spanish dances which were not too good even when they were new.

This is a typical example of the motives and the vested interests behind the growth, the pushing, and the touting of "ethnicity."

An interesting article was published in the British magazine *Encounter* (February 1975). It is entitled "The Universalisation of Ethnicity" and is written by Nathan Glazer, a well-known American sociologist. It is quite revealing of the modern intellectuals' attitude toward the spread of ethnicity—more revealing in what Mr. Glazer does *not* say than in what he does.

He observes: "The overwhelming majority of people . . . are born into a religion, rather than adopt it, just as they are born into an ethnic group. In this respect both are similar. They are both groups by 'ascription' rather than 'achievement.' They are groups in which one's status is immediately given by birth rather than gained by some activities in one's life."

This is eminently—and horribly—true. There is a great deal to be said about the horrifying approach of a world dominated by people who prefer "ascription" to "achievement," and who seek a physiologically determined, automatically given status rather than a status they have to earn. Mr. Glazer does not say it; he merely reports.

He is disturbed by the relationship of "ethnic group" to "*caste,*" but treats it merely as a problem of definitions. But, of course, castes are inherent in the notion of ethnicity—castes of superiors and inferiors, determined by birth, enforced and perpetuated by law, dividing people into "aristocrats," "commoners," etc., down to "untouchables."

Mr. Glazer makes a true and profoundly important statement: "The United States is perhaps unique among the states of the world in using the term 'nation' to refer not to an ethnic group but to all who choose to become Americans." But he draws no conclusions from it. Yet it is extremely significant that the United States was the archenemy and the destroyer of ethnicity, that it abolished castes and any sort of inherited titles, that it granted no recognition to groups as such, that it recognized only the right of the individual to *choose* the associations he wished to join. Freedom of association is the opposite of ethnicity.

Mr. Glazer does not raise the question of the original American philosophy and the relationship of its destruction to the rise of ethnicity. The focus of his interest lies elsewhere. He writes: "The Socialist hope for a trans-national class struggle, based on class identification, never came to pass. Instead, it has been replaced by national and ethnic conflicts." And: "In most countries national interests and ethnic interests seem to dominate over class interests." Mr. Glazer is baffled by this development. He offers some tentative explanations with which he himself is not satisfied, such as: "The trends of modernisation, even while they do destroy some bases of distinctive culture and distinctive identity, create a need for a *new kind of identity* related to the old, intimate type of village or tribal association." A modern, technological society, which includes nuclear bombs and space travel—to be run by villages or by tribal associations?

Mr. Glazer himself tends to dismiss theories of this sort, and admits that he cannot find an explanation. "This is the heart of the darkness. Why *didn't* the major lines of conflict within societies become class conflicts rather than ethnic conflicts? . . . In most developing countries Marxism remains the ideology of the students and often of the ruling group—but *ethnicity* is the focus around which identity and loyalty have been shaped." Mr. Glazer comes closer to an answer when he observes that ethnicity has "an irrational appeal," but he takes it no further. He says instead:

> It would seem that the rallying cries that mobilise the classes have, in recent decades, had less power than the rallying cries that mobilise the races, tribes, religions, language-users—in short, the Ethnic Groups. Perhaps the epidemic of ethnic conflicts reflects the fact that leaders and organisers believe they can get a more potent response by appealing to *ethnicity* than they can by appealing to Class Interest.

True, leaders and organizers do believe this—but why? The answer to Mr. Glazer's questions lies in the fact that Marxism is an *intellectual* construct; it is false, but it is an *abstract* theory—and *it is too abstract for the tribalists' concrete-bound, perceptual mentalities.* It requires a significantly high level of abstraction to grasp the reality of "an *international* working class"—a level beyond the power of a consciousness that understands its own village, but has trouble treating the nearest town as fully real. No, the level of men's intelligence has not deteriorated from natural causes; it has been pushed down, retarded, stultified by modern anti-intellectual education and modern irrationalist philosophy.

Mr. Glazer does not see or is not concerned with any part of this answer. It is obvious that he is disturbed by the spread of ethnicity, but he tries to hope for the best—and this leads him, in conclusion, to a truly unspeakable statement. After proposing some sort of solution in the form of "either guaranteed shares for each group, or guaranteed rights for each individual and each group," he continues: "The United States in the past seemed to find the approach in terms of 'guaranteed rights' more congenial than the approach in terms of guaranteed shares; but recently Americans have begun to take individual rights less seriously, and to take group shares more seriously." After I recovered from feeling sick at my stomach, I asked myself: What Americans has Mr. Glazer been observing or associating with? I do not know—but his statement is libel against an entire nation. His statement means that Americans are willing to sell their rights for money—for a "share of the pie."

In his last paragraph Mr. Glazer observes that there was time when "the problems of Ethnicity, as a source of conflict within nations and between nations, have generally appeared as simply a left-over, an embarrassment from the past. It is my conviction they must now be placed at the very centre of our concern for the human condition."

He is right to fear such a prospect.

There is no surer way to infect mankind with hatred—brute, blind, virulent hatred—than by splitting it into ethnic groups or tribes. If a man believes that his own character is determined at birth in some unknown, ineffable way, and that the characters of all strangers are determined in the same way—then no communication, no understanding, no persuasion is possible among them, only mutual fear, suspicion, and hatred. Tribal or ethnic rule has existed, at some time, in every part of the world, and, in some country, in every period of mankind's history. The record of hatred is always the same. The worst kinds of atrocities were perpetrated during ethnic (including religious) wars. A recent grand-scale example of it was Nazi Germany.

Warfare—permanent warfare—is the hallmark of tribal existence. A tribe—with its rules, dogmas, traditions, and arrested mental development—is not a productive organization. Tribes subsist on the edge of starvation, at the mercy of natural disasters, less successfully than herds of animals. War against other, momentarily luckier tribes, in the hope of looting some meager hoard, is their chronic emergency means of survival. The inculcation of hatred for other tribes is a necessary tool of tribal rulers, who need scapegoats to blame for the misery of their own subjects.

There is no tyranny worse than ethnic rule—since it is an unchosen serfdom one is asked to accept as a value, and since it applies primarily to one's mind. A man of self-esteem will not accept the notion that the content of his mind is determined by his muscles, i.e., by his own body. But by the bodies of an unspecified string of ancestors? Determinism by the means of production is preferable; it is equally false, but less offensive to human dignity. Marxism is corrupt, but clean compared to the stale, rank, musty odor of ethnicity.

As to the stagnation under tribal rule—take a look at the Balkans. At the start of this century, the Balkans were regarded as the disgrace of Europe. Six or eight tribes, plus a number of subtribes with unpronounceable names, were crowded on the Balkan peninsula, engaging in endless wars among themselves or being conquered by stronger neighbors or practicing violence for the sake of violence over some microscopic language differences. "Balkanization"—the breakup of larger nations into ethnic tribes—was used as a pejorative term by the European intellectuals of the time. Those same intellectuals were pathetically proud when they managed, after World War I, to glue most of the Balkan tribes together into two larger countries: Czechoslovakia and Yugoslavia. But the tribes never vanished; they have been popping up in minor explosions all along, and a major one is possible at any time.

In the light of tribalism's historical record, it is ludicrous to compromise with it, to hope for the best or to expect some sort of fair "group shares." Nothing can be expected from tribalism except brutality and war. But this time, it is not with bows and arrows that the tribes will be armed, but with nuclear bombs.

As a tiny preview of what tribalism would mean in a modern, technological civilization, a story in *The New York Times* of January 23, 1977, reports that the French-speaking Canadians of Quebec had demanded the use of French in all official dealings, including at airports, but "a federal court upheld a ban by the federal Ministry of Transport on the use of French for landings at Montreal's two international airports. (English is the language accepted at airports in every nation of the world.)"

Let me remind you of the recent terrible collision of two planes in the Canary Islands. Although all the personnel involved spoke English perfectly, the investigations seem to indicate that the collision was caused by linguistic misunderstandings. But what is that to the Canadians of Quebec, or to Idi Amin of Uganda, or to any other ethnic tribalists who might demand that *their* language be spoken by every plane pilot in the world? Incidentally, that collision took place because the small airport was overcrowded with planes that could not land at a nearby major airport: the major airport had been bombed by ethnic terrorists who were seeking the independence of the Canary Islands from Spain.

How long would the achievements of a technological civilization last under this sort of tribal management?

Some people ask whether local groups or provinces have the right to secede from the country of which they are a part. The answer is: on ethnic grounds, no. Ethnicity is not a valid consideration, morally or politically, and does not endow anyone with any special rights. As to other than ethnic grounds, remember that rights belong only to individuals and that there is no such thing as "group rights." If a province wants to secede from a dictatorship, or even from a mixed economy, in order to establish a free country—it has the right to do so. But if a local gang, ethnic or otherwise, wants to secede in order to establish its own government controls, it does not have that right. No group has the right to violate the rights of the individuals who happen to live in the same locality. A wish—individual or collective—is not a right.

Is there a way to avoid the rebirth of global tribalism and the approach of another Dark Ages? Yes, there is, but only one way—through the rebirth of the antagonist that has demonstrated its power to relegate ethnicity to a peaceful dump: capitalism.

Observe the paradoxes built up about capitalism. It has been called a system of selfishness (which, in *my* sense of the term, it *is*)—yet it is the only system that drew men to unite on a large scale into great countries, and peacefully to cooperate across national boundaries, while all the collectivist, internationalist, One-World systems are splitting the world into Balkanized tribes.

Capitalism has been called a system of greed—yet it is the system that raised the standard of living of its poorest citizens to heights no collectivist system has ever begun to equal, and no tribal gang can conceive of.

Capitalism has been called nationalistic—yet it is the only system that banished ethnicity, and made it possible, in the United States, for men of various, formerly antagonistic nationalities to live together in peace.

Capitalism has been called cruel—yet it brought such hope, progress and general good will that the young people of today, who have not seen it, find it hard to believe.

As to pride, dignity, self-confidence, self-esteem—these are characteristics that mark a man for martyrdom in a tribal society and under any social system except capitalism.

If you want an example of what had once been the spirit of America—a spirit which would be impossible today, but which we must now struggle to bring to a rebirth—I will quote from an old poem that represents the opposite of the abject self-abasement of ethnicity. It is a poem called "The Westerner" by Badger Clark.

He begins with "My fathers sleep on the Eastern plain and each one sleeps alone"—he acknowledges his respect for his forefathers, then says:

> But I lean on no dead kin.
> My name is mine for fame or scorn,
> And the world began when I was born,
> And the world is mine to win.

Gender Tribalism

Peter Schwartz

All forms of collectivism rest on a certain metaphysics. The collectivist tenets—in economics, that production is primarily a social effort; in politics, that the group, not the individual, has rights; in ethics, that the individual must sacrifice his interests to the needs of society; in epistemology, that the judgment of an individual mind is subordinate to the collective consensus—all stem from a deeper premise: that the individual is impotent to cope with reality. The individual, on this premise, cannot sustain his life on his own, and must depend upon the group for survival.

This viewpoint, as applied to women, is what feminism essentially promulgates.

Of all the supposedly demeaning views of women for which feminists condemn our "patriarchal" society, none is remotely as denigrating as that held by feminism itself. It is, today, uniquely feminists who depict women as congenitally helpless, endlessly "victimized" creatures.

It is feminists who declare that, without government aid, women are compelled to accept only 75 percent of what men are paid—that their advancement at work is blocked by a "glass ceiling," which only the weight of government can shatter—that women cannot be expected to hold full-time jobs unless government provides day-care services for their children—that women cannot get hired for the better jobs or admitted into the better schools, except through "affirmative-action" preferences—that women cannot attain self-esteem as long as *Playboy*-type material (which, a court rules, has "a negative impact on the individual's sense of self-worth and acceptance") is legally permitted to be sold.[1]

The message of such feminist stands is that the individual woman cannot succeed in life by her own efforts and on her own merit. She is at the mercy of forces she cannot control, unable to obtain work, education or self-respect without the succor of a (governmental) nursemaid.

This is not merely a journalistic description of what feminists see as an unfortunate condition of women at present. This is, rather, a part of their basic philosophy—a philosophy that holds metaphysical powerlessness to be woman's normal state.

And it is a state that feminists actively *foster*. They want women to believe that the way to attain one's goals is to rely, not on individual merit, but on the power of the group. According to feminism, acquiring the specific abilities necessary for success in some area should be of little concern to women. In fact, they should dismiss the very need for such abilities. What they should count on, instead, is the fact of their gender.

For example, the average woman scores lower on the Medical College Admissions Test (because of deficiencies in her knowledge of science) than the average man. Should women who want to be doctors come to the logical conclusion that they need to study harder? Should women be advised to master science, so that they can be accepted on the same basis as men, irrespective of gender? No, say the feminists; the only conclusion to be drawn is that not enough women are being admitted—so the qualifications must be changed.[2]

If a woman wants to be, say, a firefighter, the feminists do not encourage her to make sure she measures up to the demanding physical standards. What matters most, she is told, is that there be a representative contingent of her gender at the firehouse. And if she does not meet the standards? She should not have to, feminists retort; women are rightly due their quota of such jobs.

With all their prattle about female "empowerment," feminists disavow the only legitimate meaning of that term: i.e., the individual woman's self-created power to make herself into a value, the power to make an employer *want* to promote her or a school *want* to enroll her—as a mutually beneficial exchange, based on her objective ability, not as a sacrificial accommodation to her gender. But that would be too independent an approach for the feminists to sanction.

Their implicit message to women is: "You cannot succeed on

your own—but you don't have to; your collective will get you what you want."

Ironically, when the contemporary feminist movement began, in the 1960s, people believed that its message was the exact opposite. They believed that women were being urged to abandon the traditional "hausfrau" mentality—i.e., the assumption (held by females no less than by males) that women were incapable of dealing with existence outside the confines of the kitchen and the bedroom. People believed that women were being urged to seek their own careers, to reject unchosen duties to others, to assert a moral right to the pursuit of their own happiness, to embrace the real world by becoming airline pilots, neurosurgeons, music composers and CEOs.

But the collectivism at the heart of the movement quickly surfaced, revealing feminism's true nature. It became clear that women were expected to obtain all these new positions, not by *earning* them qua individuals, but by demanding them qua females. It became clear that the hausfrau image, far from being rejected, was being endorsed by feminism—in an updated, uglier form.

Whereas the old hausfrau mentality said that women could not perform the more demanding jobs as competently as men, this same mentality now says that women should not be *required* to. Now, the fact of gender supposedly *entitles* women to their "fair share" of corporate vice presidencies, irrespective of ability. Now, under this "neo-hausfrauism," women don't have to earn any reward—they just have to call upon Momma State to grab it for them. Now, as before, the conclusion for women is: gender determines all.

It is only the perverse influence of modern collectivism that permits such moral debilitation to be termed "liberation."

In pushing this philosophy, feminism attracts the very worst among women. It draws all those who want to be absolved of responsibility for their lives. Every housewife who feels guilty for having forever given up her pursuit of a career—every mindless scrub nurse who regrets having abandoned her ambition for something more—every bitter woman in a dead-end job or a dead-end life—are all reassured that their plight is not their fault. The individual woman cannot succeed—feminist doctrine proclaims; so she is not to be reproached for her failures.

One type of woman, however, *is* to be reproached: the woman of true independence. The woman who wants to judge and be judged according to individual merit—who scorns the crutch of "affirmative action," who succeeds on her own and who is proud of it—is chastised as a traitor to her tribe. She would never have achieved anything—feminists resentfully insist—had it not been for the collective efforts of all women.

Feminism rests upon dependency. It tenaciously recruits—and molds—dependent, self-abnegating women. It inculcates in them a belief in their metaphysical helplessness—and then waits for them to become docile members of the flock.

Feminism wants to enshrine the very mentality from which it claims to "liberate" women. It seeks to re-channel the hausfrau mentality—the desire to be provided for—by simply switching the object of dependence from husbands to the "Sisterhood."

The leaders of feminism advocate the creed of the social worker. The social worker exists, not to help people escape from trouble, but to persuade them that life inherently *is* trouble—from which escape is impossible without the help of the social worker. Feminists want to instill a similar state of mind, by convincing the individual woman that she is doomed to frustration and failure—unless she hitches her wagon to the collective caravan of womanhood.

At the root of this malign conception of women lies a premise about free will. Feminists implicitly believe that women have no genuine volition and that their choices in life are not freely made.

Thus, according to feminism, a woman is never to feel guilty, no matter how low she may have sunk. Has she thrown her life away in a loveless marriage, in drug addiction, in prostitution, in violent crime? She could not help it, feminists tell her. Her choices are not the cause of her misery. Society did not *allow* her to do anything else. It is society, not she, that needs changing. And the only true "choice" a woman can make, therefore, is a collective one: to stand in solidarity with her female comrades.

The heroines of the feminist movement are not the women who achieve productive lives by their own efforts, but those who announce how empty and impossible their lives would have been without the maternalistic aid of a feminist-sensitive state. The woman who has no real self to assert—who pleads to be taken care of by her "sisters"—who preaches loyalty to quotas and subservience to the collective—who declares that the source of her unhappiness is not her own irrational choices in life but a tyrannical culture—it is she who is held up as a model to be emulated.

Because feminism regards volition as a myth, women are consistently portrayed as victims. Since they are not held responsible for any failure to attain some end, every frustrated whim of theirs is taken as a sign of victimization. It is taken as evidence that women are being denied their rightful share of the goods. "Feminist consciousness"—says one author—"is consciousness of *victimization*."[3] (Emphasis in original.)

The actual "victimizer" is, of course, reality itself. If a woman wants to be hired for a certain position or to gain entry into a certain school, not because she qualifies for it, but because she belongs to a class whose desires are not being fulfilled—then it is reality that is the barrier. For it is reality that demands objective qualifications. It is reality that presents us with the unbending law of causality, the law which states that a job can be done only by those who can do it. It is objectivity—the need to adhere to the requirements of reality—that is feminism's real enemy.

But feminists dismiss the very concept of an objective reality, because the volitionless woman cannot survive in such a world. She cannot accommodate herself to a universe that makes such rigid demands upon her. She wants the "flexibility" of the nonobjective. She feels ineffectual in an objective reality—so feminism repudiates it for her.

"Feminist analysis"—says a professor at the University of New Mexico Law School—"begins and ends with the principle that objective reality is a myth."[4]

Thus feminists denounce the "exclusionary" means by which society evaluates doctors, lawyers, soldiers. Why, they ask, should women be judged by objective standards? And if one answers: because reality and reason mandate it—their reply is: Why should women be bound by reality and reason? Why can't a woman be allowed to construct a more malleable world, a world she feels is more hospitable to her wishes? Why shouldn't she be judged, for example, by her compassion for the ill, rather than her ability to perform surgery—or by her aptitude for telling stories rather than for logically analyzing legal principles—or by her capacity to bond with her fellow soldiers rather than to run an obstacle course in full military gear?

As the president of City College of New York, complaining about a lack of "diversity" in universities, writes: "Institutions of higher learning in the United States are products of Western society in which masculine values like an orientation toward achievement and objectivity are valued over cooperation, connectedness and subjectivity."[5]

Why, feminists wonder, should even immutable facts stand in the way of women's egalitarian desires? For instance, why should women pay more for annuities just because they have longer life expectancies? Why should they pay different medical insurance premiums just because they incur pregnancy-related costs?[6] Why should females not be members of the Dallas Cowboys and the Vienna Boys Choir? As one feminist organization claims: "There is no such thing as fair and unfair discrimination."[7]

In this war between women and objectivity—between whims and reality—it is considered "discriminatory" to give priority to the latter combatant.

But since reality per se is not very responsive to political protests, feminists direct their grievances against the party they blame for "inventing" such an unyielding universe: men.

It is men who push the idea of objectivity—feminism argues—as a means of keeping women subjugated. It is men who arbitrarily refuse to indulge a woman's whims, as they insist that she be judged by merit, not gender. It is men who are to blame for every female who becomes a stewardess rather than a pilot, a cheerleader rather than a quarterback, a secretary rather than a vice president.

Feminists observe that males have somehow managed to succeed in reality. They have somehow been able to acquire the jobs, the wealth, the fame, the happiness. The way for women to do likewise—feminists maintain—is, not to master reality, but to harness its surrogate: the male. How? By acting like the children feminism believes they metaphysically are, and petulantly demanding that their desires be accommodated—by men. By insisting that they be given their "allowances," in the form of prescribed quotas of jobs, promotions, college admissions, etc.—to be produced and financed by men. (At least, the old hausfrau method of directly latching onto a husband for financial security was a more honest form of dependence.)

This evaluation of women as non-volitional ciphers, and of men as their vile oppressors, is implicit throughout the feminist philosophy. But there is one area in which this view is made virtually *ex*plicit: sex.

Sex between a man and a woman is not what it seems, according to feminists—i.e., it is not really voluntary. Law professor Susan Estrich, for instance, writes: "Many feminists would argue that so long as women are powerless relative to men, viewing a 'yes' as a sign of true consent is misguided."[8]

Other feminists contend that a woman cannot be held accountable for her decision to engage in sex. "There could be many reasons why a woman might not resist a man's advances so that unwanted intercourse could occur without force. The woman . . . may be confused. Her socialization may make it difficult for her to resist."[9]

In other words, women—*adult* women—are incapable of saying no when they do not want to have sex. They are the passive, deterministic products of their "socialization." Consequently, feminists say, women cannot be held responsible for having sex, any more than children can.

This idea of women as volitionless doormats obliterates the distinction between the voluntary and the forced. Do women have a rational faculty, by which they *choose* whether or not to engage in sex? Not according to feminists, who declare that "verbal coercion" constitutes rape. And what is "verbal coercion"? It is "a woman's consenting to unwanted sexual activity because of a man's verbal arguments *not including verbal threats of force*."[10] (Emphasis added.) So whenever the man utters anything indicating a desire for sex, any subsequent sexual activity, no matter how willing the woman is, may well make him criminally liable.

This is why, in incidents in which men are denounced (sometimes correctly) for "sexual misconduct"—such as the one at the Navy's 1991 Tailhook convention—no differentiation is made between actions in which the women willingly engage and actions in which they are forced to participate. To the feminist, it is all "coercive."

On this view, it is not the objective facts that are legally decisive, but the woman's subjective emotions. Says law professor Catherine MacKinnon: "I call it rape whenever a woman has sex and *feels violated*."[11] (Emphasis added.)

Facts are simply brushed aside by feminists. Since women are seen as incapable of exercising volition, the crucial distinction with respect to sex is, not between the woman's giving and withholding consent, but between her feeling and not feeling "violated"—a feeling on the basis of which men are to be indicted, tried and sentenced.

A study of college students ("Project on Campus Sexual Assault"), sponsored by *Ms.* magazine in 1985, is widely hailed as an authoritative, scientific survey of the prevalence of rape in American society. It found that over 25 percent of college-age women had been victims of rape or attempted rape. This reinforced the portrait of a patriarchal culture in which women are under constant attack by, and need constant protection from, their natural enemy, the male.

Yet it was only the survey's distorted definition of rape—based on the view of women as "socialized" puppets, unable to make their own decisions—that led to such a conclusion. For example, according to the questionnaire, if a woman accepts a drink from a man and they then willingly have sex, it may be considered rape, because the man has "impair[ed] the other person's judgment or control by administering any drug or intoxicant."[12]

In fact, of those classified by the survey as having been raped, 73 percent indicated that they themselves *did not believe that the sexual activity in question constituted rape*. And over 40 percent of the "victims" *had sex again with their "attackers*."[13]

This neo-hausfrau movement believes that women must be treated like children. They cannot be trusted to give "informed consent," they cannot be relied upon to know whether they have been raped and they need continuous parental supervision to make sure their needs are being met.

When a march on Washington was organized by the National Organization for Women to publicize "violence against women," the objects of the protest were, not just rape or battery, but *reductions in welfare spending and cutbacks in affirmative action programs*. As reported in the *New York Times*, the feminists "equated what they called 'political violence' with physical attacks."[14] A parent who beats an infant and a parent who withholds meals from an infant are both guilty of physical abuse. Similarly—feminist thinking goes—adult women are "victimized" by a denial of welfare benefits as much as by a real assault.

Just as the essence of rape, according to feminists, is not the act of physically forcing a woman to have sex, so the nature of its evil is not the coercion—but the collective "discrimination" by one class against another.

This primitive, tribalist view is most openly advocated by MacKinnon, who writes: "Sexual violation is both a practice and an index of inequality between the sexes, both a symbol and an act of women's subordinate social status to men."[15] Unable to perceive a woman as an individual even with respect to her being the target of an actual rape, MacKinnon sees the crime as being committed against the tribe. It is not that a particular woman has been attacked by a particular man—or even that physical force has been used—but that one collective has been judged "inferior" to another.

Rape should be prosecuted as a "sex equality case," MacKinnon says. In a rape trial, the central questions about the accused would include: "How does this man treat women sexually? Is he a sex bigot?" If the courts were to adopt this approach, she concludes, "At least rape would be called in law what it is in life: sex discrimination."[16]

But if the essence of rape is "discrimination"—what is the difference between sex and rape? The act of sex is undeniably "discriminatory"—it discriminates by gender. Doesn't that make it inherently evil?

Whether the claim is that "yes" equals "no," or that rape equals "inequality"—sex is transformed by feminists into the archetypal act of aggression by men against women. *Sex per se becomes rape.* And all men become guilty of it.

Rape, says one "acquaintance-rape educator," "is not some form of psychopathology that afflicts a very small number of men. In fact rape is not that different from what we see as socially acceptable or socially laudable male behavior."[17] Rape, says a noted feminist author, is "a conscious process of intimidation by which *all men* keep *all women* in a state of fear."[18] (Emphasis in original.)

What is the source of this enormous hostility toward men, and particularly toward sex between men and women? The act of sex, Ayn Rand writes, is an act of metaphysical assertion: "To a rational man, sex is an expression of self-esteem—*a celebration of himself and of existence*. . . . [I]t is his response to his own highest values in the person of another."[19] (Emphasis in original.) Sex is an affirmation of an individual's self-worth, of his or her capability to live successfully in reality and to experience the joy of such success.

What assessment of sex, then, follows from an opposite metaphysics? If sex is good because it celebrates the individual's capacity to master reality and achieve values—how must feminists, who believe that a woman fundamentally lacks that capacity, perceive sex?

To them, sex is a union, not between two partners sharing their highest values, but between two antagonistic forces: a brutal despot—who wantonly denies woman her due by insisting that she earn her place in the world: and a feckless, perpetual victim—who desperately clings to others for her basic identity and for her very survival. On this view, sex for the woman is not a joyous affirmation of her sense of self-value, but an intolerable reinforcement of her sense of helplessness—and of her resentment toward the man for *not* being helpless.

Sex, according to feminists, is sheer oppression. The woman is being dominated. She is being "taken" by her enemy. Sex is the quintessential "victimization" of woman—the woman who lacks the capacity even to assert her own will in the face of male "verbal coercion."

Feminist theorist Andrea Dworkin, who depicts sex as "wartime invasion and occupation," presents this view unabashedly: "Physically, the woman in intercourse is a space inhabited, a literal territory occupied literally: occupied even if there has been no resistance, no force; even if the occupied person said yes please, yes hurry, yes more." The fact that women may judge sex to be good makes the act all the worse, she says. These "occupied women [are] more base in their collaboration than other collaborators have ever been: experiencing pleasure in their own inferiority, calling intercourse freedom."[20]

Dworkin's is not some "lunatic fringe" viewpoint. Her odious characterization of sex follows logically from the feminist metaphysics. If the individual woman is a powerless, volitionless nonentity, then sex *is* a combination of callous invasion and abject collaboration. Dworkin is merely being more consistent, and is taking feminist ideas more seriously, than many of her feminist cohorts.

* * *

The doctrine of feminism pervades today's culture. To question and oppose its "politically correct" tenets, especially within academia, requires an independent mind. That is, it requires precisely the faculty whose existence feminism will not acknowledge—and whose force it cannot withstand.

Feminism needs to be repudiated by everyone—man or woman—who recognizes the crucial need to think, and to act, by oneself. If you understand that a human being's basic identity is *self*-created, and is not the product of gender—if you grasp the fact of your capacity to achieve your own goals by your own effort—if you indignantly reject the demand that anyone live by the guidance and the power of the collective—then do not permit the ideas of feminism to go unchallenged. Expose, and condemn, the self-effacing dependency that this "liberation" movement cultivates. Above all, let people see that the ideological battle over feminism is not between the female and the male—but between tribalism and independence.

REFERENCES

1. "Canada Court Says Pornography Harms Women," *New York Times,* February 2, 1992, p. B7

2. On the Medical College Admission Test—the only standardized test available to medical schools—women attain a mean score 88 percent that of men on the physical sciences section of the test; and 90 percent on the biological sciences. Yet in recent years, according to the Association of Medical Colleges, equal proportions of male and female applicants have been accepted to medical schools. ("Women seem to communicate better in the interview," says the associate dean of admissions at Harvard Medical School.) See Martin L. Gross, *The End of Sanity* (Avon Books, 1997) pp. 72–75.

3. Sandra Lee Bartky, *Femininity and Domination: Studies in the Phenomenology of Oppression* (Routledge, 1990), p. 15.

4. Ann Scales of the University of New Mexico Law School, quoted by David Brock in *The Real Anita Hill* (Free Press, 1993) p. 384.

5. Yolanda Moses, quoted in a New York *Post* editorial, "CUNY Does It Again," May 26, 1993, p. 18.

6. The Supreme Court has endorsed this view, ruling in 1983 that sex-segregated actuarial tables violate the Civil Rights Act of 1964 because "under the statute, even a true generalization about a class cannot justify class-based treatment."

7. An official of the National Federation of Business and Professional Women's Clubs, quoted in *The Intellectual Activist,* July 29, 1983, p. 3.

8. Quoted by Katie Roiphe in "Date Rape's Other Victim," *New York Times Magazine,* June 13, 1993, p. 30.

9. Charlene L. Muehlenhard and Jennifer L. Schrag, quoted by Norman Podhoretz in "Rape in Feminist Eyes," *Commentary,* October 1991, p. 33.

10. Roiphe, op. cit.

11. Quoted by Carol Iannone, "Sex and the Feminists," *Commentary,* September 1993, p. 31.

12. Christina Hoff Sommers, *Who Stole Feminism?* (Simon & Schuster, 1994), pp. 212–213.

13. Ibid., pp. 213–214.

14. "Thousands in Capital Protest Attacks on Women," *New York Times,* April 10, 1995, p. A1.

15. "The Palm Beach Hanging," *New York Times,* December 15, 1991, Section 4, p. 15.

16. Ibid.

17. Py Bateman, quoted by Podhoretz, op. cit., p. 30.

18. Ibid. (from Susan Brownmiller's book *Against Our Will: Men, Women and Rape,* Bantam, 1976).

19. Ayn Rand, "Of Living Death," *The Voice of Reason* (New American Library, 1998), p. 54.

20. Quoted by Podhoretz, op. cit., p. 31 (from Andrea Dworkin's book *Intercourse,* Free Press, 1988).

The Anti-Industrial Revolution

The Philosophy of Privation

Peter Schwartz

The first code of ethics that deliberately and unequivocally divorced man's actions from his interests was Immanuel Kant's. It was Kant who declared that man, to be certain that he is acting morally, must not merely ignore his interests—material or spiritual—but must willfully contradict them. It was Kant who created a formal dichotomy between that which constitutes the good and that which fulfills any need of human life.

Kant's philosophy gradually worked its way into Western culture. Now, some two hundred years later, a political movement has arisen that brazenly endorses this killer creed. It is a movement that seeks to prohibit the pursuit of human values—because of one's moral "duty" to the non-human. That movement is: environmentalism.

Many people hold a benign view of environmentalism. They regard it as a salutary force, as a sort of global sanitation department. While critical of certain "excesses," people believe that environmentalism fundamentally seeks to improve man's life by cleaning up the dirt in his water and the pollutants in his air.

But that is a dangerously superficial assessment. If one examines the conflicts between the interests of man and the "interests" of nature, it becomes clear that the former are invariably sacrificed to the latter by environmentalists. Whenever there is a hydroelectric dam to be built, it is the welfare of the snail darter or the Chinook salmon that is inviolate, and the welfare of man that is dispensable. Whenever there is a choice between cutting down trees for human use and leaving them in place for the spotted owl, it is the bird's home that environmentalists save and human habitation that goes unbuilt.

Huge tracts of Arctic land are off-limits to productive enterprises, in order not to disturb the caribou and the ice floes. Mosquito- and alligator-infested swamps (euphemistically called *wetlands*) are deemed sacred, not to be defiled by man-made drainage. (Even land that is actually growing crops can be christened wetlands, if some bureaucrat decides that vegetation typically found in swamps *could* have grown there had the crops not been planted.) The most beneficial projects, from housing developments to science observatories, are halted if there is any danger—if there is any *allegation* of danger—to some piddling species.

The incalculable damage inflicted on human beings by such prohibitions is immaterial to environmentalists. They have abandoned even the pretext of holding human happiness as their ultimate purpose. In its place, as an open secret that the public is unable to take fully seriously, is the premise that nature must remain unchanged *as an end in itself.* It is the premise that nature must be protected, not *for* man, but *from* man.

Several years ago a controversy arose concerning a new cancer-fighting drug, taxol. It was found in the bark of the Pacific yew tree. The director of the National Cancer Institute described taxol as "the most important new drug we have had in cancer for fifteen years."[1] But environmentalists insisted that the trees, which are considered scarce and are home to the spotted owl, remain largely untouched.

Al Gore, in his book *Earth in the Balance,* declares himself incapable of choosing between people and trees: "It seems an easy choice—sacrifice the tree for a human life—until one learns that three trees must be destroyed for each patient treated. . . . Suddenly we must confront some tough questions."[2]

According to an official of the Oregon Natural Resources Council: "The basic issue in our mind is that the yew [tree] is a finite resource. . . . Our concern is that there will not be any left the way we are approaching this."[3] Not be any left—*for whom?* Certainly, his concern was not that the people now dying of cancer would lack trees for their treatment; those were the very people being denied available medicine by the environmentalists. Nor was his concern that future cancer victims would go untreated; for that would imply an endorsement of a crash program to plant new trees—and to cut down every single existing one that was needed for its taxol. Toward whom, then, was this official's concern directed? Toward *no one.* Toward no human being, that is. Environmentalism wants to preserve those trees *for the sake of the trees.* It wants all the people who are suffering from cancer simply to renounce this potential cure. It wants them to accept the inviolability of the yew tree.

Environmentalists view man as the enemy. Their aim is to keep nature pristine, free from the predatory invasions of man. It is not human welfare that sets the standard by which they make their judgments.

For example, author Tom Regan argues that medical research on animals, designed to discover cures for human diseases, should be abolished. He says: "If it means that there are some things we cannot learn, then so be it. We have no basic right not to be harmed by those natural diseases we are heir to."[4]

David Foreman, founder of the organization Earth First, puts it more bluntly: "Wilderness has a right to exist for its own sake, and for the sake of the diversity of the life forms it shelters; we shouldn't have to justify the existence of a wilderness area by saying, 'Well, it protects the watershed, and it's a nice place to backpack and hunt, and it's pretty.' "[5]

David Graber, a biologist with the National Parks Service, revels in execrating human beings as trespassers upon nature. He describes himself as among those who "value wilderness for its own sake, not for what value it confers upon mankind. . . . We are not interested in the utility of a particular species, or free-flowing river, or ecosystem, to mankind. They have intrinsic value, more value—to me—than another human body, or a billion of them. Human happiness, and certainly human fecundity, are not as important as a wild and healthy planet. . . . It is cosmically unlikely that the developed world will choose to end its orgy of fossil-energy consumption, and the Third World its suicidal consumption of landscape. Until such time as Homo sapiens should decide to rejoin nature, some of us can only hope for the right virus to come along."[6]

(And speaking of viruses, they too have "rights." According to Rutgers ecologist David Ehrenfeld, the world's remaining supply of the smallpox virus should not be exterminated, since it preys only on human beings.[7])

Taking this illogic one step further, there are now "ecoterrorists," who use violence against loggers and other "intruders" upon nature's domain. A spokesman for the Green Party of Germany says: "We in the Green movement aspire to a cultural model in which the killing of a forest will be considered more contemptible and more criminal than the sale of six-year-old children to Asian brothels."[8] And according to an activist with Earth First, injuring or even murdering such "forest-killers" is justifiable self-defense: "The holocaust against the environment and its species is the same as any holocaust against humans."[9] (Earth First's apt slogan? "Back to the Pleistocene"—the glacial era of one million years ago; it is no accident that the Unabomber was openly sympathetic to the goals of this group.)

But if "wilderness has a right to exist for its own sake"—then man does not. Man survives only by altering nature to satisfy his own needs. Man cannot survive, as animals do, by automatically adapting to the natural surroundings in which he happens to find himself. Nature's vast wilderness, if passively accepted, is *inimical* to his survival. Man must transform the naturally given into a truly *human* environment. He must produce the values his life requires—he must grow food and build supermarkets, chop down trees and erect condominiums, mine ore and design jet planes, isolate organisms and manufacture vaccines. None of these values exists ready-made in nature. Man brings all of them into being only by transmuting his "natural environment."

To live as a human being requires that one regard nature as nothing but a *means* toward one's ends. Every cart, rowboat and space shuttle man has constructed violates the "right" of land, sea and air to maintain their "natural states." Every conscious decision to enhance human life—every attempt to rise above the animals—entails the subduing of nature and the repudiation of environmentalist doctrine. Man's life depends upon his productiveness. In Ayn Rand's words, it depends on a "process by which man's consciousness controls his existence, a constant process of acquiring knowledge and shaping matter to fit one's purpose, of translating an idea into physical form, of remaking the earth in the image of one's values."[10]

But if man lives only by a process of remaking the earth—what is the implication of the environmentalist demand that he renounce this process?

Environmentalism insists that man give up the value of material comfort and the expectation of material progress. He must distrust modern science and modern technology, since they only distance him from nature. He must forgo nuclear power and genetic engineering, luxury cars and food additives, Styrofoam cups and disposable diapers. He must stifle his inventiveness and shrink his cognitive horizons. His ancient ancestors managed to get by without an agglomeration of artificial gadgets—so must he. The essence of this message is that man should accept the only type of existence in true "harmony" with nature: an existence free of the man-made. Which means: for most, an early death; for the others, a life of backbreaking toil and bare subsistence.

The Worldwatch Institute, an environmentalist think tank, offers a stark concretization of this ideal: "The Eskimo's scrupulous use of every scrap of seal or walrus in the face of absolute scarcity might serve as a symbol for all in the years ahead. Conspicuous and excessive consumption of energy and food should be discouraged by law and by social pressure, thus reducing demand."[11]

All the imprecations against "excessive consumption"—all the exhortations to "recycle," to "conserve energy," to "save the earth"—have, as their motivation, a vision of the crudely primitive state of this Eskimo. That is the environmentalist nirvana.

But why do people accept this? Why do the citizens of a modern, industrial society not recoil in horror at the attempt to establish privation as a virtue? Because of two insidious ideas pushed by environmentalists—one metaphysical, the other ethical. The first is that production cannot be "sustained"; the second, that it is unjust to "exploit" nature.

The first idea springs from the old collectivist belief that wealth is created not by the individual, but by the tribe. This belief severs the act of production from the (individual's) faculty of reason. It was updated by Karl Marx, who maintained that the industrial factories and offices are somehow "just here," waiting to be coaxed by proletarian sweat and muscle into discharging their riches.

Environmentalists agree with this view of production as a mindless process. Production, they believe, consists in serendipitously finding the goods—in digging into the earth and uncovering what nature generously yields up. The goods are nature's beneficent gift to us. In the act of production, man is just a bit player, while nature is the star.

But whereas Marx implied that wealth is generated automatically, the environmentalist says it is not. The environmentalist holds that since production is not an act of reason, we cannot assume that the golden eggs will magically continue to appear. Instead, he says, with every scrap of wealth we greedily extract, with every clearing we plow and every bath we run, we "diminish" nature. By persistently trying to improve our environment to suit our ends, we are exceeding nature's willingness to nurture us. We are not allowing her to "replenish" herself. We are not allowing her to set a "sustainable" pace.

Production, therefore, is a hopeless effort. We are running out, the environmentalists cry. Of what? Of everything. The attempt to maintain our present level of wealth—let alone to increase it—is futile. Nature's fragile "ecosystem" simply will not allow it. We must resign ourselves to our impoverishment, because the mother lode is being exhausted.

Marx said the goods are here somehow—so society should seize them. Whereas the environmentalists say the goods are here somehow, but will not be here tomorrow—so society should "conserve" them.

It is not their own policies that are lowering our living standards—environmentalists disingenuously declare. The cause, rather, is the built-in limitations of nature. And the only solution is for us to reconcile ourselves to that fact. That is, since nature has only so much to give, we must stop seeking more. This injunction to make do with less is then resignedly accepted by the public because, it believes, there is no alternative.

Now consider the enormity of what is being evaded by the proponents of this metaphysics of scarcity. The Western world enjoys a material abundance at the end of the twentieth century that is orders of magnitude greater than what existed, say, in the tenth. The population is vastly larger, yet there are vastly more goods per person. Why? Certainly, natural resources have not miraculously multiplied. There is no greater quantity now of iron, or rainfall, or sand or petroleum. Rather, man's *mind* has been at work. Man has taken iron and made it into tools. He has taken waterfalls and made them into generators of electricity. He has transformed grains of sand into computer chips, and oozing black glop into gasoline. A continuous reshaping of nature has occurred. Man has given value to the raw materials that had always existed but had been worthless—worthless, because they had been part of nature's environment, not man's.

This is the essence of production: taking the elements of nature, rearranging their form—and generating prosperity. It is a conceptual, quintessentially *human* process. Wealth does not exist as a fixed, static quantity. It is the creation of a dynamic, boundless mind. And it has no inherent limitations.

The doomsday stories about running out of some "finite resource" (including those coming from the Malthusian predecessors of today's environmentalists) are endless; all of them ignore the causal connection between reason and production. For example, in 1908 the U.S. Geological Survey stated that the maximum future supply of crude oil in the U.S. was 22.5 billion barrels; eighty-seven years' worth of consumption later, there were over 22 billion barrels *just in unused, proven reserves.* In 1914 the U.S. Bureau of Mines said that future American production of oil could total no more than 5.7 billion barrels; in the following eighty years, over 160 billion barrels were produced. In 1939 the Department of the Interior forecast that our oil supplies would last only another thirteen years; some thirty years later, the rate of production alone had almost tripled.[12]

If one recognizes the intellectual root of production, one realizes the arbitrariness of extrapolating from present reserves to a remote future—even with respect to "non-renewable" resources. Goods are produced by rational men acting according to their knowledge and their evaluations. Proven reserves are merely the quantity of some good that it is currently worthwhile to know is available when needed. But the finitude of a given stockpile is no basis for assuming that, when it is used up, scarcities may ensue. There is simply no rational value in locating now all the sources of raw material for the goods that the market will demand only in some far-off future—just as no one would take pains to identify today the particular store from which he will buy a new television set in ten years when his current one wears out. (As the time approaches—*if* television has not been replaced by some superior product—he will make the effort to find a specific outlet from which to purchase what he needs.)

This is why no "finite resources" have ever disappeared, even though they have been in use for millennia. The value of some mineral is not intrinsic in its sheer existence. Its value is a consequence of the fact that man has recognized how it can be made to fill a human need. Every step of creating this value, from discovering how to mine it to inventing new uses for it, is an act of reason. As more of the known quantity of the good is used up and it becomes scarcer, its value grows, and it then becomes rational to search for more supply—it becomes rational to develop improved means of production—it becomes rational to devise better and cheaper substitutes. All of this prevents a good from simply being forever depleted. (Indeed, in a free market the known reserves often *expand* over time. For example, between 1950 and 1994 the U.S. reserves of "finite" zinc rose 271 percent; and of "finite" iron ore, 527 percent.[13])

Only a view of production as mere mechanical motion would make someone believe that what does not exist today will not come into existence tomorrow. That is an unwarranted conclusion, even assuming that the level of knowledge and technology remains unchanged. It is doubly unwarranted given that one cannot know what cognitive advances will be made tomorrow, or what new developments *those* advances will make feasible on the day after tomorrow.

Knowledge is hierarchical. Earlier knowledge makes possible later knowledge. In a continual expansion of thought, every new idea is the key to countless newer ones. Every new thought is another step up the cognitive ladder, providing a wider, more efficient perspective from which to look out on reality—a perspective not attainable from the lower rung. Physical goods are the material product of those thoughts, and will therefore increase as knowledge increases. As long as man is politically free—free to think, and free to act on his ideas—there will be no shortage of physical goods, any more than there can be of intellectual goods.

The irony is that environmentalists sense the connection between reason and production (which is what makes them try to obscure it). This impels them to argue that we are running out of not only physical goods—but *ideas* as well.

The Worldwatch Institute, for example, in discussing "the depletion of physical resources," states: "[S]cientific advances in the near future will not be made as frequently or as cheaply as in the past. The known conceptual ground has been worked over pretty thoroughly, and subsequent explorers will find rich research veins less exposed and harder to exploit"[!][14] (One can only be grateful that our genetic engineers and our computer designers—to indicate just two of the many areas that have seen major scientific advances in recent years—were not deterred by such inanity.)

This is a perfectly consistent application of environmentalism. There is no fundamental difference between the act of producing food and the act of producing ideas. The mind is the source of each. To deny its efficacy in the first, therefore, is to deny it in the second.

The contention that a precarious scarcity is our fate—that unless we content ourselves with living in igloos and hunting for walrus, we are endangering the very planet—paves the way for another, more lethal notion.

After arguing that privation is metaphysically inescapable, environmentalists proceed to insist that it is also *desirable.* That is, having maintained that production is not the work of reason, they go on to denounce it as theft—theft from one's neighbors, theft from future generations, theft from the earth itself. And this is the second crucial assertion on which their case depends: namely, that production—the " exploitation" of nature—is morally wrong.

Why, they ask, should you be allowed to extirpate nature's wealth simply to gratify your desires? Who are you to claim such a right for your own selfish purposes? Who are you to declare that you have rights but that nature does not?

According to environmentalism, there is no moral legitimacy to valuing yourself above the rest of nature. "Ecological egalitarianism," as one author hails it, "accords nature ethical status at least equal to that of humans."[15]

In other words, first environmentalism proclaims that the Spartan life of the primitive Eskimo is unavoidable—then, that it is one's moral duty to aspire to it. First you are told that the quest for prosperity is mindless self-destruction—then, that sustaining your measly existence ought not take precedence over some swampland's divine right to wetness.

Only one code of ethics could make such a viewpoint possible: the code of altruism, the code that brands the pursuit of self-interest as evil. This belief is environmentalism's most potent weapon. What, after all, is more manifestly selfish than the act of production itself, in which you remake nature to serve your values? At its core, environmentalism is the demand that you surrender your comfort, your well-being, your *self.* Stop caring about your desire to be happy—it admonishes—and start worrying about how to please the snail darters and the spotted owls.

Altruism is the doctrine that man has no moral right to exist for his own sake. Taken from the Latin *alter* (or "other"), it is the doctrine that the sole justification for your life is your willingness to sacrifice it to others. Environmentalism is altruism unadulterated and uncamouflaged. In the past, the call for sacrifice was made on behalf of other human beings, such as the poor and the sick. Now, in a faithful extension of the altruist maxim, the term "others" is merely being broadened. Now, we are being urged to sacrifice the human to the non-human.

And if it *is* evil to live for your own sake, how can you resist such a demand? If self-abnegation is noble, what could be more praiseworthy than to subordinate your existence to that of the bugs, the weeds, and the mud?

The premise of self-sacrifice is embedded in the deceptive meaning now attached to the very term "environment." Logically, there can be no concept of an "environment" that is not the environment *of* someone (or something)—any more than there can be "property" that exists independently of the owner of the property. "Environment" is a relational concept. It properly refers to the surroundings *of* some entity as they relate *to* that entity.

But that is not how the environmentalist employs the term. He subverts it to denote an "environment" severed from any relationship to man—which then enables him to mislead people into *evaluating* it apart from any relationship to man.

That is, he initially counts on its correct meaning, so that people accept a need to care about the fate of the "environment"—which they assume in some way is *their* environment and is linked to *their* fate. This is why the movement's focus is pointedly on the "environment," rather than on the non-relational concept "nature." But once a confused public has been taken in, environmentalists repackage "environment" to denote something upheld as existing separately from human beings.

Cashing in on the altruist ethics, they condemn as wrong—as selfish—the view that any human value must be a value to *man.* Just as they want you to believe it is wrong to *define* "environment" only in relation to man, they want you to believe it is wrong to *evaluate* it only in relation to man. It is erroneous, they say, to believe that the only "environment" worth protecting is one that is useful to human beings. A vein of iron ore, or a forest, or a sunrise should be regarded as values, they say, not because it benefits man, but because it "benefits" nature. These things have "value"—the environmentalist declares—apart from any connection to, or evaluation by, human beings.

According to the tenets of altruism, you should "value" that which holds no significance for your life—*because* it holds no significance for your life. So while nature's bogs and bugs may not be of any value to you, the precept of self-sacrifice commands: *that* is why you should treat them as though they are.

Thus, even the putative treasures of environmentalists—such as parks set aside as enclaves of uncommercialized, unindustrialized nature—are not permitted to be used as sources of enjoyment for man.

For example, when Yellowstone Park was devastated by fire in 1988, firefighting efforts were prohibited for weeks. Park officials allowed the fire to rage out of control, because it had begun naturally (through lightning). By the time firefighters were finally permitted to contain the conflagration, well over one million acres had burned, at a cost of 150 million dollars. What was the motive behind this lunacy? "Fire is a benign rather than a malignant force," explained Yellowstone's chief naturalist. He and other park officials viewed their primary responsibility during the disaster, not as preventing further damage by nature's fire, but as safeguarding the grounds against "unnatural" encroachments. As a news report in the *New York Times* described it: "They said they were trying to protect pristine areas from the destructive effects of bulldozers, fire engines and irrigation pipes."[16]

Yellowstone Park was regarded not as a value to man, but as a "value" to and for its natural self. So why not let it burn down, as long as the flames were part of its "natural" state? The head of the Glacier Institute put the philosophic issue this way: "It comes down to what we expect those lands to be. Is the park primarily for human use or their recreation? Or is the park to be maintained in its original state, letting fires do what they're going to do?"[17]

In other words: is man morally entitled to use nature to benefit himself—or must he become nature's self-sacrificing menial?

It is obvious which alternative environmentalists choose. Technology—which represents the conquest of nature by the human mind—is therefore an object of fear and hatred. It is routinely denounced by environmentalists. They greet every technological advance—from food preservatives to growth hormones to cloning—with a knee-jerkful of scare stories. Technological achievements are psychological threats to the environmentalist. They stand as testimony to the fact that man is both capable and worthy of living. To the nature-venerator, who cries that man can be neither, this is a terrifying reproach. So he reacts by trying to suppress technology (while rationalizing that he harbors only "practical" concerns about human safety).

Environmentalism is a systematic campaign to make man feel puny. It is a screed against self-esteem. It wants man to proclaim his own insignificance and to tremble before the mountains and the mites.

Today's man is told by environmentalists that he—like his primitive ancestors—must hold nature in quivering awe. He is to be, not the ruler of nature, but its obedient thrall. That is, he is to worship nature—*as a God.*

Environmentalism amounts to a modern, secularized form of religion. It is an ideology that instructs man to prostrate himself before a superior, ineffable force. It is an ideology that declares the human mind too feeble to grasp the complexities of an inscrutable world, or "ecosystem." It is an ideology propelled by the desire to have man subordinate himself to a hallowed power—a power which must be placated and paid homage, if man is to receive the gracious bounty upon which his existence depends.

This mysticism is now openly avowed within the environmentalist movement. For instance, New Left mandarin Tom Hayden taught a course at Santa Monica College on "Environment and Spirituality." It began with a discussion of the Bible, and ended with the prospects for what he called a new "earth-oriented religion." Hayden explained: "We need to see nature as having a sacred quality, so we revere it and are in awe of it. That forms a barrier to greed and exploitation and overuse."[18]

The Ecoforestry Institute, in a full-page ad opposing the logging of trees, says about forests: "They have an *intrinsic value* beyond objective measure. A society that sees them only as a resource to be exploited, as a crop to be marketed, has lost its sense of the sacred. Saving America's forests is more than an economic or ecological issue. It is a spiritual one as well."[19] (Emphasis in original.)

This unearthly fusion of religion and environmentalism originated with the New Left. As Paul Ehrlich writes: "It is probably in vain that so many look to science and technology to solve our present ecological crisis. Much more basic changes are needed, perhaps of the type exemplified by the much-despised 'hippie' movement—a movement that adopts most of its religious ideas from the non-Christian East. It is a movement wrapped up in Zen Buddhism, physical love and a disdain for material wealth."[20]

Predictably, the representatives of environmentalism and of religion are forging overt ties. For example, the late scientist Carl Sagan issued "an appeal for joint commitment in science and religion." It was a call for transforming environmentalism into a religious crusade. "We are close to committing—many would say we are already committing—what in religious language is sometimes called Crimes against Creation," he said. Environmentalism "must be recognized from the outset as having a religious as well as scientific dimension. . . . Thus there is a vital role for both religion and science. We hope this appeal will encourage a spirit of common cause and joint action to help preserve the Earth."[21] (This was signed by a number of prominent scientists, including Hans Bethe and Stephen Jay Gould, and by over two hundred religious leaders across the globe—from the dean of the Harvard Divinity School to the Secretary-General of the National Council on Islamic Affairs to the abbot of the Zen Community of New York.)

Even Pope John Paul II has taken up the cause. Contrary to those who regard Christianity as incompatible with environmentalism, the pope sees their fundamental unity. He has declared that world peace is threatened by "a lack of due respect for nature, by the plundering of natural resources and by a progressive decline in the quality of life. . . . Today, the dramatic threat of ecological breakdown is teaching us the extent to which greed and selfishness—both individual and collective[!]—are contrary to the order of creation, an order which is characterized by mutual interdependence. . . . The commitment of believers to a healthy environment for everyone stems from their belief in God the Creator, from their recognition of the effects of original and personal sin, and from the certainty of having been redeemed by Christ."[22]

Both the Church and environmentalism condemn the conception of nature as something to be refashioned by and for man. Both believe that man must repudiate the virtue of productiveness and of pride. Whether the commandment is to make use of nature in service to God or to make use of nature in service to endangered species—man is rendered a servant. Either way, the principle is the same: man must sacrifice his selfish enjoyment of earthly comforts in deference to a "higher" power.

There remains one final issue to be examined in judging environmentalism: its claim to science. In trumpeting the dangers of particular industrial products and activities, environmentalists typically invoke all kinds of empirical evidence. How, then, can their allegations be summarily dismissed? Isn't the honest opponent of environmentalists obligated to investigate, and refute, all their evidence? How can one ignore the copious research, the clinical studies, the laboratory experiments, the complex computer models—all supposedly proving the dire consequences of various technologies? Isn't cold, hard science on the side of environmentalism?

The answer is: no—and the very question reflects the environmentalists' worst perversion of all. Their scientific garb is a masquerade. It is designed to hide the fact that their claims do not rest on scientific evidence, but on the opposite: on a sweeping *rejection* of the methodology of science. Consider, for example, the environmentalists' case against Alar.

Alar is a chemical developed in the early 1960s that improves the appearance of apples and delays their ripening. In 1989, it became the target of a campaign to ban it, orchestrated by the Natural Resources Defense Council. The NRDC announced that it had conducted tests revealing that Alar causes cancer in people. The news media heralded the story of a greedy manufacturer foisting his toxic product upon unsuspecting, apple juice–drinking children. Alarmed farmers, grocers, and parents began avoiding apples. The apple-growing industry lost over 200 million dollars. The manufacturer was compelled to remove Alar from the market.

But what was the scientific basis for these claims? The NRDC tests did indeed show that Alar produced tumors in mice—in doses equivalent to what a human being would absorb by eating fourteen tons of apples a day for seventy years. (And mice fed *half* that amount—the equivalent of seven tons a day for seventy years—produced no tumors at all.)[23]

An earlier study of rodents by the Environmental Protection Agency also supposedly showed a link between Alar and cancer. Yet according to the EPA's own data, the average human exposure to the allegedly carcinogenic chemical was .000047 milligrams per kilogram of body weight (mg/kg); the mice in the EPA study, however, were given doses of 7 mg/kg (for males) and 13 mg/kg (for females)—a level *148,000 to 276,000 times* that of human exposure. (And even at that level, none of the *rats* in the study was stricken with cancer.)[24]

This is considered sufficient grounds for panicking the public and crippling an industry.

Or consider the pesticide DDT. It was banned in the U.S. in 1972, largely because it was said to be carcinogenic. That conclusion was based on studies that found DDT to cause benign liver tumors in mice (and nothing at all in other experimental animals)—and even then, only at doses *100,000 times higher* than what a person would absorb by ingesting DDT through residues in food.[25]

It is now accepted practice in environmentalist circles to assume that if *some* quantity of a substance is harmful, then *any* quantity is. But is there any substance on earth about which this context-dropping claim cannot be made? Everything can become deadly in sufficiently large doses—including water, or air, or organically grown soybeans. If a one-ton piano crashing down on you is fatal, does this imply that a one-ounce feather floating onto your shoulders once a day for eighty-eight years is also a threat? Potatoes contain arsenic; lima beans contain cyanide; nutmeg contains a hallucinogen; broccoli contains a substance that causes cancer in animals.[26] Should these be outlawed? None of the environmental "scientists" cares to publicize an obvious fact: the dosage level makes all the difference between safety and danger.

They don't care to publicize this—because they have an agenda other than the presentation of the truth. Dishonesty, as one of these pseudo-scientists explains, is their best policy: "We have to offer up scary scenarios, make simplified, dramatic statements, and make little mention of any doubts we may have. Each of us has to decide what the right balance is between being effective and being right."[27]

Virtually any claim about some industrial danger is given instant publicity by environmentalists, while evidence of the benefits (or of the falsehood of the allegation of danger) is systematically disregarded. Paul Ehrlich, for example, has made a living out of issuing apocalyptic statements that the world is running out of food. In 1968 he wrote: "The battle to feed all of humanity is over. In the 1970s the world will undergo famines—hundreds of millions of people are going to starve to death in spite of any crash programs embarked upon now. At this late date nothing can prevent a substantial increase in the world death rate. . . . We must have population control at home, hopefully through a system of incentives and penalties, but *by compulsion if voluntary methods fail.*"[28] (Emphasis added.)

Yet reality's repeated debunking of Ehrlich's predictions (to say nothing of the horrifying totalitarianism of his proposed "solution") has not diminished his status as an influential prophet. His regularly updated scenarios of doom are still taken seriously by the environmentalists; his well-known book *The Population Bomb* has gone through more than two dozen printings.

With respect to DDT, the promoters of "eco-hysteria" ignore a study in which *people* were fed DDT every day for up to twenty-seven months—with no harmful results. They ignore the fact that during the period of heaviest DDT use in the United States, from 1944 to 1972, deaths from liver cancer *dropped* 30 percent.[29]

And, most tellingly, they ignore the *benefits* of DDT (and the consequent harm created by its prohibition). They ignore the fact that before the advent of DDT, malaria was rampant. In Sri Lanka (then Ceylon), for example, there were 2.8 million cases of malaria in 1948. By 1963, because DDT killed the insects bearing the disease, the number had dropped to 17! But in the late 1960s, the spraying was halted due to the growing attacks on DDT; by 1969 the number of malaria cases in Sri Lanka had gone back to 2.5 million. In India, about 75 million cases of malaria occurred in 1951; ten years later (after DDT was introduced) the figure had fallen to 50,000; by 1977, however, it had risen to at least 30 million.[30] Today, millions of people a year are dying from malaria as a result of environmentalists' hostility toward pesticides. (But of course the truth about DDT is unimportant when compared with the need for "being effective.")

The environmentalist utilizes science, not to discover the facts, but to obfuscate them. After stripping away the veneer of rationality, one will discover that the hallmark of the catastrophe claim is the half-truth and the out-of-context fact.

When environmental "scientists" claim, for instance, that thousands of highly acidic and fishless lakes in the Northeast (the most severe cases of which are in the Adirondacks) are proof of the destructiveness of "acid rain" caused by coal-burning electric utilities—they neglect to mention: that most of the acidic lakes in the Adirondacks were acidified by natural organic acids; or that the average Adirondack lake is more *alkaline* now than one hundred fifty years ago; or that highly acidic, fishless waters exist naturally in regions with *no* industrial activity, such as the Rio Negro in the Amazon Basin (a river system the size of the Mississippi River).[31]

When environmental "scientists" claim that man-made chlorofluorocarbons (CFCs) have depleted the stratosphere of ozone, leaving us more exposed to the sun's ultraviolet radiation—they neglect to mention: that during the period when the ozone layer was presumably diminishing, the levels of ultraviolet radiation at the earth's surface were *falling*[32]; or that, at its peak, the world output of CFCs was 1.1 million tons annually, while *300* million tons of natural chlorine reach the atmosphere each year through the evaporation of seawater alone[33]; or that a 5 percent drop in ozone—which is of a magnitude that elicits grim calculations of increased skin cancers—would, according to those very calculations, result in a rise in radiation equivalent to that experienced by someone who merely moves sixty miles closer to the equator (say, from Santa Barbara to Los Angeles).[34]

When environmental "scientists" claim that overpopulation is exhausting the earth's capacity to sustain its inhabitants—they neglect to mention: that such conclusive yardsticks as per-capita food production and life expectancy are showing regular *increases*[35]; or that life improves most where industrialization is strongest; or that finding space for a growing population is such a non-problem that if all 5.8 billion earthlings relocated to Texas tomorrow, the resultant population density (22,000 people per square mile) would not be even *half* the current density of, say, Paris.[36]

This whole warped approach is the antithesis of science and objectivity. It is not scientific truth that environmentalists seek to discover—it is not reality that they hold as an absolute—it is not reason that shapes their conclusions. Reason is only an obstacle to the goals of these "scientists"—and some of them readily admit it.

For instance, author Jonathan Schell discusses the nature of the evidence necessary to form conclusions about environmental matters. He writes that scientists should "disavow the certainty and precision they normally insist on. Above all, we need to learn to act decisively to forestall predicted perils, even while knowing that they may never materialize. . . . Scientists need to become connoisseurs and philosophers of uncertainty. . . . The incurable uncertainty of our predicament, far from serving to reassure us, should fill us with unease and goad us to action."[37]

Let's translate this: Despite the lack of rational evidence for some claim of impending doom, we should nonetheless assume that it is true. Certainty and precision may be appropriate in dealing with other issues, but not environmental ones. The knowledge we have about some technology's vast benefits is to be outweighed by the *absence* of knowledge we have about its alleged harmfulness. It does not matter, therefore, that these "philosophers of uncertainty" do not know whether their statements are true. As long as a prediction of theirs can "fill us with unease," it should be acted on, whether it can be scientifically proved or not.

The aim of the environmentalists' studies and experiments, then, is not the identification of accurate, scientific knowledge, but the inculcation of a state of hysterical ignorance. Blind emotion, not reason, is to be our guide in coming to conclusions.

I am not a scientist, and I have not thoroughly investigated these issues. I cannot say that I have conclusive proof that CFCs are not threatening the ozone layer or that factory emissions are not changing the earth's temperature. But what I can say about the environmentalists' claims is something more fundamental: they warrant no cognitive attention—because they are not *attempts* at cognition. They are arbitrary vociferations. They do not represent efforts to reach objective truths. Therefore, as utterances issued not to illuminate reality but to distort it, they should not be admitted into the realm of science.

In this respect, the environmentalist methodology is identical to that of the "Scientific Creationists."

The Creationists' claims about errors in the theory of evolution are not based on science. The Creationists do not want to discover the *facts* about the origin of life. They use science merely as a facade, to disguise the fact that the Bible is the source of their beliefs and that their only agenda is a religious one. They do not seek genuine evidence for their position, because they do not accept any *necessity* for evidence. No facts or arguments will sway them, because their viewpoint does not rest on facts and arguments: it rests on faith. None of their "refutations" of evolution, therefore, qualifies as science.

Once the Creationists' basic method has been discredited, one need not scrutinize every new assertion they come up with. One need not disprove such assertions—indeed, one should not even try to, since it only legitimizes them—in order to defend the validity of evolution. The only rational response to all Creationist "arguments" is to dismiss them as being outside the realm of the rational. They simply deserve no cognitive respect—including even the respect of identifying them as "true" or "false."

The statements of environmentalists ought to be accorded the same *a*scientific status. Just as when you wish to determine the facts about evolution, the pronouncements of Creationists should be irrelevant to your search; so too, if you wish to determine the facts about a particular environmental question, you should do so independently of the declarations made by environmentalists. (Yes, it may turn out that some allegation of theirs happens to be true—by accident, as a parrot's squawkings may coincidentally parallel some fact of reality. If this occurs, and one ascertains it by rational means, appropriate steps should be taken to alleviate the danger—steps that logically *cannot* include any renunciation of technological progress.)

If and when there is genuine evidence that something manmade is harmful to human health or damaging to property, the victim is entitled to legal remedies—on the basis of standard laws that have long existed. These are the same kinds of laws that prevent your neighbor from starting a fire or releasing tear gas in his backyard if it will reach yours. If you can show that you were hurt by someone's actions, your rights should be protected by law. But you must meet one requirement: you must be able to prove your case objectively.

To environmentalists, this requirement is an unacceptable impediment. They do not want to be bound by the strictures of logic and science in their efforts to stifle production. Reason is not the method suited to their ends. They want to "disavow certainty and precision"—and to have government regulators accept their unproved assertions on faith.

The way to assess environmentalism, therefore, is not as a scientific issue, but as a *moral* one. In response to all the claims about the harm posed by various technologies, one must ask a basic question: "Harmful—by what standard?" For according to the standard of man's life here on earth, technology as such is beneficial—wealth as such is beneficial—material progress as such is beneficial. According to a rational standard, no *actual* threats to human welfare could justify the destruction of that upon which man's welfare depends—namely, production, technology, and freedom. The solution to any such threats must embrace improved production, better technology, more capitalism.

But environmentalists do not hold such a standard. What they find "harmful" is man's liberation from a life of primitive toil and bare subsistence. To them, the "harm" lies in the very existence of technology, wealth, and progress; it lies in the fact of industrialization per se. Paul Ehrlich, for instance, declares: "We've already had too much economic growth in the United States. Economic growth in rich countries like ours is the disease, not the cure."[38]

According to the group Earth First. "If radical environmentalists were to invent a disease to bring human populations back to sanity, it would probably be something like AIDS. It has the potential to end industrialism, which is the main force behind the environmental crisis."[39]

This is why environmentalists show no concern for all the suffering and deaths resulting from the *absence* of technology. This is why they do not care about their "ideal" Eskimo's lack of indoor plumbing, central heating, electricity, dentistry, and heart-transplant technology. This is why they are untroubled by the demonstrable evils resulting from all the roads and oil refineries and nuclear plants *not* built—not built, because of the environmentalist desire to protect nature from man.

This is also why, whatever dangers environmentalists claim to find, their answer is always to denounce progress and to search for "nature-friendly" alternatives. If acid rain is supposedly destroying our lakes, they direct us not to neutralize it easily with some alkaline—but to shut down the factories. If topsoil is supposedly being eroded, they direct us not to invent methods of more efficient farming—but to stop harvesting the crops. If there is too much traffic, they direct us not to build better highways—but to stop making the cars. Whatever the alleged problem, their incessant "solution" is: de-industrialize.

Environmentalists believe that "chemicals" are bad, additives are bad, artificial flavoring is bad, preservatives are bad, synthetic fibers are bad—that "interfering" with the processes of nature is inherently immoral. They ban food additives that supposedly cause cancer—yet are indifferent to the natural presence of the identical substances in foods. They condemn DDT—yet disregard the fact that we ingest 10,000 times more naturally produced pesticides than man-made ones.[40] They praise societies that wallow in the filth and disease that characterize a non-technological "harmony" with nature—yet condemn those that enjoy the cleanliness and health resulting from modern sewage systems, washing machines, refrigeration, and polio vaccines. Whatever is a product of human design, in other words, is by that fact baneful; whatever is natural is by that fact benign.

This view of the man-made as intrinsically noxious is simply the corollary of the premise that nature is intrinsically good. The environmentalists' perverse standard of value is: the human is the harmful—and the way to achieve human "welfare" is to do away with the human.

Environmentalism seeks the renunciation of all progress and pleasure. Its goal is not the elimination of air pollution or filthy water—or anything else actually harmful to man. (If there *are* people animated by such concerns, they should form a new pro-technology/anti-dirt organization; but they should *not* ally themselves with the Paul Ehrlichs, the David Grabers, and the David Foremans, whose dictatorial aims are only abetted by unthinking "fellow-travelers.")

Environmentalists do not want to promote human happiness, or even the "happiness" of other species. Those who are callously indifferent to the millions of people who die annually because DDT has been banned will not be moved to moral outrage at the "injustice" of some spotted owl losing its nest. What environmentalists desire is not the welfare of the non-human—but the misery of man.

This is true of all manifestations of altruism. It is not the poor whom altruists wish to lift up (if it were, they would advocate laissez-faire capitalism); it is rather the productive whom they wish to bring down. But when the demand for self-sacrifice takes the form of environmentalism, the desire to destroy becomes more overt. In that form, there is far less pretense of pursuing any human values. There is only the snarling demand for universal deprivation.

The philosophic inspiration for all this is Immanuel Kant. It was Kant, the primary secularizer of religion, whose characteristic approach was to propound a mysticism dressed up as rationality. It is environmentalism that has thoroughly implemented his philosophy.

Kant postulated a "noumenal" world—a non-material world unknowable to man, a world that transcends human perception and human interests, a world that represents "true reality" because it is "unfiltered" by human consciousness. Environmentalism proceeds to postulate an ineffable "ecosystem"—a dimension whose arcane workings are accessible only to those possessing the faculty described by the Ecoforestry Institute as a "sense of the sacred," a dimension in which it is considered "unnatural" for man to engage in what his life requires—productive activity—a dimension that remains "real" only as long as it is unsullied by human values.

Kant maintained that reason can give us only a distorted picture of reality, that the mind is unreliable and can never be in touch with existence "as it really is." Environmentalism too maintains that man's mind is incapable of grasping, and thereby governing, nature, that only if we "disavow certainty and precision" can we apprehend the actual devastation industrialization is sowing, that rational science blinds us to the truth that the squashing of some insect or the trampling of some shrub may bring a fragile planet crashing into oblivion.

And obviously, environmentalism's exhortations to sacrifice for nature—to surrender our self-interest, not for religion's promise of bliss in some afterworld nor for Marx's assurance of prosperity in some indefinable future, but to surrender it as our rewardless obligation to the snail darters and the wetlands, to surrender everything human to anything non-human—what is that, but Kant's "categorical imperative" to submit to moral duty, for no reason and for no human end, but for the sake of submission as an end in itself?

The method that Kant instituted, and that environmentalism has adopted, consists of a continual inversion of the rational and the irrational. It consists of Kant's proclamation that whatever man perceives is not real, *because* he perceives it, and that whatever is of value to man is not moral, *because* it is a value. And it consists of environmentalism's final corruption: the declaration that production is destruction—the declaration that whatever wealth we produce makes us poorer, *because* we have produced it.

Kant used the prestige of reason—to undermine reason and objectivity; environmentalism uses the prestige of science—to undermine science and production. Both insidiously pose as advocates of the rational—Kant, by pretending that it is not really reason that he is negating; environmentalists, by pretending that it is not really production (but only "unsustainable" production) that they are attacking. Both, at root, seek to render human life and happiness impossible.

The single basic truth uttered by environmentalists is about themselves: they want to crush what they regard as the evil of self-interest. Their ideology has taken hold not in spite of its opposition to the requirements of man's life—but *because* of it, because it has latched firmly onto the prevailing cultural premise of self-sacrifice. In their campaign for privation, this moral evaluation is their strongest weapon.

It is time to disarm them.

There is only one practical way of fighting environmentalism: by morally defending man. The apologetic attempts to oppose environmentalist laws by showing how much better off the "environment" would be through private, non-bureaucratic efforts, are—like the appeasing attempts to fight the welfare state by arguing that capitalism is more compassionate toward the homeless—doomed to failure. Instead, what needs to be upheld, proudly and unequivocally, is the principle that there is no value in nature apart from that which is of value to man, which means: there *is* no "environment"—other than the environment of man.

The men who live by that premise—the men who make civilization and progress possible—are choking on the philosophic pollution of environmentalism. They need to be freed from the suffocating clutches of the worshipers of a virgin earth. They need to breathe air—the liberating air of industrialization. They need to be left free to produce—to continue creating the magnificent abundance that has lifted humanity out of the caves and jungles of the pre-industrial era. And who are these individuals? Everyone who understands, and glories in, the fact that man lives by reshaping nature to serve his values.

REFERENCES

1. Dr. Samuel Broder, director of the National Cancer Institute, quoted in "Trees Yield a Cancer Treatment, But Ecological Cost May Be High," *New York Times,* May 13, 1991, p. A1.
2. Al Gore, *Earth in the Balance* (Houghton Mifflin, 1992), pp. 105–106.
3. Wendell Wood, quoted in "Trees Yield a Cancer Treatment, But Ecological Cost May Be High," *New York Times,* May 13, 1991, p. A14.
4. Tom Regan, quoted by David Hardy, in *America's New Extremists: What You Need to Know About the Animal Rights Movement* (Washington Legal Foundation, 1990), p. 8.
5. D. Petersen, "The Plowboy Interview," *Mother Earth News,* Jan./Feb. 1985, p. 21.
6. David Graber, "Mother Nature as a Hothouse Flower," *Los Angeles Times Book Review,* Oct. 22, 1989, pp. 1, 9.
7. Cited by Joel Schwartz in "Apocalypse Now," *Commentary,* Aug. 1990, p. 56.
8. Carl Amery, quoted in *Trashing the Planet* (Regnery Gateway, 1990), by Dixy Lee Ray, p. 169.
9. Darryl Cherney, quoted in "Militant Environmentalists Planning Summer Protests to Save Redwoods," *New York Times,* June 19, 1990, p. A18.
10. Ayn Rand, *Atlas Shrugged* (Signet, 1957), p. 946.
11. Robert Fuller, "Inflation: The Rising Cost of Living on a Small Planet," Worldwatch Paper no. 34, Jan. 1980 (Worldwatch Institute).
12. "Doomsday and Inflation," *The Intellectual Activist,* May 1, 1980, p. 4. Oil data from: *U.S. Crude Oil, Natural Gas, and Natural Gas Liquid Reserves* (U.S. Energy Information Administration, 1995); *Historical Statistics of the United States: Colonial Times to 1970* (U.S. Dept. of Commerce, 1975); *Sta-*

tistical Abstract of the United States (U.S. Dept. of Commerce, 1996).

13. *Mineral Facts and Problems* (U.S. Dept. of the Interior, 1956); *Mineral Commodity Summaries* (U.S. Dept. of the Interior, 1994).
14. Fuller, op. cit.
15. Roderick Frazier Nash, quoted in "The Rights of Nature and the Death of God," by Joel Schwartz, *The Public Interest,* Fall 1989, pp. 3–4.
16. "Ethic of Protecting Land Fueled Yellowstone Fires," *New York Times,* Sept. 22, 1988, pp. A1, A24.
17. Ibid.
18. "Chronicle," *New York Times,* Aug. 3, 1991, p. 20.
19. Ad by Ecoforestry Institute of the U.S. (Portland, Oregon), *New York Times,* May 25, 1993, p. A9.
20. Paul Ehrlich, *The Population Bomb* (Ballantine, 1968), p. 171.
21. Carl Sagan, "Guest Comment: Preserving and Cherishing the Earth—an Appeal for Joint Commitment in Science and Religion," *American Journal of Physics,* July 1990, p. 615.
22. Pope John Paul II, "World Day of Peace Message," 1990 (published by the Vatican, Dec. 1989).
23. Dixy Lee Ray, *Trashing the Planet* (Regnery Gateway, 1990), pp. 78–79.
24. Eric W. Hagen and James J. Worman, *An Endless Series of Hobgoblins* (Foundation for Economic Education, 1995), pp. 10–11, 19.
25. Ray, op. cit., p. 73.
26. Elizabeth M. Whelan and Frederick J. Stare, *Panic in the Pantry* (Prometheus, 1992), pp. 66–76.
27. Stephen Schneider, quoted in "Our Fragile Earth," by Schell, op. cit.
28. Ehrlich, op. cit., p. xi.
29. Ray, op. cit. pp. 72–73.
30. Ibid., p. 69; also, Julian L. Simon, *The Ultimate Resource 2* (Princeton University, 1996), p. 261.
31. Edward C. Krug, "Acid Rain and Acid Lakes: The Real Story" (published in *Heritage Foundation Backgrounder*), April 19, 1990, p. 13.
32. Michael Sanera and Jane S. Shaw, *Facts, Not Fear* (Regnery, 1996), pp. 167–168.

33. Ray, op. cit., p. 45.
34. Sanera and Shaw, op. cit., pp. 168–169.
35. Simon, op. cit., pp. 87, 320.
36. Calculations based on data in *Encyclopedia Americana,* 1996, Vol. 21, p. 430.
37. Jonathan Schell, "Our Fragile Earth," *Discover,* Oct. 1987, pp. 47–50.
38. Paul Ehrlich, quoted in "Journalists and Others for Saving the Planet," by David Brooks, *Wall St. Journal,* Oct. 5, 1989, p. A28.
39. From an Earth First newsletter, cited by Ray, op. cit., p. 168.
40. Hagen and Worman, op. cit., p. 101.

BIBLIOGRAPHY

It is difficult for the conscientious reader to find books that treat environmental issues objectively. The following is a list of some titles meeting that standard:

Animal Scam (Regnery Gateway, 1993), Kathleen Marquardt
An Endless Series of Hobgoblins (Foundation for Economic Education, 1995), Eric W. Hagen and James J. Worman
Environmental Overkill (Regnery Gateway, 1994), Dixy Lee Ray
Facts, Not Fear (Regnery, 1996), Michael Sanera and Jane S. Shaw
Panic in the Pantry (Prometheus, 1992), Elizabeth M. Whelan and Frederick J. Stare
Rational Readings on Environmental Concerns (Van Nostrand Reinhold, 1992), Jay H. Lehr, ed.
Science Under Siege (William Morrow, 1996), Michael Fumento
The State of Humanity (Blackwell, 1995), Julian L. Simon, ed.
Toxic Terror (Prometheus, 1993), Elizabeth M. Whelan
Trashing the Planet (Regnery Gateway, 1990), Dixy Lee Ray
The True State of the Planet (Free Press, 1995), Ronald Bailey, ed.
The Ultimate Resource 2 (Princeton University, 1996), Julian L. Simon

Multicultural Nihilism

Peter Schwartz

In order to rise from the cave, man had to grasp the fact of values. Every step forward entailed the knowledge not only of how to take that step, but of why it was a value—of why it was a step *forward.* It was not enough for men to learn, for example, how to hunt with knives or spears; they had to evaluate this knowledge and conclude that hunting with weapons was *better* than hunting with bare hands. Across the entire span of history, man had to comprehend such truths—the truth that planting crops was better than foraging off the land, that indoor plumbing was better than outhouses, that electricity was better than candlelight, that science was better than superstition. Not just "different," but better—*objectively* better.

Mankind advanced only because some individuals originated better ways of doing things (and because the rest of society came to see the validity of those innovations). When some exceptional prehistoric man conceived the uses of fire, he understood the advantage of cooked meat over raw meat. His achievement was not regarded as the biased product of a "heat-centrist," who was insensitive to those who preferred their mastodon uncooked. In order to advance, men had to discern that certain products had *value*—i.e., that they were worth creating, worth using, and worth defending.

The history of mankind is the history of the creation of values. The recognition that some things further human life and are therefore good, while other things do not and are therefore bad, is what made civilization possible. It is this premise that enabled man to progress from numerology to mathematics, from astrology to astronomy, from alchemy to chemistry—and from the cave to the skyscraper.

It is this progression that today's dominant intellectuals wish to undo.

Nothing is objectively better than anything else, they assert. Anyone who elevates Western civilization above primitive, voodoo-worshiping tribes—anyone who admires the skyscraper and scorns the cave—is looking at life through a distorting, "Eurocentric" prism.

These intellectuals are the multiculturalists. They argue, not for the obvious proposition that many cultures exist, but for the invidious proposition that all are equal in value. Every culture is "different," they say—but none is superior. And what is the ultimate goal of this ideology? To *reverse* the process of civilization, by wrenching man back to a primeval state of existence.

Multiculturalism's major battleground is the classroom. There, beneath its bromidic protestations about wanting to change the educational curricula only to "broaden" the content and expose students to "different" ways of life, its hostility toward rational values is readily revealed.

In New York City, for example, a local school board decided to comply with the multiculturalists' dictate to teach students about other cultures. But the board wanted to present such information in the context of the superiority of American ideals. It passed a resolution stating: "We reject the notion that all cultures should be taught in an atmosphere of moral equivalency."[1]

This offended the multiculturalists, who refused to tolerate the upholding of certain values over others. The school chancellor, for one, denounced the board's stand: "I firmly believe it is possible to gain an appreciation of American culture and values without derogating other cultures."[2] (In other words, a teacher must refrain from suggesting any deficiency in a culture that practices, say, slavery or cannibalism—and, further, must persuade the class that such moral neutrality is consistent with "an appreciation of American culture and values.")

A school board in Florida made a similar attempt to comply with the ostensible aims of multiculturalism. It designed a program to instruct students about other cultures—and simultaneously to "instill an appreciation of our American heritage and culture, such as: our republican form of government, capitalism, a free enterprise system" and "other basic values that are superior to other foreign or historic cultures." An irate teachers union declared that this violated the spirit of multiculturalism. The union threatened to sue the school board for ignoring a state law that students must be taught to "eliminate personal and national ethnocentrism so that they understand that a specific culture is not intrinsically superior or inferior to another."[3]

What multiculturalism seeks is not to broaden, but to shrink our knowledge of the cultures of the world. That is, it seeks to expunge our awareness of the *value* of an American or Western—or rational—way of life, and the *dis*value of its antipodes. Multiculturalism wants to do away with all such discriminations. It wants to erase the distinction between the two opposite ends of the normative scale, i.e., between the primitive and the civilized.

But multiculturalists are not promiscuous valuers, indiscriminately granting equal validity to whatever people choose and asking only for universal tolerance of all choices. They are not blandly indifferent to values. Rather, their charges of "intolerance" and "exclusion" are consistently targeted against one specific category of choices. They regularly criticize Americans for "insensitivity" toward the "Third World," but never criticize, say, Rwandans for insufficiently appreciating the culture of capitalism. They condemn colleges for teaching that the Great Works of Western minds are better than the scrawlings of random jungle dwellers—but they do not seem to find the reverse view unacceptable.

The discriminations that multiculturalism rejects are those in which a civilized, Western culture is held as superior to a primitive one—i.e., in which the rational is valued while the irrational is not—i.e., in which an actual value is being embraced and a non-value spurned. That is the only "intolerance" they find intolerable. When multiculturalists vilify Christopher Columbus for "corrupting" the Indians, they are attacking the view that the culture Columbus represents is *good,* that reason and science are *better* than mysticism and savagery, that life in the advanced, productive Renaissance societies of Europe was objectively superior to life in the barbarous, warring tribes of the New World.

All the "multi-ethnic" assaults on the educational curriculum are variants of this antagonism toward the non-primitive. Multiculturalists recommend, for example, the teaching of "ethnomathematics," as a way to persuade failing minority students that the most primitive forms of mathematics (such as "African sand drawings") are as valid as the most advanced.[4] New York State high schools are now required to teach that the Iroquois Indians (who were paid by England during the Revolutionary War to direct their scalp-taking proclivities exclusively toward the colonies) inspired the American Constitution.[5] A University of Pennsylvania professor derides American colleges for emphasizing reading and writing, which "are merely technologies of control" and are "martial law made academic"; he demands, instead, a greater focus on the "voices of newly emerging peoples" who challenge "Western hegemonic arrangements of knowledge" and who uphold the ancient oral tradition (as manifested, for example, in "rap music").[6]

The motive for upholding such blatant non-values is to undercut authentic values. The multiculturalist cannot abide the idea that the mathematics of today is good, while primitive "African sand drawings" are worthless. Who are we to make such assessments?—the multiculturalist snarls. Who are we to laud Columbus, or to regard the modern physician as superior to the tribal medicine man, or to deem the skill of reading and writing more desirable than the capacity to narrate folktales? Who are we to say that the Western is better than the non-Western, the scientific better than the non-scientific, the rational better than the irrational?

Multiculturalism is the debased attempt to obliterate values by claiming that they are indistinguishable from non-values. Multiculturalism is an assault not simply against the evaluation of cultures, but against values *as such.* It is an assault on the sine qua non of human life—against the identification of something as *good.*

A prime illustration of this is the notorious "Specific Manifestations of Oppression." This is a circular distributed by the Office of Student Affairs at Smith College. It declares that "people can be oppressed in many ways and for many reasons because they are perceived to be different." To name this, "new words tend to be created to express the concepts that the existing language cannot."[7] One such neologism of oppression, cited in the circular, is:

"*Ethnocentrism*"—which is defined as: "oppression of cultures other than the dominant one in the belief that the dominant way of doing things is the superior way."[8]

But "dominant" means only "prevailing over others." What if a culture prevails over others because it is *in fact* better, and because people comprehend that fact? In America, for instance, the prevailing culture endorses freedom rather than dictatorship, and the laws of science rather than the myths of the occult. Is this "oppressive" to the cultures that deny freedom? Is it "oppressive" to conclude that surgery cures illnesses and should be applauded, while faith healing does not and should be scorned? How have these students come to be so detached from reality that they find it inconceivable that one "way of doing things" may actually be superior to another? Can't one judge some viewpoints to be right, and therefore to be *better* than those that are wrong?

To the multiculturalist, however, nothing can give rise to such differentiations. The belief that one idea is better than another—regardless of whether it is based on rational evidence or not—is inherently "oppressive." To the multiculturalist, *to evaluate is to tyrannize.*

Here is another example from the Smith College flyer:

"*Lookism*"—which is defined as: "the construction of a standard for beauty/attractiveness; and oppression through stereotypes and generalizations of both those who do not fit the standard and those who do."[9]

A stereotype, which is an oversimplified, and hence false, generalization, is precisely what "lookism" is *not* objecting to. Stereotyping would entail, for example, the belief that all beautiful people are successful and happy. The falsity of some stereotype, however, is not grounds for attacking generalization itself—which "lookism" does. There are many valid generalizations about "beauty," such as: "Beauty is preferable to ugliness." And *that* is exactly the kind of generalization multiculturalism wants to suppress. For that is an *evaluation,* which follows from the judgment of beauty as something good, which itself follows from the identification of a standard of value. What multiculturalism fundamentally opposes is a standard—*any* standard—by which some things are recognized as values and others as non-values.

This virulence fully erupts in a third neologism listed in the manifesto:

"*Ableism*"—which is the "oppression of the differently abled, by the temporarily abled."[10]

This term encompasses all human capacities—physical, intellectual, moral. It reflects the wish to nullify any rational basis for judging, and thus for distinguishing among, human beings. It is a wholesale onslaught against the means by which man achieves his ends, and against the ends themselves.

If it is "oppression" to discriminate between those having a particular ability and those lacking it, then indeed—as multiculturalists demand—sports competitions should not be restricted to the athletically able, nor college diplomas to the alphabetically able. *No* "discriminatory" standards, then, should ever be applied. Mortgage loans should not be reserved for those with a means of repaying them; driver's licenses should not be issued only to the sighted; burial plots should not be limited to the dead. Indeed, isn't the very evaluation of life over death an insensitive prejudice—the prejudice of "lifeism"? Who, after all, is morally entitled to decide that being among the "temporarily existing" is preferable to joining the "differently existing"?

This antipathy to values is why the concept "racism" has come to be perverted by multiculturalism. Objectively, this term refers to the (false) belief that an individual's character is determined by his racial lineage. Multiculturalists, however, attach to "racism" a very different content. They define "racism," not as discrimination on the basis of race, but as discrimination per se. They denounce the racist essentially for labeling some people as superior to others; *why* he does so is immaterial. Discriminating between blacks and whites, according to the multiculturalist, is the same as discriminating between geniuses and fools, heroes and villains, creators and killers. All evaluative distinctions—which means: *values as such*—are viewed as despotic.

To concretize this, consider the import of an incident at the University of Pennsylvania. An undergraduate member of a "diversity education" committee was concerned about some aspects of the school's multicultural program. She sent a note to the administration, in which she expressed a "deep regard for the individual and my desire to protect the freedoms of all members of society."[11]

This generated an acrimonious response on the part of one university administrator. He returned her note, with her word "individual" underlined and with the following comment from him: "This is a red flag phrase today, which is considered by many to be *racist.* Arguments that champion the individual over the group ultimately privilege the 'individuals' belonging to the largest or dominant group."[12] (Emphasis added.)

By any rational analysis, racism and individualism entail opposite philosophies. The former evaluates people by the collective attribute of race; the latter, according to each person's own characteristics. Why, then, would multiculturalism equate the two? Because they both *evaluate*—i.e., they *differentiate* some people from others based on some standard. The fact that racism rests on an irrational standard, while individualism rests on a rational one, is meaningless to the multiculturalist. To him, the very use of standards is anathema.

An egalitarian leveler does not raise a drug-besotted bum into a moral ideal. He *has* no moral ideal. His defense of the non-ambitious and non-productive is mere window-dressing for his real motive: the desire to squash the productive and the ambitious—a desire he pursues by insisting that we not discriminate between the productive and the non-productive, and that a bum and a Bill Gates should therefore enjoy equal comforts in life.

The egalitarian is far worse than, say, the devout religionist who condemns the rich. For the latter is upholding an alternate set of values, albeit an irrational one. He calls for the forswearing of wealth because he believes in the supreme value of a non-material, supernatural dimension. Egalitarianism, however, is a lower species of irrationalism. It is stark nihilism. It reveres no values—it seeks only the destruction of values. It promotes a leveling for the sake of leveling, an eradication of value as an end in itself, or—as Ayn Rand puts it—"a hatred of the good for being the good."[13]

This is the philosophic mantle multiculturalism has donned. Multiculturalists uphold the primitive not because they believe it to be a superior value—but because it is *inferior*, because it is a non-value. They want to annihilate what they regard, not as evil—but as *good*. They do not embrace a standard of value according to which ugliness and disability are esteemed. The multiculturalist esteems nothing. He does not love non-beauty and non-ability; he is moved only by a hatred for the beautiful and the able. He wants to exterminate beauty and ability *because* they are good, because on some level he *does* grasp their value—but his only response to value is venomous hostility.

* * *

This is what underlies the insidious tenet known as "diversity." This is what explains the seeming incongruity between multiculturalism's repudiation of all values and its ardent advocacy, as an unquestioned absolute, of the value of "diversity."

Why would anyone consider "diversity" a value? While there are many contexts in which it can be desirable, it is never a rational goal in and of itself. One can argue, for example, that diversifying one's investments is good, so that risk is minimized. But the premise is not that diversity as such is better than non-diversity; it is that diversified *investments* are better than non-diversified ones (which premise itself rests on the value of investment, of financial security, of wealth, etc.).

But how could "diversity" per se be good, irrespective of what is being diversified? Is unimpaired health, for example, a shortcoming, which should be "diversified" by exposure to disease? Is knowledge to be "balanced" by ignorance? Or sanity by periodic bouts of madness? What, then, is the meaning of the crusade for "diversity"?

Its supporters claim that the purpose of "diversity" is to provide the antidote to policies of "exclusion." To understand what they actually want "diversified," and what they want not to be "excluded," let us look at the notion of racial "diversity."

Is racial "diversity" being advocated in order to prevent the racist exclusion of minorities from some sphere? Clearly not. For if it were, multiculturalists would become instant champions of merit. If their goal in the workplace, for instance, were to keep employers from discriminating on the basis of skin color, multiculturalists would insist that every employee be judged solely by his qualifications. They would excoriate any company that granted any importance to race. They would not care what percentage of which race was "represented" anywhere. They would unhesitatingly endorse the hiring of a qualified white over a less qualified black. They would regard race as irrelevant. And they would realize that the only way to ensure that it never becomes relevant is to adhere to a rigorous standard of merit.

But multiculturalists do not want race to be irrelevant. Instead, they call for a "diversity" in which race is the salient consideration. They demand that certain quotas of minorities be employed. And if those hired by this method are not sufficiently qualified—well, they say, the need for racial "diversity" is paramount.

But why? For decades the liberals fought to have race ignored.

"Color-blindness" was their professed ideal. They denounced those who judged any member of a minority not by his objectively important characteristics, but by the *unimportant* one of race. Yet now, while they aver that no race is superior to another, they are more obsessed with skin color than any redneck racist. Why?

The answer is: precisely *because* race is unimportant—i.e., *because* it is a non-value.

A policy of disregarding race and of evaluating each individual according to his abilities is unacceptable to multiculturalists. A company that eschews all forms of racial discrimination does not elicit praise from them. To the contrary, if it does not actively recruit personnel based on race—if it is "color-blind" and hires only by merit—it elicits antagonism. Such a company is admonished to adopt a "diversity" program and to meet some arbitrary ethnic quota.

But if a workforce has been assembled by ignoring race and by hiring only qualified people, there is just one way to "diversify" it: by using *un*qualified (or less qualified) people. If the best-qualified individuals available have been hired, then substituting employees of a particular race is like substituting employees of a particular eye color or ear length. It can be done only by hiring the less competent. What is being counteracted and "diversified," therefore, is the standard of judging workers. That standard—the standard of objective qualifications—is being "balanced" with its opposite. Hiring by ability is being "diversified" with hiring by non-ability.

In the 1970s, liberals began pushing for "affirmative action" for racial minorities. Because blacks were portrayed as lacking—lacking education, lacking jobs, lacking wealth—society was told to sacrifice for their sake by giving them preferential treatment in various areas. It was the sheer fact of their need, not any positive value they possessed, that formed the basis for such treatment.

But even then, the liberals did not explicitly disavow a standard of value. Rather, they claimed that "affirmative action" would enable the "disadvantaged" eventually to meet a rational standard. By getting a preferential boost, the argument went, minorities would acquire the same values that the "advantaged" whites held—i.e., they would gradually attain the same abilities, pass the same tests, perform the same work and thus enjoy the same rewards.

Today's "diversity" doctrine, however, repudiates even that tenuous link to values. Now, the very premise that ability should be the standard by which workers are judged is condemned as "exclusionary" and "racist." Now, it is labeled "ableism." Now, the contention is that blacks should be preferentially hired, not to help them meet a job's objective standards, but as a means of defying the standards themselves.

Why—the multiculturalist demands—should blacks adopt the standards of whites? Why should grades rather than ethnic heritage determine who graduates? Why is an applicant's performance on an employment test better grounds for being hired than his "street smarts"? Why is English better than "Ebonics"? Why should the corporate world regard a computer programmer as better than someone who can interpret the messages of ancient tom-tom drums? There *is* no "better," multiculturalists assert—there is only "diversity."

It is unquestionably true that to espouse a standard of value is to be "exclusionary": it is to exclude the *non*-valuable. Any yardstick debars whatever fails to measure up. To hire according to ability is to reject the incompetent. *This,* not racial discrimination, is the only type of "exclusion" multiculturalism wants to do away with.

And that requires doing away with standards as such. The "diversity" or "balance" multiculturalists uphold, therefore, is one between a standard of value and a *non*-standard—between a standard and an *anti*-standard. Since they, unlike earlier racists, do not regard one race as better than another, they are not offering the characteristic of race as an alternative standard. Race is self-avowedly unimportant to the multiculturalist. It is a non-value, serving only to *undercut* standards. Those who use it are saying, in effect: "Why restrict employment or college admissions to those who meet a standard of value? Why not entirely transcend standards by 'diversifying'?"

The only motive for elevating a non-value is to nullify a real value. The exponents of racial "diversity" are not seeking a mixture of races achieved within a context of objective justice and of rational evaluation; justice and rationality are mercilessly anti-egalitarian and anti-"diversity." Instead, the goal is a "diversity" of justice and injustice, of rationality and irrationality, of judging by ability and judging by race.

The "diversity" dictum, therefore, means that people are to be "evaluated" according to a non-value. It means that the standard of ability is no better than the *non*-standard of race. It means that people are to be hired not because they are able, nor because they will become able, but because the able must be "diversified" with the non-able. It means that the qualified and the unqualified—those who offer some human value and those who do not—are never to be differentiated. *That* is the mixture mandated by "diversity."

Thus, we now have the United States Defense Department issuing an employment policy stating that "in the future special permission will be required for the promotion of all white men without disabilities." And we have the Federal Aviation Administration giving its supervisors the guideline that "the merit promotion process . . . need not be utilized if it will not promote your 'diversity' goals."[14]

Promote people *because* they are disabled—promote them *because* they have no merit—promote them not for what they possess but for what they *lack.* Uphold an anti-value, precisely *because* it negates genuine values. That is the multicultural catechism. Ability must be "diversified" with non-ability, and those who have no value to offer—those who have only disvalues to offer—must not be "excluded." So if an applicant is rejected on the grounds that he does not meet the standard of ability, he is being wrongly "excluded," according to multiculturalists; but if someone who does meet that standard is rejected on the grounds that he fails to meet the non-standard of race, he is being rightly dismissed as an obstacle to "diversity."

This is why "diversity" is invoked always to undercut some value, never to strengthen it. "Diversity" is appealed to, for example, as an argument for schools to devote more attention to the "linguistically challenged"; it is never used to justify more classes for the academically gifted, so that schools might "diversify" upwards rather than downwards. There is never any clamor on campuses to "diversify" the orthodoxy of "political correctness" with viewpoints that categorically oppose, say, feminism or affirmative action. (To say nothing of the deathly silence about "diversifying" the anti-reason, anti-egoism curricula in philosophy departments with the ideas of, say, Objectivism.) Such proposals are nonexistent because "diversity" means: destroying the valuable by incorporating the non-valuable.

Racial minorities are merely convenient pawns in this egalitarian campaign. They have been *defined* by liberal propaganda as permanent, helpless deficients. They have been unjustly made into proxies for the hopeless and the unable—proxies for the absence of value—which reinforces the multicultural claim that to judge people according to their objective value is inherently to exclude blacks. The multiculturalists want the public to believe that without "diversity" quotas, minorities will fail. (And thus the many capable, independent, successful blacks—who happen to be the greatest victims of "diversity"—hold no interest for the left, which pretends they do not exist.)

The demands of "diversity" now extend well beyond race. From condemning the rules of grammar for being intolerant of "linguistic diversity" to mandating the inclusion of mutes in oratory contests, the multiculturalist declares: do not "discriminate." Standards, he cries, are "Eurocentric" chains of oppression, while "diversity" is liberation. Liberation from what? From reality's insistence that value is in fact better than non-value.

This philosophy underlies the strange meaning multiculturalists attach to the term "culture." The characteristics by which they group people—e.g., race, language, ancestry—are ones that can be important only to the crudest, most primitive, tribal mentality. To any rational individual, these characteristics are insignificant—which, again, is exactly why they are selected. They are perversely designated as defining characteristics of some group *because* they lack value. And to magnify the perversion, they are said to constitute "cultures."

A genuine culture represents the ideas and values that a particular group of people has chosen. Whether it is the most advanced, technologically driven civilization, whose achievements are consciously and enthusiastically embraced by members of that society—or the most stagnant, tradition-mired tribe, whose members slavishly follow the choices of their ancestors—a culture is a volitional product. A culture is that which people have chosen and which influences their basic way of life.

But multiculturalism deliberately highlights that which is *un*chosen and which has virtually *no* influence on a people's way of life. It focuses on two aspects of man: on purely physiological traits (such as race and gender) and on random characteristics that are readily interchangeable with one another (such as one's language being French rather than English, or one's address being in Serbia rather than in Croatia). The physiological traits are those that no one has any choice over; the others consist of those that no reasonable individual would deem important enough to *bother* making a choice over. But to the multiculturalist, the less authentic value some attribute has for a group of people, the more it defines a "culture."

The irrationality of old-fashioned racism pales before that of multiculturalism, which holds that there are separate "cultures" of blacks, of Hispanics, of gays, of the handicapped—characteristics that are distinctive by virtue of their being non-values that are (supposedly) non-chosen. (Which is, incidentally, why today's left is so insistent that homosexuality is beyond anyone's choice; there would be no officially sanctioned "gay culture" if that orientation were seen as volitional.)

The multiculturalist designates the unchosen as the core of your identity. Concomitantly, he belittles that which *actually* shapes your character and values: the volitional—which means, fundamentally: your faculty of thinking. Individual thought is a myth, says the multiculturalist. Your ideas are simply part of your unchosen ethnic makeup. Like every collectivist, the multiculturalist subscribes to a (subjectivist) version of determinism. He believes that each "culture"—i.e., each ethnic tribe—has a unique mental content shared by, and only by, the members of that tribe. He ethnicizes all ideas by dogmatically labeling them as: black principles of science, women's theories of law, gay musicology, white interpretations of history, etc.

The most glorious cultural accomplishments are cavalierly disvalued by multiculturalism. From the Greeks' cultivation of reason and happiness, to the Enlightenment's development of science and individual freedom, to the Industrial Revolution's mastery of nature through technology and entrepreneurship—across a range of discoveries and inventions providing inestimable value to every rational individual, of any race, color, and gender—the multiculturalist's scornful response is: "These are the products of white European males, and so are irrelevant to the concerns of non-whites, non-Europeans, and non-males."

While multiculturalists are obviously collectivists, they are different in one significant respect from other versions of collectivism: they are also modern egalitarians.

Egalitarianism is the doctrine that openly demands a leveling of all men, so that no one may enjoy anything that others lack. Wealth, brains, talent, looks—whatever the value is, no one may benefit from it unless all do so identically. As Ayn Rand describes it, egalitarians seek "not *political,* but *metaphysical* equality—the equality of personal attributes and virtues, regardless of natural endowment or individual choice, performance and character."[15]

Multiculturalists zealously endorse this philosophy. They realize that there can be no metaphysical equality based on values. They know there can be an equality only of *non-values*—an equality obtained by cutting down whoever tries to rise. And they implement this process of leveling in two stages.

First, they demand that the individual surrender his identity to his ethnic tribe. This crushes all legitimate self-value. Then, to eradicate even any sense of pseudo-value men might acquire through tribal membership, they demand that one collective sacrifice itself to another—that any tribe of "haves" immolate itself for the sake of any tribe of "have-nots."

Thus, if white males constitute a non-egalitarian proportion of corporate CEOs, or if Asians make up a non-egalitarian ratio of university students, their interests must be sacrificed to those of other "cultures." The non-whites or the non-Asians are the recipients of these benefits, not because they embody any value—but because they *don't,* and because the code of diversity allows no discrimination between a value and a non-value. Special preference is given to those "cultures" whose workers do not deserve promotion, or whose students do not deserve admission, *because* they don't deserve it. Multiculturalists, in other words, *do not claim that any distinctive group represents the good.*

This is a major departure from the views of earlier collectivists. Marx, for example, maintained that while the individual was nothing, the proletariat was history's noble embodiment of the good. Hitler told his followers to obliterate their egos for the sake of the Aryan collective—which, he said, personified the human ideal. The earlier racists in America's South held whites to be morally and intellectually superior to blacks. All these collectivists held some group as the standard of value.

Multiculturalism, however, is a full-scale renunciation of value. It is the first ideology to overtly weld egalitarianism and collectivism. It is adamantly collectivist—while eschewing the claim that any collective is genuinely better than any other. It believes that the individual has no value—and neither does any group (to which he must subordinate himself).

(This is what led the University of Pennsylvania official to make such a bizarre criticism of individualism. Leaving aside his inability to think in terms of anything other than groups, he recognized that under individualism, the "dominant [i.e., objectively better] group" triumphs, while under collectivism—an *egalitarian* collectivism—the better is sacrificed to the worse.)

Some may regard it as paradoxical that multiculturalism proclaims this universal equality of all "cultures," while simultaneously invoking special privileges for certain groups. Some even conclude that the egalitarianism is merely a facade, which enables its proponents to further the interests of the specific groups they favor.

This is a grave error. In fact, the call for "equality" and the call for "preferential treatment" are the same thing.

Egalitarianism wants to level everyone, which means: to drag the best down to the status of the worst. It contends that the hardworking individual is not entitled to a more enjoyable life than that of the irresponsible moocher. Society must treat the two identically. How? By rewarding the parasite and penalizing the producer, until the inequalities are eliminated. Both parties are subject to the same egalitarian principle: namely, that the "haves" ought to be drained until universal equality—i.e., universal "have-not-ism"—is attained. If the rational and the irrational are to be treated alike, this *means* that the latter must be given objectively "preferential" treatment.

And that is multiculturalism's goal. It consistently demands that values be "diversified" with non-values. It promotes "preferential treatment" for certain "cultures"—not for those it regards as superior, but for those that do not meet *any* standard of value, so that they become "equal" to those that do.

This is what makes multiculturalism far more radical, and more consistent, than old-style cultural relativism. The relativists held that each society is entitled to concoct its own standard of value. Despite this false notion, however, they still believed that values, once concocted, are to be pursued and non-values shunned. They held that whatever a culture chooses is "good" for that culture, and should therefore be defended by that culture.

Multiculturalists, by contrast, renounce the very idea of "good"—even a subjective notion of it. They preach, not a moral equivalence of everything and everyone, but a militantly *a*moral equivalence—i.e., a system under which a value is never to be deemed preferable to a non-value.

The nihilistic view of "culture" and "identity"—as defined by unchosen and insignificant attributes—is the means by which multiculturalism fully severs any connection between man and value. The greater its incongruity with authentic, rational values, the more a "culture" is extolled, and the more each individual is urged to efface himself within it. The meaning and the essence of multiculturalism is the worship of *anti*-values—of that which is patently inimical to human life.

There is no clearer, or more loathsome, illustration of this than the ongoing controversy about a cure for deafness.

Deafness is a terrible curse, particularly when the victim is a child. Deafness imposes upon children a world in which the learning of language—the tool of conceptual thought—is agonizingly difficult. But medicine has recently developed a surgical procedure, called a cochlear implant, to restore hearing in many deaf children. This operation represents an incalculable, life-saving blessing. It is a breakthrough that any parent of a deaf child should passionately embrace.

Yet there is organized opposition to it—among the deaf.

The National Association of the Deaf has denounced the procedure as "invasive surgery on defenseless children." As described in *The New York Times:* "Leading advocates of the deaf say it is brutal to open a child's skull and wind wires through the inner ear, or cochlear, just to rob that child of a birthright of silence."[16]

The editor of *Silent News,* a periodical published for the deaf, says: "I think it is wrong for a hearing parent to deny a deaf child his cultural identity and force him to be hearing."[17]

An article in *The Atlantic* explains the metaphysics of this viewpoint: "Deafness is not a disability. Instead, many deaf people now proclaim, they are a subculture like any other. They are simply a linguistic minority (speaking American Sign Language) and are no more in need of a cure for their condition than are Haitians or Hispanics."[18]

That article is titled: "Deafness as Culture."

Here is the full flowering, and full evil, of the multiculturalist philosophy. Here is a naked assault on the irreplaceable value of hearing—on the grounds that anti-value requires cultural preservation.

The multiculturalist bristles at the idea that it is *better* to be able to hear than not. That idea is a manifestation of oppression, he asserts. Hearing and deafness, he says, are merely characteristics of two different "cultures"—and "different" can never imply "better." So if a hearing person is not considered to be malfunctioning, if he is not a candidate for corrective surgery—why, then, should the deaf person be? Performing this implant, the multiculturalist declares, is discriminatory. It is a repudiation of deaf culture and of what one author hails as "deaf pride." It is "ableism." It is, perhaps, "audioism." After all, why should the capacity to hear be universally valued? Why shouldn't there be auditory "diversity" among people?

As the editors of *Deaf Life* magazine explain this: "An implant is the ultimate denial of deafness, the ultimate refusal to let deaf children be Deaf."[19] This is precisely correct. The implant is a medical denial that deafness is incurable, and a moral denial that deafness is desirable. But the "culturalists" of the deaf prefer to cling to their illness. Deafness, they have been taught, is their cultural birthright. It is what defines their identity, in conservation of which they willingly—*enthusiastically*—consign innocent children to the horrors of a lifetime of deafness.

And to compound this depravity, the deaf are then urged to take pride in their pathology. In an unspeakable act of corruption, deaf children are exhorted to take pride, not in their ability to overcome their handicap, but in their *refusal* to overcome it—in their wish to *remain* stricken—in their desire to venerate deafness—in their enshrinement of disability qua disability—in their grotesque devotion to the multicultural dogma that hearing cannot be superior to deafness.

The goal of multiculturalism is to undermine all values, and all aspiration to values. Not to improve the plight of minorities, or the uneducated or the deaf—but to bring everyone down, majority and minority, intelligent and ignorant, healthy and sick alike, in fervent pursuit of "non-discrimination" between that which sustains human life and that which does not.

But the target of multiculturalism's nihilism goes beyond evaluation. It extends to the root of evaluation: cognition itself. The multiculturalist attacks not just values, but the means of *knowing* any value—of knowing *anything.* On the very same grounds of ethnic egalitarianism, he allows no epistemological discrimination between logic and illogic, between reason and mysticism. Instead, he says, these alternatives represent nothing more than . . . "ethnic preferences."

This is the deeper meaning of multiculturalism's belief in ethnic determinism. Each "culture" is said to have its unique method of mental functioning. Adopting the basic premise of Marx's and Hitler's "polylogism," multiculturalists interpret a commitment to reason and to objectivity as merely a white male prejudice.

"Nothing that passes through the human mind doesn't have its origin in sexual, economic and racial differentiae," says a professor at Duke University.[20] Scientific inquiry is dismissed by feminists as a "male way of knowing," and Isaac Newton's epochal work, *Principia,* is denounced by them as a "rape manual."[21] Various "feminist scholarship guidelines," established by New Jersey for its schools, reveal the current gender-perspective on science: "[M]ind was male. Nature was female, and knowledge was created as an act of aggression—a passive nature had to be interrogated, unclothed, penetrated, and compelled by man to reveal her secrets."[22]

The very pursuit of knowledge is now derided as "logophallocentrism." Or, as feminist theorist Catherine MacKinnon succinctly, and graphically, puts it: "To know has meant to fuck."[23]

For generations philosophers have taught that logic is impotent and rational man a myth; multiculturalists are simply exploiting the resultant epistemological confusion. The practical goal of their crude "ethnicizing" of thought is the same as that of all attempts to "persuade" the public that reason is unreliable: to sap people's will to fight irrationality—the irrationality that the "persuaders" then feel free to perpetrate.

Why don't people rise up in righteous indignation against racial quotas and "ethnomathematics" and the exaltation of deafness in children? Why is such senselessness allowed to persist? Only because people have been intellectually disarmed. They have been told that dismissing multiculturalism as senseless reflects an "ethnocentric" bias toward reason. While most people do not agree with such tripe, they have no answer to it—their philosophers have refused to give them answers—and so they are helpless. They will despair, but they will not fight.

In the face of this intellectual pacifism, multiculturalism is able to mount its distinctive assault on reason. Its stratagem comprises two lines of action which, at first, seem self-contradictory. On the one hand, multiculturalism emphasizes differences, such as racial ones. Indeed it revels in them, zealously dividing people all the way down to sub-sub-sub-ethnicities. On the other hand, it vehemently refuses to acknowledge differences, such as those between the deaf and the hearing, or the qualified and the unqualified. It condemns as "exclusionary" any attempt to focus on human differences.

This apparent anomaly, however, represents a consistent viewpoint. It reflects the multiculturalist's desire to revert to a preconceptual stage. The differences that he accepts—e.g., those of race and gender—are ones that are known on a purely *perceptual* level. As long as he can regard such characteristics as narrow, brute facts, he approvingly acknowledges differences among people. What he disparages, however, are *conceptual* differentiations.

That is, the multiculturalist is quite willing to discriminate perceptually—as an animal does—between the sheer facts of, say, hearing and not hearing a sound. What he opposes is conceptually identifying those two facts—i.e., abstracting what is essential about them, relating them to other relevant knowledge, understanding the causes and consequences of each fact, judging that man's life is greatly expanded by the ability to hear and, most crucially, *making the normative differentiation that hearing is therefore good and deafness bad.*

The volitional act of evaluation is possible only to a conceptual mind; to a perceptual mentality, there are just raw, disconnected data. "Different, not better" is the rallying cry of the concrete-bound mind. It is the cry of the multiculturalist, who first ejects conceptualization from human consciousness—and then eliminates evaluation from human life.

The multiculturalist aggressively celebrates perceptual differences among people because they are pivotal to his purpose: dividing mankind into various tribes. To the multiculturalist, each one of the brute differences he observes—black skin/white skin, male bodies/female bodies—constitutes a tribe, or a herd, or a "culture."

The garden-variety altruist says: "We are all brothers, and each of us is our brother's keeper"; the multiculturalist adapts this by saying: "We are all primitive tribalists, and each of us is our tribe's keeper." He wants people to exult in their tribal differences, in their being black or gay or deaf. This is how the individual is made a slave to his tribe. The black teenager, for example, is told to avoid studying hard at school because that would amount to "thinking white." The deaf child is told to surrender any chance at hearing, because that would betray his "culture of deafness." Those who engage in campaigns to find remedies for disabilities—such as actor Christopher Reeve, who suffers from a spinal-injury paralysis—are damned (as "offensive to people who have learned to live with their disabilities") and pitied ("I feel sorry for [Reeve] because he wants to be cured") by a growing horde of "disability activists."[24]

This is how multiculturalists seek to render the individual non-existent. They want to establish the tribe as the moral lawgiver—the tribe as the exacter of sacrifices—the tribe as the shaper of one's identity—the tribe as the primary unit of reality. There are no individuals, multiculturalism insists—there is only the tribal organism, of which each man is an interchangeable, dispensable cell.

All "cultural" differences are to be kept inviolate, according to multiculturalists—which means that tribalism, which they hail as "diversity," is to be eternally preserved. They want each tribe to wallow mindlessly in the crude characteristics that set it apart from other tribes—without being instructed that some alternative is *better*. They know that to convey such an evaluation would be to destroy the tribal identity. They know that to hold such an evaluation is to urge the deaf to try to become hearing, the ugly to become attractive, the illiterate to become literate. It is to tell them that their tribal designations should be repudiated, and that each individual ought to pursue his own, rational values.

This is what the multiculturalist rabidly resists. "Don't tell me about good and bad," he cries. "I just want to preserve my tribe's special differences. Why should everyone strive to hear and to be handsome and literate and able—that would be anti-diversity."

This is unadulterated egalitarianism—upheld as a means of embalming tribal differences. It is egalitarianism, designed to perpetuate a life of stagnation and to ratify the inertia of a consciousness that dreads escaping from collective bondage. It is egalitarianism, sought by those who recoil, in terror, from the prospect of assuming responsibility for questioning tribal customs and for thinking and living independently. It is egalitarianism, cherished by those who have no desire to make their lives any better—because they cling to the belief that the very idea of "better" is oppressive.

If, however, each tribe is to be lauded for its distinctive primitiveness, then this calcified mentality feels safe. Then—since those differences are not to be conceptually processed and evaluated, and since the need for "diversity" forbids denying to one group what any others have—all will be granted the "security" of universal, tribal "equality": the same graduation rates, the same income levels, the same number of cochlear implants.

Because multiculturalism wants to invalidate the rational mind, it denounces conceptual discriminations among people. Whenever one judges that, in a given context, essential differences exist—that the elderly are different from the young, that the competent are different from the incompetent, that human beings are different from animals—one is condemned as an "ageist," an "ableist," a "speciesist." There is an unending litany of such egalitarian "anti-concepts"[25] to describe virtually any act of cognitive discrimination.

Multiculturalists refuse to distinguish the essential from the non-essential. They refuse to grasp that, say, men and women ought to be treated as essentially different in some contexts—e.g., with respect to romantic love or clothing design—and as essentially similar in others—e.g., with respect to their intellectual capacity or their ability to drive a car. The multiculturalist refuses to understand that the deaf are essentially different from others when it comes to, say, ability to communicate and essentially similar when it comes to, say, possession of political rights.

To a mind frozen on the perceptual level, there *are* no essential, as against non-essential, characteristics. The stunted multicultural mentality sees only a proliferation of tribal traits and asks only one question: are all tribes being treated identically or are some being "discriminated" against?

Because values are based on facts, this egalitarianism is ultimately not moral, but epistemological. It espouses a certain cognitive approach to reality—an approach that abjures conceptual discriminations between essentially different things. The diversity doctrine, by advocating non-discrimination between value and non-value, is simply an application of this wider anti-conceptual premise. By keeping man's consciousness on the level of an animal's, multiculturalism aborts the cognitive *means* of making such a distinction.

Multiculturalism wants to drag man back to a primitive mode of functioning. It is an ideology intended to make man into a barbarian—mentally and thereby existentially. If fully adopted, this can mean only one thing in practice: full-scale tribal warfare, leading to wholesale extermination that would surpass Hitler's wildest longings.

When ethnic subjectivism reigns, there can be no other result—and no other purpose. If there are no objective truths and no objective methods for discovering them—if reasons, arguments, and logic are "cultural biases"—then all human interaction reduces ultimately to the wishes, and the weapons, of one tribe versus those of another.

On any matter, then, the only relevant consideration becomes the identities of the tribes involved. If you apply for admission into college, you will be asked: Which tribe are you from and how many of that tribe have already been accepted? If you present the most eloquent arguments in support of your ideas, you will be asked: To which tribe do you belong and which tribes are affected by your beliefs?

Tribalism reduces men to the status of beasts snarling over a piece of meat. It makes it impossible for people to deal with one another rationally, particularly with respect to disagreements and conflicts. If an O.J. Simpson is put on trial, there will be no such thing as objective evidence by which to prove guilt. There will be only the perception that a member of one tribe is being prosecuted by those of another—and only one possible verdict: the tribe regarded as representing the "have-nots" must prevail over the "haves."

The tenets of law and reason, which are products of a conceptual age, will no longer constrain people. People will act like the pack of animals multiculturalism has taught them to become. If a community decides it does not like a certain jury verdict—or a supermarket's price of milk—what course of action will it pursue? It will see only that one tribe has been aggrieved by another and will choose violent retribution as its response.

Multiculturalism is the abject repudiation of centuries of civilization. It marks the retrogression to an existence in which individuals no longer seek independently—i.e., conceptually—to identify the true and the good, but rather become a swarm of savages, unthinkingly accepting their chieftains' edicts and ceaselessly feeding at one another's throats. Multiculturalism is paving the road that leads, in the end, back to the cave.

America used to be known by a cogent sobriquet: the melting pot. This named the fact that, when coming to America, immigrants of various nationalities, languages, and ancestries would discard their backgrounds and unite in a common embrace of freedom. They did so because they understood that freedom was essential to their lives, while the accidents of their pasts were not. They grasped that the values represented by America, not those of their ethnic heritage, constituted their true culture and bound together all who accepted them. The melting-pot metaphor represented the principle of integration—politically, socially, and epistemologically.

Today, this is a "politically incorrect" description of America. Now our schoolchildren are taught that an "ethnic mosaic" is the proper metaphor. *Dis*integration has become the guiding premise, and tribal balkanization its logical manifestation.

The antidote to this return to primitivism is a return to the "melting pot"—a return to a time in which liberty and progress were unobstructed. To be more precise, the antidote requires a huge leap forward. It requires a commitment to the philosophy of individualism, which, tragically, America never fully had, even at the start. It requires the conviction that, in all moral and political issues, the individual is the primary unit—that man's defining characteristic is his rational mind—that the objective standard of value is man's life—and that, of all the cognitive discriminations his life necessitates, the one between value and non-value is the most crucial.

If enough voices were to articulate such a philosophy, the phenomenon of multiculturalism would quickly vanish. Forced to face the bright, unyielding light of reason, it would sink back into the primordial ooze from which it arose.

REFERENCES

1. "Cortines Vows To Stop Board's 'America Best' Plan," New York *Post,* June 22, 1994, p. 20.
2. Ibid.
3. "School Board Will Recognize Other Cultures, but as Inferior," *New York Times,* May 13, 1994, p. 16.
4. Claudia Zaslavsky, "Integrating Mathematics with the Study of Cultural Traditions" (paper presented at the International Conference of Mathematical Education in Budapest, Hungary, summer 1988).
5. William A. Henry III, *In Defense of Elitism* (Doubleday, 1994), p. 45.
6. Dinesh D'Souza, *Illiberal Education* (The Free Press, 1991), pp. 6–7; and "Illiberal Education," *The Atlantic,* Mar. 1991, p. 53.
7. John Taylor, "Are You Politically Correct?", *New York* magazine, Jan. 21, 1991, p. 34.
8. Ibid.
9. Ibid.
10. Ibid.
11. Ibid., p. 35.
12. Ibid.
13. Ayn Rand, "The Age of Envy," *Return of the Primitive* (Meridian, Revised Edition, 1997), p. 130.
14. Paul Craig Roberts, "The Rise of the New Inequality," *Wall St. Journal,* Dec. 6, 1995, p. A20.
15. Rand, op. cit., p. 140.
16. "Pride in a Soundless World: Deaf Oppose a Hearing Aid," *New York Times,* May 16, 1993, pp. 1, 22.
17. Ibid.
18. Edward Dolnick, "Deafness as Culture," *The Atlantic* magazine, Sept. 1993, p. 37.
19. Ibid., p. 43.
20. Dinesh D'Souza, "Illiberal Education," *The Atlantic* magazine, March 1991, p. 63.

21. Christina Hoff Sommers, *Who Stole Feminism?* (Simon & Schuster, 1994), p. 66.
22. Taylor, op. cit., p. 38.
23. Hoff Sommers, op. cit.
24. "Eager To Bite the Hands That Would Feed Them," *New York Times,* June 1, 1997, pp. 1, 6 (Section 4).
25. See Ayn Rand's discussion of "anti-concepts" in " 'Extremism,' or the Art of Smearing," *Capitalism: The Unknown Ideal* (Signet, 1967), p. 173.

The Anti-Industrial Revolution

Let us begin by translating an abstract idea into concrete, specific terms. A current trend proclaims that technology is man's enemy and should be restricted or abolished. Let us project what this idea would mean in practice.

Suppose that you are a young man in the year 1975. You are married, have two children and own a modest home in the suburbs of a large city. Let us observe a normal, average day of your life.

You get up at five a.m., because you work in the city and must be at the office at nine. You always had a light breakfast, just toast and coffee. Your electric percolator is gone; electric percolators are not manufactured any longer, they are regarded as an item of self-indulgent luxury: they consume electric power, which contributes to the load of power stations, which contributes to air pollution. So you make your coffee in an old-fashioned pot on an electric—no, an oil-burning stove; you used to have an electric one, but they have been forbidden by law. Your electric toaster is gone; you make your toast in the oven; your attention wanders for a moment and you burn the toast. There is no time to make another batch.

When you had a car, it took you three-quarters of an hour to get to the office; but private automobiles have been outlawed and replaced by "mass transportation." Now it takes you two hours and a half. The community bus can make the trip in a little over an hour, when it is on time; but you never know whether it will be on time, so you allow for half-an-hour's delay. You trudge ten blocks through the bitter gusts of a cold morning wind to your community bus stop, and you stand waiting. You have no choice—there are no other means of transportation—and you know it; so does the bus company.

When you reach the city, you walk twelve blocks from the bus terminal to the office building. You make it on time. You work till noon, then eat, at your desk, the lunch you have brought from home. There used to be six restaurants in the two blocks around the building; but restaurants are notorious sources of pollution—they create garbage; now there is only one restaurant, and it is not too good, and you have to stand in line. Besides, you save money by packing your own lunch. You pack it in an old shoe-box; there are no metal boxes: the mining of metal has been severely curtailed; there are no plastic bags—a self-indulgent luxury; there are no Thermos bottles. Your sandwich is a little stale and your coffee is cold, but you are used to that.

In the later hours of the afternoon, you begin to watch the clock and to fight against the recurring attacks of your enemy: boredom. You have worked for the company for eight years; for the past three years, you have been office manager; there is no promotion to expect, no further place to go; business expansion has been arrested. You try to fight the boredom by telling yourself that you are an unusually lucky fellow, but it does not help much. You keep saying it because, under the boredom, there is a nagging fear which you don't want to acknowledge: that the company might go out of business. You know that paper consumes trees, and trees are essential for the preservation of life on earth, and forests must not be sacrificed for the sake of self-indulgent luxuries. The company you work for manufactures paper containers.

By the time you reach the bus terminal again, on your way home, you reproach yourself for being exhausted; you see no reason for it. Your wife—you keep telling yourself—is the real victim. And she is.

Your wife gets up at six a.m.—you have insisted that she sleep until the coal furnace, which you lighted, has warmed the house a little. She has to cook breakfast for your son, aged 5; there are no breakfast cereals to give him, they have been prohibited as not sufficiently nutritious; there is no canned orange juice—cans pollute the countryside. There are no electric refrigerators.

She has to breast-feed your infant daughter, aged six months; there are no plastic bottles, no baby formulas. There are no products such as "Pampers"; your wife washes diapers for hours each day, by hand, as she washes all the family laundry, as she washes the dishes—there are no self-indulgent luxuries such as washing machines or automatic dishwashers or electric irons. There are no vacuum cleaners; she cleans the house by means of a broom.

There are no shopping centers—they despoil the beauty of the countryside. She walks two miles to the nearest grocery store and stands in line for an hour or so. The purchases she lugs home are a little heavy; but she does not complain—the lady columnist in the newspaper has said it is good for her figure.

Since there are no canned foods and no frozen foods, she starts cooking dinner three hours in advance, peeling and slicing by hand every slimy, recalcitrant bit of the vegetables. She does not get fruit very often—refrigerated freight cars have been discontinued.

When you get home, she is trying not to show that she is exhausted. It is pretty difficult to hide, particularly since there are no cosmetics—which are an extra-self-indulgent luxury. By the time you are through with dinner and dishwashing and putting the children to bed and a few other chores, you are both free. But what are you to do with your brief evening? There is no television, no radio, no electric phonograph, no recorded music. There are no drive-in movies. There is a movie theater in a town six miles away—if you catch the community bus in time. You don't feel like rushing to catch it.

So you stay at home. You find nothing to say to your wife: you don't want to depress her by discussing the kinds of things that crowd your mind. You know that she is keeping silent for the same reason. Junior did not eat much dinner: he has a sore throat; you remember vaguely that diphtheria had once been virtually eliminated, but epidemics of it have been recurring recently in schools around the country; seventy-three children died of it in a neighboring state. The last time you saw your father, he complained about pains in his chest; you hope desperately that it is not a heart ailment. Your mother died of a heart ailment at the age of fifty-five; the old doctor mentioned a device that could have saved her, but it was a product of a very, very advanced technology, which does not exist any longer: it was called a "pacemaker."

You look at your wife; the light is dim—electricity is rationed and only one bulb per room is allowed—but you can see the slump of her shoulders and the lines at the corners of her mouth. She is only thirty-two; she was such a beautiful girl when you met her in college. She was studying to be a lawyer; she could have combined a career with the duties of a wife and mother; but she could not combine it with the duties of heavy industry; so she gave it up. In the fifteen hours of this day, she has done the work of a dozen machines. She has had to do it—so that the brown pelican or the white polar bear might not vanish from this earth.

By ten o'clock, you feel a desperate longing for sleep—and cannot summon any other desire. Lying in bed, by the side of your wife who feels as you do, you wonder dimly what it was that the advocates of a return to nature had been saying about the joys of an unrestrained sexuality; you cannot remember it any longer. As you fall asleep, the air is pure above the roof of your house, pure as arctic snow—only you wonder how much longer you will care to breathe it.

This, of course, is fiction.

In real life, there is no such thing as a gradual descent from civilization to savagery. There is a crash—and no recovery, only the long, drawn-out agony of chaos, helplessness and random death, on a mass scale. There is no such thing as retrogressing "a little." There is no such thing as a "restrained progress." You are hearing many voices today that object to an "unrestricted technology." A *restricted* technology is a contradiction in terms.

What is not fiction, however, are the countless ways in which your life—and any meaning, comfort, safety or happiness you may find in life—depends on technology. The purpose of the far too brief example I gave you was to prompt you to make a similar, personal inventory of what you would lose if technology were abolished—and then to give a moment's silent thanks every time you use one of the labor- and, therefore, time- and, therefore, life-saving devices created for you by technology.

If someone proposed to reduce you to the state I described, you would scream in protest. Why don't you? It *is* being proposed loudly, clearly and daily all around you. What is worse, it is being proposed in the name of *love* for mankind.

There are three major reasons why you, and most people, do not protest. (1) You take technology—and its magnificent contributions to your life—for granted, almost as if it were a fact of nature, which will always be there. But it is not and will not. (2) As an American, you are likely to be very benevolent and enormously innocent about the nature of evil. You are unable to believe that some people can advocate man's destruction for the sake of man's destruction—and when you hear them, you think that they don't mean it. But they do. (3) Your education—by that same kind of people—has hampered your ability to translate an abstract idea into its actual, practical meaning and, therefore, has made you indifferent to and contemptuous of ideas. *This* is the real American tragedy.

It is these three premises that you now have to check.

The attack on technology is being put over on you by means of a package deal tied together by strings called "ecology." Let us examine the arguments of the ecologists; their motives will become clear as we go along.

Under the title "The Ravaged Environment," a survey of the ecological crusade was published in *Newsweek* on January 26, 1970. In spite—or, perhaps, because—of its sympathy with that crusade, it is an accurate survey: it captures the movement's essence, spirit and epistemological style.

The survey begins by declaring that man "has come face to face with a new man-made peril, the poisoning of his natural environment with noxious doses of chemicals, garbage, fumes, noise, sewage, heat, ugliness and urban overcrowding."

Observe the odd disparity of the things listed as perils: noxious chemicals, along with noise and ugliness. This mixture occurs in all the arguments of the ecologists; we shall discuss its motives later.

The perils—the survey keeps stressing—are not merely local, but global, they affect the whole of the earth and threaten the survival of all living species. What kinds of examples are given and on the grounds of what evidence?

"In the shallow waters of the Pacific Ocean off Los Angeles, sea urchins—a small sea animal—are enjoying a population boom, thanks to the organic materials in sewage being washed out to sea. Normally, the sea urchins' population levels are tied to the quantity of kelp on the ocean bottoms; the animals die off when they have eaten all the kelp, thus allowing new crops of the seaweed to grow. But now that the sewage is available to nourish the sea urchins, the kelp beds have not had a chance to recover. In many places the kelp, for which man has found hundreds of uses (it is an ingredient of salad dressing and beer) has disappeared altogether.

"There is, of course, no way of calculating the exact effects of the loss of kelp on its particular ecosystem."

An "ecosystem" is defined as "the sum total of all the living and non-living parts that support a chain of life within a selected area." How do the ecologists select this area? How do they determine its interrelationship with the rest of the globe, and over what period of time? No answer is given.

Another example: "Right now some ecologists are worried about the possible effect on the Eskimo of the great oil race on Alaska's remote North Slope. Oil spills in the ever-frozen sea, they fear, would be trapped in the narrow space between water and ice, killing first the plankton, then the fish and mollusks that feed on the plankton, then the polar bears, walrus, seals and whales that feed off sea life, and finally threatening the Eskimos who live off these animals.

"The net outcome of the current research, hopefully, will be a better understanding of the potential consequences of man's tampering with any ecosystem."

Consider the *actual* consequences of this particular example. Without any effort on their part, the Eskimos are to receive fortunes in oil royalties, which will enable them to give up their backbreaking struggle for mere subsistence and to discover the comfort of civilized life and labor. If—and it is only an "if"—the ecologists' fears came true, the Eskimos would have the means to move to a better background. Or are we to assume that the Eskimos prefer their way of life to ours? If so, why are they entitled to a preference, but we are not? Or shall we assume that the Eskimos have inalienable rights, but Thomas Edison does not? Or are the Eskimos to be sacrificed to the polar bears, walruses, seals and whales, which are to be sacrificed to the fish and mollusks, which are to be sacrificed to the plankton? If so, why? But we will come back to these questions later.

"Non-human environments," the survey declares, "have a remarkable resiliency; as many as 25 or even 50 per cent of a certain fish or rodent population might be lost in a habitat during a plague or disaster, yet the species will recover its original strength within one or two years. It's man-made interference—or pollution—that can profoundly disturb the ecosystem and its equilibrium."

Bear this in mind: factories represent pollution—plagues do not.

"The worst fears of land conservationists concern not the accidental spoilage of land by wastes, but its exploitation by man to build mines, roads and cities. In time he may encroach so far on his greenery that he reduces the amount of air he has to breathe."

Have you ever looked at a map of the globe and compared the size of the area of industrial sites and cities to the size of the area of untouched wilderness and primeval jungles? And what about the greenery cultivated by man? What about the grains, the fruit trees, the flowers that would have vanished long ago without human care and labor? What about the giant irrigation projects that transform deserts into fertile, green lands? No answer.

"Louisiana's state bird, the brown pelican, has vanished from its shores," the survey laments, blaming the bird's extinction on DDT.

The dinosaur and its fellow-creatures vanished from this earth long before there were any industrialists or any men—and environmental "resiliency" never brought them back. But this did not end life on earth. Contrary to the ecologists, nature does not stand still and does not maintain the kind of "equilibrium" that guarantees the survival of any particular species—least of all the survival of her greatest and most fragile product: man.

But love for man is *not* a characteristic of the ecologists. "Man has always been a messy animal," the survey declares. "Ancient Romans complained of the sooty smoke that suffused their city, and in the first century Pliny described the destruction of crops from climate changes wrought by the draining of lakes or deflection of rivers."

Such events did not occur in the period that followed the fall of Rome: the Dark Ages.

Would you regard the following as an expression of love for man? This deals with another alleged pollution created by cities: noise. "Nor can the harried urban inhabitant seek silence indoors. He merely substitutes the clamor of rock music for the beat of the steam hammers, the buzz of the air conditioner for the steady rumble of traffic. The modern kitchen, with its array of washing machines, garbage-disposal units and blenders, often rivals the street corner as a source of unwanted sound."

Consider the fate of a human being, a woman, who is to become once again a substitute for washing machines, garbage-disposal units and blenders. Consider what human life and suffering were like, indoors and out, prior to the advent of air conditioning. The price you pay for these marvelous advantages is "unwanted sound." Well, there is no unwanted sound in a cemetery.

Predictions of universal doom are interspersed with complaints of this kind. And nowhere, neither in this survey nor elsewhere, does one find any scientific evidence—no, not to prove, but even to support a valid hypothesis of global danger. But one does find the following.

". . . some scientists," the survey declares, "like to play with the notion that global disaster may result if environmental pollution continues unchecked. According to one scenario, the planet is already well advanced toward a phenomenon called 'the greenhouse effect.' Concentrations of carbon dioxide are building up in the atmosphere, it is said, as the world's vegetation, which feeds on CO_2, is progressively chopped down. Hanging in the atmosphere, it forms a barrier trapping the planet's heat. As a result, the greenhouse theorists contend, the world is threatened with a rise in average temperature which, if it reached 4 or 5 degrees, could melt the polar ice caps, raise sea level by as much as 300 feet and cause a worldwide flood. Other scientists see an opposite peril: that the polar ice will expand, sending glaciers down to the temperate zone once again. This theory assumes that the earth's cloud cover will continue to thicken as more dust, fumes and water vapor are belched into the atmosphere by industrial smokestacks and jet planes. Screened from the sun's heat, the planet will cool, the water vapor will fall and freeze, and a new Ice Age will be born."

This is what bears the name of "science" today. It is on the basis of this kind of stuff that you are being pushed into a new Dark Age.

Now observe that in all the propaganda of the ecologists—amidst all their appeals to nature and pleas for "harmony with nature"—there is no discussion of *man's* needs and the requirements of *his* survival. Man is treated as if he were an *unnatural* phenomenon. Man cannot survive in the kind of state of nature that the ecologists envision—i.e., on the level of sea urchins or polar bears. In that sense, man is the weakest of animals: he is born naked and unarmed, without fangs, claws, horns or "instinctual" knowledge. Physically, he would fall an easy prey, not only to the higher animals, but also to the lowest bacteria: he is the most complex organism and, in a contest of brute force, extremely fragile and vulnerable. His only weapon—his basic means of survival—is his mind.

In order to survive, man has to discover and produce everything he needs, which means that he has to *alter* his background and adapt it to his needs. Nature has not equipped him for adapting himself to his background in the manner of animals. From the most primitive cultures to the most advanced civilizations, man has had to *manufacture* things; his well-being depends on his success at production. The lowest human tribe cannot survive without that alleged source of pollution: fire. It is not merely symbolic that fire was the property of the gods which Prometheus brought to man. The ecologists are the new vultures swarming to extinguish that fire.

It is not necessary to remind you of what human existence was like—for centuries and millennia—prior to the Industrial Revolution. That the ecologists ignore or evade it is so terrible a crime against humanity that it serves as their protection: no one believes that anyone can be capable of it. But, in this matter, it is not even necessary to look at history; take a look at the conditions of existence in the undeveloped countries, which means: on most of this earth, with the exception of the blessed island which is Western civilization.

The wisest words I read on the subject of pollution and ecology were spoken by the ambassador of one of those countries. At a United Nations symposium, Oliver Weerasinghe, ambassador from Ceylon, said: "The two-thirds of mankind who live in developing countries do not share the same concern for the environment as the other one-third in more affluent regions. *The primary problem for these developing areas is the struggle for the bare necessities of life.* It would, therefore, not be realistic to expect governments of these areas to carry out recommendations regarding environmental protection which might impede or restrict economic progress." (*Industry Week,* June 29, 1970. Italics mine.)

In Western Europe, in the preindustrial Middle Ages, man's life expectancy was 30 years. In the nineteenth century, Europe's population grew by 300 percent—which is the best proof of the fact that for the first time in human history, industry gave the great masses of people a chance to survive.

If it were true that a heavy concentration of industry is destructive to human life, one would find life expectancy declining in the more advanced countries. But it has been rising steadily.

Here are the figures on life expectancy in the United States (from the Metropolitan Life Insurance Company):

1900—47.3 years
1920—53 years
1940—60 years
1968—70.2 years (the latest figures compiled)

Anyone over 30 years of age today, give a silent "Thank you" to the nearest, grimiest, sootiest smokestacks you can find.

No, of course, factories do not have to be grimy—but this is not an issue when the survival of technology is at stake. And clean air is not the issue nor the goal of the ecologists' crusade.

The figures on life expectancy in different countries around the globe are as follows (from *The New York Times Almanac*, 1970):

England — 70 years
India — 50 years
East Africa — 43 years
Congo — 37 years
South Vietnam — 35 years

If you consider, not merely the length, but the kind of life men have to lead in the undeveloped parts of the world—"the *quality* of life," to borrow, with full meaning, the ecologists' meaningless catch phrase—if you consider the squalor, the misery, the helplessness, the fear, the unspeakably hard labor, the festering diseases, the plagues, the starvation, you will begin to appreciate the role of technology in man's existence.

Make no mistake about it: it is *technology* and *progress* that the nature-lovers are out to destroy. To quote again from the *Newsweek* survey: "What worries ecologists is that people now upset about the environment may ultimately look to technology to solve everything . . ." This is repeated over and over again; technological solutions, they claim, will merely create new problems.

". . . a number of today's environmental reformers conclude that mankind's main hope lies not in technology but in abstinence—fewer births and less gadgetry. . . . The West Coast has also spawned a fledgling 'zero GNP growth' movement. Harvey

Wheeler, of Santa Barbara's Center for the Study of Democratic Institutions, believes the U.S. may reach a point—perhaps in ten years—when 'the present rate of growth is absolutely disastrous and economic growth may well have to be eliminated altogether.' "

And: "Russell Train [one of President Nixon's advisers] warns that improving the quality of life will entail unpopular cutbacks on luxuries. 'People have shown no inclination,' he points out, 'to give up the products of affluence—TV sets and gadgets.' "

You have probably seen on television, as I have, the younger adherents of the ecological crusade, the hippie types who scream, denouncing modern "luxuries," with special emphasis on the *electric toothbrush,* which, they claim, contributes to pollution by consuming electricity. Leaving aside the fact that this toothbrush, as any dentist will tell you, is an extremely valuable tool of health care, because it provides gum massage, let us consider its consumption of electricity.

An average household light bulb consumes 100 watts of electricity. This bulb is used approximately 8 to 10 hours a day, which means a daily consumption of 800 to 1000 watt-hours. Compare this figure with the following: a General Electric Cordless Toothbrush consumes *2 watts* of electricity when being recharged. Whatever the motives of those hippies' attacks, concern for air pollution is not one of them.

The immediate—though not the ultimate—motive is made quite clear in the *Newsweek* survey. "To a man they [the ecologists] maintain that a national population plan must be invoked, primarily through a national land-use plan." "The battle against pollution must also overcome the jurisdictional lines that carve the planet into separate sovereignties." The ecologists' programs cannot be accomplished "without some fairly important modifications of the American tradition of free enterprise and free choice." The "obstacles to reform [are] man's traditional notions of growth, sovereignty, individualism and time." "What is needed, the ecologists suggest, is a rebirth of community spirit, not only among men but among all of nature." How they intend to impose a "community spirit" on nature, where living species exist by devouring one another, is not indicated.

The immediate goal is obvious: the destruction of the remnants of capitalism in today's mixed economy, and the establishment of a global dictatorship. This goal does not have to be inferred—many speeches and books on the subject state explicitly that the ecological crusade is a means to that end.

There are two significant aspects in this New Left switch of the collectivists' line. One is the open break with the intellect, the dropping of the mask of intellectuality worn by the old left, the substitution of birds, bees and beauty—"nature's beauty"—for the pseudoscientific, super-technological paraphernalia of Marx's economic determinism. A more ludicrous shrinking of a movement's stature or a more obvious confession of intellectual bankruptcy could not be invented in fiction.

The other significant aspect is the reason behind this switch: the switch represents an open admission—by Soviet Russia and its facsimiles around the world and its sympathizers of every political sort and shade—that collectivism is an industrial and technological failure; that *collectivism cannot produce.*

The root of production is man's mind; the mind is an attribute of the individual and it does not work under orders, controls and compulsion, as centuries of stagnation have demonstrated. Progress cannot be planned by government, and it cannot be restricted or retarded; it can only be stopped, as every statist government has demonstrated. If we are to consider nature, what about the fact that collectivism is incompatible with man's nature and that the first requirement of man's mind is freedom? But observe that just as the ancient mystics of spirit regarded the mind as a faculty of divine origin and, therefore, as unnatural, so today's mystics of muscle, observing that the mind is not possessed by animals, regard it as unnatural.

If concern with poverty and human suffering were the collectivists' motive, they would have become champions of capitalism long ago; they would have discovered that it is the only political system capable of producing abundance. But they evaded the evidence as long as they could. When the issue became overwhelmingly clear to the whole world, the collectivists were faced with a choice: either turn to the right, in the name of humanity—or to the left, in the name of dictatorial power. They turned to the left—the New Left.

Instead of their old promises that collectivism would create universal abundance and their denunciations of capitalism for creating poverty, they are now denouncing capitalism *for creating abundance.* Instead of promising comfort and security for everyone, they are now denouncing people for being comfortable and secure. They are still struggling, however, to inculcate guilt and fear; these have always been their psychological tools. Only instead of exhorting you to feel guilty of exploiting the poor, they are now exhorting you to feel guilty of exploiting land, air and water. Instead of threatening you with a bloody rebellion of the disinherited masses, they are now trying—like witch doctors addressing a tribe of savages—to scare you out of your wits with thunderously vague threats of an unknowable, cosmic cataclysm, threats that cannot be checked, verified or proved.

One element, however, has remained unchanged in the collectivists' technique, the element without which they would have had no chance: altruism—the appeal for self-sacrifice, the denial of man's right to exist. But observe the shrinking of plausibility with the expansion of the scale: some forty years ago, Franklin D. Roosevelt exhorted this country to sacrifice for the sake of an underprivileged "one-third of a nation"; fifteen years later, the sacrifice was stretched to include the "underprivileged" of the whole globe; today, you are asked to sacrifice for the sake of seaweeds and inanimate matter.

To the credit of the American people, the majority do not take the ecology issue seriously. It is an artificial, PR-manufactured issue, blown up by the bankrupt left who can find no other grounds for attacking capitalism. But the majority, as in so many other issues, remain silent. And this, precisely, is the danger. "The uncontested absurdities of today are the accepted slogans of tomorrow." They are accepted by default.

It is possible, however, that the leftists may have outsmarted themselves, this time. The issue may be stolen from them and dissolved by American common sense, which may take them at their word, accept the semiplausible bait and reject the rest of the ecological package deal.

What is the semiplausible bait? The actual instances of local pollution and dirt, which do exist. City smog and filthy rivers are not good for men (though they are not the kind of danger that the ecological panic-mongers proclaim them to be). This is a scientific, *technological* problem—not a political one—and it can be solved *only* by technology. Even if smog were a risk to human life, we must remember that life in nature, without technology, is wholesale death.

As far as the role of government is concerned, there are laws—some of them passed in the nineteenth century—prohibiting certain kinds of pollution, such as the dumping of industrial wastes into rivers. These laws have not been enforced. It is the enforcement of such laws that those concerned with the issue may properly demand. Specific laws—forbidding specifically *defined* and *proved* harm, physical harm, to persons or property—are the only solution to problems of this kind. But it is not solutions that the leftists are seeking, it is controls.

Observe that industry has been made the scapegoat in this issue, as in all modern issues. But industry is not the only culprit; for instance, the handling of the sewage and garbage disposal problems, which is so frequently here denounced, has been the province of the local governments. Yet the nature-lovers scream that industry should be abolished, or regulated out of existence, and that more power should be given to the government. And as far as the visible dirt is concerned, it is not the industrial tycoons who strew beer cans and soda-pop bottles all over the highways of America.

Since the enormous weight of controls created by the welfare-state theorists has hampered, burdened, corrupted, but not yet destroyed American industry, the collectivists have found—in ecology—a new excuse for the creation of more controls, more corruption, more favor-peddling, more harassment of industry by more irresponsible pressure groups.

The industrialists, as usual, will be the last to protest. In a mixed economy, the industrialists will swallow anything and apologize for anything. Their abject crawling and climbing on the "environmental" bandwagon is consistent with their policy of the past four or five decades, inculcated by Pragmatism: they would rather make a deal with a few more bureaucrats than stand up and face the issue in terms of philosophical-moral principles.

The greatest guilt of modern industrialists is not the fumes of their factory smokestacks, but the pollution of this country's intellectual life, which they have condoned, assisted and supported.

As to the politicians, they have discovered that the issue of pollution is pay dirt and they have gone all out for it. They see it as a safe, non-controversial, "public-spirited" issue, which can mean anything to anyone. Besides, a politician would not dare oppose it and be smeared from coast to coast as an advocate of smog. All sorts of obscure politicians are leaping into prominence and onto television screens by proposing "ecological" reforms. A wise remark on the subject was made by a politician with whom I seldom agree: Jesse Unruh of California. He said: "Ecology has become the political substitute for the word mother."

The deeper significance of the ecological crusade lies in the fact that it does expose a profound threat to mankind—though not in the sense its leaders allege. It exposes the ultimate motive of the collectivists—the naked essence of *hatred* for achievement, which means: hatred for reason, for man, for life.

In today's drugged orgy of boastfully self-righteous swinishness, the masks are coming down and you can hear all but explicit confessions of that hatred.

For example, five years ago, on the occasion of the East Coast's massive power failure and blackout, *Life* magazine published the following in its issue of November 19, 1965: "It shouldn't happen every evening, but a crisis like the lights going out has its good points. In the first place, it deflates human smugness about our miraculous technology, which, at least in the area of power distribution and control, now stands revealed as utterly flawed . . . and it is somehow delicious to contemplate the fact that all our beautiful brains and all those wonderful plans and all that marvelous equipment has combined to produce a system that is unreliable."

Currently, the *Newsweek* survey criticizes the spectacular progress of the United States, as follows: "The society's system of rewards favored the man who produced more, who found new ways to exploit nature. There were no riches or prestige for the man who made a deliberate decision to leave well enough alone—in this case, his environment." Observe that this "system of rewards" is treated as if it were an arbitrary whim of society, not an inexorable fact of nature. Who is to provide the riches—or even the minimum sustenance—for the man who does not choose "to exploit nature"? What is "prestige" to be granted for—for nonproduction and nonachievement? For holding man's life cheaper than his physical environment? When man had to "leave well enough alone"—in prehistoric times—his life expectancy was 15 to 20 years.

This phrase, "to leave well enough alone," captures the essence of the deaf, blind, lethargic, fear-ridden, hatred-eaten human ballast that the men of the mind—the prime movers of human survival and progress—have had to drag along, to feed and to be martyred by, through all the millennia of mankind's history.

The Industrial Revolution was the great breakthrough that liberated man's mind from the weight of that ballast. The country made possible by the Industrial Revolution—The United States of America—achieved the magnificence which only free men can achieve, and demonstrated that reason is the means, the base, the precondition of man's survival.

The enemies of reason—the mystics, the man-haters and life-haters, the seekers of the unearned and the unreal—have been gathering their forces for a counterattack, ever since. It was the corruption of philosophy that gave them a foothold and slowly gave them the power to corrupt the rest.

The enemies of the Industrial Revolution—its displaced persons—were of the kind that had fought human progress for centuries, by every means available. In the Middle Ages, their weapon was the fear of God. In the nineteenth century, they still invoked the fear of God—for instance, they opposed the use of anesthesia on the grounds that it defies God's will, since God intended men to suffer. When this weapon wore out, they invoked the will of the collective, the group, the tribe. But since this weapon has collapsed in their hands, they are now reduced, like cornered animals, to baring their teeth and their souls, and to proclaiming that man has no right to exist—by the divine will of inanimate matter.

The demand to "restrict" technology is the demand to *restrict* man's mind. It is nature—i.e., reality—that makes both these goals impossible to achieve. Technology can be destroyed, and the mind can be paralyzed, but neither can be restricted. Whether and wherever such restrictions are attempted, it is the mind—not the state—that withers away.

Technology is applied science. The progress of theoretical science and of technology—i.e., of human knowledge—is moved by such a complex and interconnected sum of the work of individual minds that no computer or committee could predict and prescribe its course. The discoveries in one branch of knowledge lead to unexpected discoveries in another; the achievements in one field open countless roads in all the others. The space exploration program, for instance, has led to invaluable advances in medicine. Who can predict when, where or how a given bit of information will strike an active mind and what it will produce?

To restrict technology would require omniscience—a total knowledge of all the possible effects and consequences of a given development for all the potential innovators of the future. Short of such omniscience, restrictions mean the attempt to regulate the unknown, to limit the unborn, to set rules for the undiscovered.

And more: an active mind will not function by permission. An inventor will not spend years of struggle dedicated to an excruciating work if the fate of his work depends, not on the criterion of demonstrable truth, but on the arbitrary decision of some "authorities." He will not venture out on a course where roadblocks are established at every turn, in the form of the horrendous necessity to seek, to beg, to plead for the consent of a committee. The history of major inventions, even in semi-free societies, is a shameful record, as far as the collective wisdom of an entrenched professional consensus is concerned.

As to the notion that progress is unnecessary, that we know enough, that we can stop on the present level of technological development and maintain it, without going any farther—ask yourself why mankind's history is full of the wreckage of civilizations that could not be maintained and vanished along with such knowledge as they had achieved; why men who do not move forward, fall back into the abyss of savagery.

Even a primitive, preindustrial economy, run primarily on muscle power, cannot function successfully through the mere repetition of a routine of motions by passively obedient men who are not permitted to think. How long would a modern factory last if it were operated by mechanics trained to a routine performance, without a single engineer among them? How long would the engineers last without a single scientist? And a scientist—in the proper meaning of the term—is a man whose mind does not stand still.

Machines are an extension of man's mind, as intimately dependent on it as his body, and they crumble, as his body crumbles, when the mind stops.

A stagnant technology is the equivalent of a stagnant mind. A "restricted" technology is the equivalent of a *censored* mind.

But—the ecologists claim—men would not have to work or

think, the computers would do everything. Try to project a row of computers programmed by a bunch of hippies.

Now observe the grim irony of the fact that the ecological crusaders and their young activist followers are vehement enemies of the status quo—that they denounce middle-class passivity, defy conventional attitudes, clamor for action, scream for "change"—and that *they are cringing advocates of the status quo in regard to nature.*

In confrontation with nature, their plea is: "Leave well enough alone." Do not upset the balance of nature—do not disturb the birds, the forests, the swamps, the oceans—do not rock the boat (or even build one)—do not experiment—do not venture out—what was good enough for our anthropoid ancestors is good enough for us—adjust to the winds, the rains, the man-eating tigers, the malarial mosquitoes, the tsetse flies—do not rebel—do not anger the unknowable demons who rule it all.

In their cosmology, man is infinitely malleable, controllable and dispensable, nature is sacrosanct. It is only man—and his work, his achievement, his mind—that can be violated with impunity, while nature is not to be defiled by a single bridge or skyscraper. It is only human beings that they do not hesitate to murder, it is only human schools that they bomb, only human habitations that they burn, only human property that they loot—while they crawl on their bellies in homage to the reptiles of the marshlands, whom they protect from the encroachments of human airfields, and humbly seek the guidance of the stars on how to live on this incomprehensible planet.

They are worse than conservatives—they are "conservationists." What do they want to conserve? Anything, except man. What do they want to rule? Nothing, except man.

"The creator's concern is the conquest of nature. The parasite's concern is the conquest of men," said Howard Roark in *The Fountainhead.* It was published in 1943. Today, the moral inversion is complete; you can see it demonstrated in action and in explicit confessions.

The obscenity of regarding scientific progress as "aggression" against nature, while advocating universal slavery for man, needs no further demonstration.

But some of those crusaders' vicious absurdities are worth noting.

Whom and what are they attacking? It is not the luxuries of the "idle rich," but the availability of "luxuries" to the broad masses of people. They are denouncing the fact that automobiles, air conditioners and television sets are no longer toys of the rich, but are within the means of an average American worker—a beneficence that does not exist and is not fully believed anywhere else on earth.

What do they regard as the proper life for working people? A life of unrelieved drudgery, of endless, gray toil, with no rest, no travel, no pleasure—above all, no pleasure. Those drugged, fornicating hedonists do not know that man cannot live by toil alone, that pleasure is a necessity, and that television has brought more enjoyment into more lives than all the public parks and settlement houses combined.

What do they regard as luxury? Anything above the "bare necessities" of physical survival—with the explanation that men would not have to labor so hard if it were not for the "artificial needs" created by "commercialism" and "materialism." In reality, the opposite is true: the less the return on your labor, the harder the labor. It is much easier to acquire an automobile in New York City than a meal in the jungle. Without machines and technology, the task of mere survival is a terrible, mind-and-body-wrecking ordeal. In "nature," the struggle for food, clothing and shelter consumes all of a man's energy and spirit; it is a losing struggle—the winner is any flood, earthquake or swarm of locusts. (Consider the 500,000 bodies left in the wake of a single flood in Pakistan; they had been men who lived without technology.) To work only for bare necessities is a *luxury* that mankind cannot afford.

Who is the first target of the ecological crusade? No, not big business. The first victims will be a specific group: those who are young, ambitious and poor. The young people who work their way through college; the young couples who plan their future, budgeting their money and their time; the young men and women who aim at a career; the struggling artists, writers, composers who have to earn a living, while developing their creative talents; any purposeful human being—i.e., the best of mankind. To them, *time* is the one priceless commodity, most passionately needed. *They* are the main beneficiaries of electric percolators, frozen foods, washing machines and labor-saving devices. And if the production and, above all, the *invention* of such devices is retarded or diminished by the ecological crusade, it will be one of the darkest crimes against humanity—particularly because the victims' agony will be private, their voices will not be heard, and their absence will not be noticed publicly until a generation or two later (by which time, the survivors will not be able to notice anything).

But there is a different group of young people, the avant-garde and cannon fodder of the ecological crusade, the products of "Progressive" education: the purposeless. These are the concrete-bound, mentally stunted youths, who are unable to think or to project the future, who can grasp nothing but the immediate moment. To them, time is an enemy to kill—in order to escape a confrontation with inner emptiness and chronic anxiety. Unable to generate and carry out a goal of their own, they seek and *welcome* drudgery—the drudgery of mere physical labor, provided, planned and directed by someone else. You saw it demonstrated on their so-called "Earth Day," when young people who did not take the trouble to wash their own bodies, went out to clean the sidewalks of New York.

These youths have some counterparts among the group they regard as their antagonists: the middle class. I once knew a hard-working housewife whose husband offered to buy her a dish-washing machine, which he could easily afford; she refused it; she would not name her reason, but it was obvious that she dreaded the emptiness of liberated time.

Combine the blank stare of that housewife with the unwashed face and snarling mouth of a hippie—and you will see the soul of the Anti-Industrial Revolution.

These are its followers. The soul of its leaders is worse. What do the leaders hope to gain in practice? I shall answer by quoting a passage from *Atlas Shrugged*. It was published in 1957—and I must say that I am not happy about having been prophetic on this particular issue.

It is a scene in which Dagny Taggart, at a conference with the country's economic planners, begins to grasp their motives.

> Then she saw the answer; she saw the secret premise behind their words. . . . These men were moved forward, not by the image of an industrial skyline, but by the vision of that form

of existence which the industrialists had swept away—the vision of a fat, unhygienic rajah of India, with vacant eyes staring in indolent stupor out of stagnant layers of flesh, with nothing to do but run precious gems through his fingers and, once in a while, stick a knife into the body of a starved, toil-dazed, germ-eaten creature, as a claim to a few grains of the creature's rice, then claim it from hundreds of millions of such creatures and thus let the rice grains gather into gems.

She had thought that industrial production was a value not to be questioned by anyone; she had thought that these men's urge to expropriate the factories of others was their acknowledgment of the factories' value. She, born of the industrial revolution, had not held as conceivable, had forgotten along with the tales of astrology and alchemy, what these men knew in their secret, furtive souls: . . . that so long as men struggle to stay alive, they'll never produce so little but that the man with the club won't be able to seize it and leave them still less, provided millions of them are willing to submit—that the harder their work and the less their gain, the more submissive the fiber of their spirit—that men who live by pulling levers at an electric switchboard, are not easily ruled, but men who live by digging the soil with their naked fingers, are—that the feudal baron did not need electronic factories in order to drink his brains away out of jeweled goblets, and neither did the rajahs of the People's State of India.

(*January–February 1971*)